Praise for *All This*

"The story of John Suthers' life includes one of the most remarkable journeys of public service in Colorado's history."

Hank Brown
former US Senator and
President of the University of Colorado

"From a fascinating personal story to an extraordinary career in public service, John Suthers' fast paced autobiographical account is a must read for anyone interested in how to overcome adversity and succeed in life. John's life story is pervaded with the redeeming values of faith, fidelity, resilience, and good humor. It's a formula for hope and success."

R. James Nicholson
former US Secretary of Veterans Affairs,
US Ambassador to the Vatican and
Chairman of the Republican National Committee

"If you wrote a manual on what you want in our public officials—integrity, dedication, and principle centered leadership—this book would be it. It's a must read for anyone in public service, or anyone contemplating it.

Jason Dunn
former US Attorney,
District of Colorado

"People are asking where leaders of character have gone, especially in public life. They need to read this book. In describing his remarkable journey John Suthers provides insight as to how government can work to serve the people. He is a leader with honor and integrity who has made it his life's work to be a good public servant and to become a good ancestor."

Major General Jack Briggs (Ret.)
CEO, Colorado Springs
Rescue Mission

"*All This I Saw, and Part of It I Was* is a fascinating and very personal account of a life spent 'in the arena.' At times both touching and funny, it's a great story about moving from adversity to accomplishment. John Suthers' memoir is of special interest to anyone interested in Colorado Springs history over the past half century."

Matt Mayberry
Director, Colorado Springs
Pioneers Museum

"John Suthers' autobiography is both entertaining and inspiring. His experience is unparalleled. His insights on issues and personalities are revealing, and sometimes humorous. John is a humble and dedicated public servant who has touched many lives. I consider him an American hero."

Admiral James McPherson (Ret.)
former Executive Director, National Association of
Attorneys General, Judge Advocate General of the
Navy and General Counsel of the Army

"In his autobiography, John Suthers shows why he is widely regarded as a consummate public servant. His honor, integrity, intelligence, and humor have made him a difference maker in his state and our country. It's been my honor to stand with him on issues that matter."

Lawrence Wasden
former Attorney General of Idaho and
President, National Association of
Attorneys General

"Strength of character defines John Suthers through the challenges he faced as a young man and his remarkable career that has spanned beyond his hometown and the courtrooms of Colorado. His autobiography will make you cry and laugh as you follow his family history and his decades-long involvement with important issues and interesting personalities. As people look for leadership from their public officials, they need look no further than the example set by John Suthers with his bedrock values of faith, family, integrity and service."

Cory Gardner
former US Senator

"A candid and surprisingly entertaining look into the life of an American prosecution legend. Principled, disciplined, devout, and ethical, this book reveals why John Suthers remains a trusted political leader by people across the political spectrum. Great read."

George Brauchler
former District Attorney,
18th Judicial District of Colorado

ALL THIS I SAW
AND PART OF IT
I WAS

A MEMOIR

JOHN SUTHERS

Edited by Laurie Knight
Cover Design by: Kristina Edstrom

PEAK PRESS

An Imprint for GracePoint Publishing (www.GracePointPublishing.com)

GracePoint Matrix, LLC
624 S. Cascade Ave, Suite 201
Colorado Springs, CO 80903
www.GracePointMatrix.com
Email: Admin@GracePointMatrix.com
SAN # 991-6032

Library of Congress Control Number: 2021918431

ISBN: (Paperback) 978-1-955272-97-1
eISBN: 978-1-955272-98-8

Books may be purchased for educational, business, or sales promotional use.
For bulk order requests and price schedule contact:
Orders@GracePointPublishing.com

To my wife, Janet, my life partner, whose love and support has made me a better person and a better ancestor than I ever could have been without her.

Table of Contents

Foreword i

The Title: All This I Saw, and Part of It I Was iii

Preface iv

Chapter I October of 1951: Where Have You Gone Joe DiMaggio? . 1

Chapter II "Many People's Lives Would Be Seriously Disrupted" ... 7

Chapter III "I Wasn't Expected, I Was Selected" 23

Chapter IV I Lived with Ozzie and Harriet 31

Chapter V I Survived Catholic School 45

Chapter VI Sic Transit Gloria Mundi 53

Chapter VII Even the "Goose" Couldn't Strike Me Out 61

Chapter VIII God, Country, Notre Dame 67

Chapter IX The Paper Chase 79

Chapter X The Straight Arrow Takes a Bride 89

Chapter XI The Prosecution Never Rests 97

Chapter XII "I Love You, Daddy" 107

Chapter XIII The Practice 117

Chapter XIV The District Attorney 129

Chapter XV "I Just Want to Be a Good Ancestor" 165

Chapter XVI The Director of Corrections 177

Chapter XVII The United States Attorney 197

Chapter XVIII General Suthers 235

Chapter XIX The Mayor 313

Chapter XX The Final Chapter 359

Acknowledgments 363

Foreword

All This I Saw, and Part of It I Was is a compelling story of an adopted son who, having suffered the death of his father at an early age, becomes determined to make a difference in his life. In his childhood and his Catholic education John Suthers was the beneficiary of love, discipline, and values. The lessons he learned found root in the fertile mind of a young man searching for answers. His success at Notre Dame and the University of Colorado Law School was the natural result of his focus and personal dedication. He was preparing for a career devoted to serving others.

What follows in the book is of one of the most remarkable journeys of public service in Colorado's history. Seeking, in his words, to become "a good ancestor," he repeatedly eschews lucrative opportunities in favor of public service. The scope and variety of issues he encounters along the path from district attorney to head of corrections, to United States Attorney, to Colorado Attorney General, and to mayor of a large city, is remarkable. What is truly unique is his constant willingness to rise above the partisan politics that plagues our current times. In our contemporary culture, people pursue celebrity status. John's life story is about turning adversity into hard work and pursuing the common good.

This inspiring story is told in a straightforward manner that describes actors in state and federal politics with insight, honesty, and frankness. Complex issues are explained in clear and understandable terms. Some of the issues confronted are among the most controversial of our times. This book suggests some solutions, not just problems. In that regard it's an important read for everyone interested in public affairs.

We all expect that those who step forward to lead us should place the public interest above their selfish concerns. The privilege of serving our country, our state, and our community is one that should command the best of each of us. Unfortunately, too many leaders fail to meet this mark. When you finish this book, I believe you'll be inspired by what one individual can accomplish by being committed to service of others above self. Hopefully, young people who read it will be inspired to seek out their own path to become a good ancestor.

Hank Brown
Former U.S Senator and
President of the University of Colorado

The Title: All This I Saw, and Part of It I Was

On July 31, 1871, a small crowd gathered in what is now downtown Colorado Springs for a ceremony in which the first stake was driven into the ground marking the founding of the city I would call home for my entire life. At the time, there wasn't a building or a tree for miles around. At the ceremony, General James Cameron, who had been hired by General William Palmer, the founder of Colorado Springs, to oversee the building of the city, gave a short speech. He spoke remarkably prophetic words about how the beauty and climate of the Pikes Peak region would draw people from all over the world. He concluded his remarks by telling all those present that in future decades they could look back and reflect on the growth and prosperity of Colorado Springs and say to themselves, *all this I saw, and part of it I was.*

I've not been able to determine if this choice of words originated with Cameron. A local historian told me he thought the words were the title of a memoir by a Union general in the Civil War. Given Cameron's background that seems logical, but I've never been able to confirm it.

In this book I'm looking back on my seven decades as a resident of Colorado and Colorado Springs and as a citizen of the United States. I'm carrying out General Cameron's directive. I chose these words for the title of this autobiography not just because of their connection to the history of Colorado Springs, but because they appropriately reflect my belief that I've been extremely fortunate to live an interesting life at an interesting time in history and to play a small part in some interesting events that occurred in Colorado Springs, the state of Colorado, and in the United States. This book contains my reflections on that life, the events I've observed, and the part I was able to play in some of them.

Preface

Let me be frank. I'm not a flamboyant guy. In fact, my family and friends frequently and humorously portray me as downright boring. I've been married to the same woman for forty-seven years. I drink very moderately, and I've never smoked anything. I don't jaywalk, and I pick up litter on the sidewalk. I've never done anything remarkable like venture into space, climb Mount Everest, or excel in sports, entertainment, or other endeavors at the highest levels. While I've held elected and appointed offices at the federal, state, and local levels, my public service has been relatively low profile.

But I believe I've led an interesting life. I was born out of wedlock and adopted as an infant. My adoptive parents died when I was young. I decided at fifteen years old, facing the trauma of my father's sudden death, that I wanted to live a life of meaning and purpose. And I set out to do so. As I reflect on the last fifty-five years, I think I've achieved my goal so far. My legal career has taken me from the local courthouse to the US Supreme Court. I achieved the legal trifecta, serving as district attorney, US attorney, and state attorney general, which allowed me to be involved in hundreds of captivating criminal cases and some of the most historic and precedent setting civil cases of our time. I had a front row seat in the war against terrorism waged after 9/11, and I was literally in the front row of the US Supreme Court in the battle over the insurance mandate in Obamacare. I also had the opportunity to serve as mayor of an ascendant American city and exercise political leadership that helped it attain unprecedented growth and

All This I Saw, and Part of It I Was

prosperity while overcoming challenges ranging from domestic terrorism to a worldwide pandemic.

I have a remarkable story to tell about how I learned the identity of my birth mother when I was thirty-nine years old, and eventually learned that I had eleven half siblings that didn't know I existed until I was sixty-nine, when I established a relationship with several of them.

Throughout my career I've held public and private sector positions that I found interesting and rewarding. I've been selective and deliberate about the career opportunities I chose to pursue. In each of those positions I've had the opportunity to observe and often play a role in some significant events that are part of the history of my city, my state, and my country. I've met a lot of very fascinating people along the way. The events and people have left me with observations about human nature and human experience.

As to why I feel the need to document my reflections on my life and the people and events which comprised it, I'd note three motivations. First, over the past three decades, when I'd relate a story to someone about an interesting legal case I'd been involved in, or the circumstances under which I determined the identity of both my birth parents and my half siblings, they'd frequently react by saying, "you really ought to write a book." Secondly, I love history and people's perspectives on it, and I believe my observations about various events, particularly in the history of Colorado and Colorado Springs, may be of interest and value to future generations. Finally, this book is for my family. I'd like my descendants to know more about their ancestor. I long ago made it my ambition to be a good ancestor, and I hope they will view me that way.

If a man is fortunate, he will, before he dies, gather up as much of his civilized heritage as he can and transmit it to his children. And to his final breath he will be grateful for his inexhaustible legacy,

knowing that it is our nourishing mother and our
lasting life.

—Will and Ariel Durant, The Lessons of History, 1968

I also want to make a point to everyone who reads this book. You don't have to have a particularly provocative personality to live a very interesting and rewarding life. But you may have to take some risks and suffer some setbacks. You may have to suffer the slings and arrows of others' opinions. You may need to realize that both success and happiness stem from how you manage your life's journey rather than whether you reach all your goals and destinations. And you'll need to understand that you have to be strong to lead a rewarding life. By documenting my life's journey, I hope I can inspire other people to make it their goal to be a good ancestor.

I conclude this preface with a caveat. The observations and reflections regarding the people and events described in this autobiography are mine alone and may not be shared by others who observed them. Undoubtedly, my critics will have a different take on certain issues and circumstances I describe or allege that I'm being selective in the matters I choose to relate. But such is the inherent reality of autobiography. Please view this book as nothing more than my personal observations and reflections on the life I've led.

Chapter I
October of 1951:
Where Have You Gone Joe DiMaggio?

For dedicated baseball fans like myself, October 1951 is considered a momentous time in the history of the game. The New York Yankees beat the New York Giants four games to two to win the World Series. It was the culmination of an amazing season. The Brooklyn Dodgers had been considered a shoo-in to win the National League pennant and led by as much as thirteen and a half games in August. But the Giants had won thirty-seven of their last forty-four games to finish the season tied with the Dodgers. A twenty-year-old rookie, Willie Mays, was instrumental in the Giants' late season surge, having overcome a one for twenty-one batting debut in the major leagues. On October 3rd, the Giants won the three-game playoff against the Dodgers, two games to one on a three-run walk-off homer by Bobby Thompson in the bottom of the ninth inning. It's called "the shot heard 'round the world" and is among the most dramatic moments in baseball history.

The October 1951 World Series would mark the last appearance in a uniform for the Yankee Clipper, Joe DiMaggio. He would announce his retirement soon thereafter. Yankee fans were disconsolate at the prospect that he would be replaced in center field by an unproven rookie named Mickey Mantle. One of my prized possessions is a picture of Joe DiMaggio together with Mickey Mantle, taken during the World Series in October of 1951.

Other interesting events were occurring in America in 1951. It was a time of incredible post-war prosperity. Americans were buying more than six million cars per year. Ninety percent of families had a refrigerator, and three-quarters had a washing machine. Households across the country were being introduced to an invention called television. Families that could afford the luxury gathered around flickering black and white screens watching programs that gave only a small hint of television's eventual role in American culture. Television ushered in a new mode of advertising that fostered mass consumerism. The lives of a generation born in the decade after World War II, to be known as baby boomers, would be shaped to a considerable extent by the invention. Long-running shows that made their debut in 1951 included *Roy Rogers and Dale Evans* and *I Love Lucy*. Those who could not afford television were still being entertained at movie theaters watching best actor of the year Humphrey Bogart in *The African Queen* and best actress Vivien Leigh in *A Streetcar Named Desire*. A science fiction thriller, *The Day the Earth Stood Still*, also debuted in 1951. Lee Strasberg became director of the Actors Studio of New York in 1951 and taught method acting to young disciples like James Dean and Marlon Brando. Actress Elizabeth Taylor and hotel heir Conrad Hilton, Jr., were divorced in February 1951. It ended the first of her eight marriages. Frank Sinatra married Ava Gardner. It was the second of his four marriages.

Songs at the top of the charts included "Be My Love" by Mario Lanza, "Cold, Cold Heart" by Tony Bennett, "Jezebel" by Frankie Lane, "Tell Me Why" by the Four Aces, and "Tennessee Waltz" by Patti Page. But American music was on the verge of a great transformation. In July of 1951 Cleveland disc jockey Alan Freed coined the term *rock and roll* to describe an emerging trend in pop music. Within the year, a show called *American Bandstand* would debut on TV in Philadelphia. In three years, Elvis Presley would hit the top of the charts.

American literature was also undergoing change in 1951 with the publication of the novel *Catcher in the Rye* by J. D. Salinger. The novel's hero and narrator, a prep school dropout named Holden Caulfield, exposed the disillusionment of the young with the phoniness of the adult world in a unique and humorous manner. In the same rebellious spirit, Jack Kerouac wrote *On the Road* in just three weeks in April 1951.

The Yankees weren't the only sports story in 1951. The great Ben Hogan won the US Open that year. The Los Angeles Rams were the National Football League champions. Richard Kazmaier of Princeton University won the Heisman Trophy. Kentucky won one of their many college basketball national championships in 1951. Florence Chadwick became the first woman to swim the English Channel in both directions. On October 5, Notre Dame played its first night football game, beating the University of Detroit 48-6 at Briggs Stadium in Detroit.

Although Jackie Robinson had broken the color barrier in Major League Baseball in 1947 and was its most valuable player in 1949, social segregation was still widespread in America. In June of 1951 a trial was held in the federal district court in Topeka, Kansas. Thirteen parents of African American children, acting through the NAACP, sued the local school board because their children were forced to attend segregated schools. They lost in the trial court. But three years later, in *Brown v. Board of Education*, the United States Supreme Court ruled in their favor, holding that segregated schools violated the equal protection clause of the Fourteenth Amendment.

In July of 1951, Julius and Ethel Rosenberg were sentenced to death following their conviction for being Communist spies. The Cold War had begun.

In 1951 a loaf of bread cost 16 cents. A new car cost an average of $1,520, and a gallon of gas cost 19 cents. A movie ticket was sixty-five cents, and a first-class postage stamp was three cents. The average new home cost $9,000. Harvard tuition was $600 per year. The average annual income in America was $3,515, and the Dow Jones Industrial Average started the year at 265. The US population was less than 155 million and the average life expectancy was sixty-eight years.

Another reality was just beginning to emerge in 1951. In World War II the United States had firmly established itself as the preeminent military/industrial power on the face of the earth. The first half of the twentieth century was a story of declining empires and the rise of new powers to fill the vacuum. After the war, the United States took the mantle of leadership of the free world from Britain and led the fight against communism. The prosperity that followed in the ensuing decades far exceeded that of the first half of the century and would ensure that baby boomers would live in what many commentators would come to call the American Century. Within forty years after 1951, the Iron Curtain would crumble, and America would be the world's sole superpower. Anyone traveling abroad in the decades after World War II would recognize the extent to which American ideas, values, movies, music, fashion, food, and other manifestations of American life had infiltrated and influenced the rest of the world. Television would be a primary means by which American culture was exported around the globe.

In 1951 Winston Churchill was once again elected prime minister of Great Britain at the age of seventy-seven. Harry Truman was president of the United States and Alben Barkley was vice president. Sam Rayburn remained Speaker of the House. The Twenty-second Amendment to the US Constitution was ratified, limiting future presidents to two terms in office. The infamous baseball great Shoeless Joe Jackson died in 1951, as did publisher William Randolph Hearst.

In October of 1951, an undeclared war was still raging in Korea. The US had intervened to stop a Chinese invasion from the north. Earlier in the year, President Truman had abruptly replaced General Douglas MacArthur, the "American Caesar," as the commander of the Allied Forces in the Far East. The American public overwhelmingly sided with MacArthur until a subsequent Senate subcommittee investigation revealed he had in fact been insubordinate. On October 17, 1951, MacArthur, still at the height of his popularity, spoke to a veteran's convention in Miami and, for the first time publicly, lashed out against the administration's policy in the conduct of the conflict in Korea. His speech was reprinted in full in the Thursday morning October 18th edition of the *New York Times*.

Something else happened on Thursday morning October 18, 1951. Something that was not reported in any newspaper. I was born at 6:22 a.m. in Mercy Hospital in Denver, Colorado, after twenty minutes of induced labor. I weighed an even six pounds and was nineteen and one-half inches long. I had blue eyes and blond hair.

The public documentary evidence of the event, which consisted only of a birth certificate issued several months after the fact, indicates that it was a normal birth in all respects. That is not entirely true. The publicly issued birth certificate does not reflect my actual parentage. In fact, the woman who actually gave birth to me never laid eyes on me. Instead, I was quickly taken from the delivery room and immediately became a ward of Catholic Charities of the Archdiocese of Denver. In that respect at least, it was an inauspicious introduction to the world.

Chapter II
"Many People's Lives Would Be Seriously Disrupted"

On a Saturday afternoon in the fall of 1990, when I was thirty-nine years old, I was speaking to a group of unwed mothers about what it was like to grow up as an adopted child. These were pregnant women who had chosen not to have an abortion and were now trying to decide whether to keep their babies or place them for adoption. It was a talk I had given several times before at the request of adoption counselors for Catholic Charities of the Diocese of Colorado Springs. From January of 1984 to January of 1989, I had been the lawyer for the diocese and worked closely with the staff at the Catholic Charities adoption agency. They were aware I was adopted and often asked me to relate my experiences to mothers considering placing a child for adoption and to couples contemplating adopting a child. Though I was then the elected district attorney in Colorado Springs, I continued to accept the invitations whenever possible. Because of my personal life experience, I was a great advocate of adoption and was glad to donate my time to such a worthy cause.

In the course of this particular discussion, I was explaining to the group why I had made no effort whatsoever to locate my natural parents. I explained that my adoptive home had been a very loving one. My parents were unable to have children of their own and adopted my sister Sharon and me from different agencies. We were told we were adopted as soon as we were able to comprehend the concept and we celebrated our adoption days as well as our birthdays. We always felt much loved. Even though my father died when I was a freshman in high school and my mother died soon after I graduated from college, I felt no desire to seek out the details of my birth or the identity of my natural parents. In contrast to another presenter who had obsessively searched out his natural mother upon learning as a sixteen-year-old that he had been adopted, I described myself to the group as a very contented adoptee.

Upon hearing my story, one of the young women in the group asked whether I would like to know my natural parents' health history in order to determine if I was prone to genetic health problems. After short reflection, I responded that I would like to have such information. At thirty-six, in the heat of my first campaign for district attorney, I experienced a sudden but ultimately temporary onset of asthma, and I wondered whether pulmonary problems awaited me as I grew older.

At the conclusion of the meeting, I was approached by an adoption counselor from Catholic Charities that I had known for several years. She explained that under current Colorado adoption laws she could probably obtain non-identifying information from Denver Catholic Charities which might contain health histories of my natural parents. I told her that would be appreciated. I frankly did not expect any follow-up to occur.

But in February 1991, I received a plain manila envelope in the mail. Inside was a three-page typed document from Catholic Charities described as Background History for John Suthers. Pertinent information contained in the document included the following passages:

> Your birth mother is described as an attractive young woman with curly brown hair, brown eyes and a fair complexion. During her pregnancy she worked for a Catholic newspaper in Denver. This employment was arranged through her parish priest in Ohio so that she could support herself while in Denver. She was born in Ohio in 1925. She is a

Roman Catholic of German-Irish descent. She has three brothers and a sister.

Your father was born in 1925 in Ohio. He is a Roman Catholic of Irish descent. During World War II, he was an ensign in the Navy… He has blond, wavy hair, blue eyes, and ruddy complexion. He is described as clean cut and extremely charming. He is the second of three children.

As to the relationship between my birth parents the document simply stated, "They had known each other for years and dated several months prior to the pregnancy."

The document also included height and weight descriptions of my parents and a brief description of their families, including my grandfathers' occupations. My maternal grandfather owned an insurance agency. My paternal grandfather owned and operated a scrap metal business. The occupations of my birth mother's four siblings were also mentioned. They were all accomplished. One of her brothers had graduated from medical school in the summer of 1951. Of course, no names were mentioned.

Finally, the document noted that my birth mother "chose not to see her child, believing that would be best." Interestingly, the document merely referred to my birth parents as being in excellent health with no other information about family health histories. It was allegedly health information that the document was intended to provide.

One piece of information contained in the document was particularly significant to me: my birth mother's employment at a Catholic newspaper in Denver. There had always been only one Catholic newspaper in Denver. The *Denver Catholic Register* had been in business for a very long time. As the attorney for the Diocese of Colorado Springs, I had done all the legal work necessary to accomplish the creation of that new diocese out of the Archdiocese of Denver effective in January 1984. As a result of that experience I had a lot of contacts in the Archdiocese of Denver and could readily make inquiries that might lead to the identity of my natural mother. At that point I remained disinclined to make the effort.

In April of 1991, I was invited to play golf with my parish priest, Father Ted Haas, and Bishop Richard Hanifan, who had been my client for the five years I represented the Diocese of Colorado Springs. During the golf game Bishop Hanifan was talking about Catholic Charities and I told him what had transpired. I asked him if he thought there would be any problem if I should ever contact the *Denver Catholic Register* and make an inquiry. He suggested I contact Jim Mauch, the executive director of the Denver Catholic Charities and ask if his agency would have a problem with an inquiry of that nature. I also asked the bishop if he knew anyone who worked at the *Register* in 1951. He immediately mentioned the name of Julie Boggs, who had worked for the newspaper for almost twenty-five years before she left in 1966 to become the personal assistant to the Archbishop of Denver. Again, I felt disinclined to act on this new information.

Approximately one month later, I attended a reception at Catholic Charities. As I turned from the food table, I noticed that the man standing next to me had a name tag that said Jim Mauch, Denver Catholic Charities. I introduced myself and eventually informed him of what had transpired. He explained that Catholic Charities, as a licensed adoption agency, simply had an obligation not to provide identifying information and that it would pose no legal problem for the agency if I followed up on the non-identifying information that I had received. He gave me the name of Monsignor Woodbridge, a retired editor of the *Register*, and suggested I contact him. That night my wife, Janet, and I had a long discussion about what had occurred. We both acknowledged that the series of events had been remarkably coincidental, and she suggested there was a certain sense of destiny about the developments. I decided to call Monsignor Woodbridge.

Woodbridge had been editor of the *Register* in the 1960s and had no relevant information about the 1951 time frame. But he did give me the names of two retired *Register* employees who had worked there in 1951—Linus Riorden and Julie Boggs. He lunched frequently with Riorden and gave me his phone number. Again, I decided to make a call.

I told the story to Riorden and asked if he had any pertinent knowledge. He said he did not and further suggested that my task would be a difficult one. He explained that in 1951, the *Register* printed about thirty-five Diocesan newspapers around the country and had more than 500 employees. He said the *Register* printed the newspaper for the Archdiocese of Cincinnati and theorized that was how the priest in Ohio made the connection with the *Register* as a place to work for a pregnant parishioner. I thanked Linus Riorden for talking to me. Almost as an afterthought he suggested, "You might give Julie Boggs a call. She knew everything that went on at the *Register*." It was the third time that I had heard her name mentioned. I asked Riorden if he knew how I could get in touch with Boggs. He said they saw each other for lunch on occasion and gave me her phone number.

After further discussion with Janet, I decided to call Julie Boggs. It was early May 1991. I introduced myself and told her I had gotten her name from Bishop Hanifan, Monsignor Woodbridge, and Linus Riorden. She was an extremely friendly and talkative woman. I subsequently learned she was somewhat of a legend among Archdiocesan employees for her candor and outspokenness. I started by saying, "Let me tell you a story," and began with the fact of my birth at Mercy Hospital on October 18, 1951, and I described the details of the events that transpired. When I related that my pregnant mother had been sent by her parish priest in Ohio to work at the *Register*, Julie became totally silent. I said, "I sense you know something about this." Julie proceeded to tell me that she had been put "in charge" of my mother. She confirmed that my mother had been sent to Colorado by a priest who was well acquainted with Monsignor John Cavanaugh, who then managed the *Register*. Julie related that she picked my mother up at the airport, helped her find an apartment on High Street in Denver, and acted as her supervisor. They grew to like each other a lot. My mother had worked as an editor at the newspaper until her pregnancy became obvious and then she worked at home. Julie said she drove my mother to the hospital on the day I was born. She stayed until the birth was complete. "Your mother never saw you," she said. "You were immediately handed over to Catholic Charities." She also drove my mother to the airport two days later for a return trip to Cincinnati.

"Your mother's name is Jeanne Fischer," Julie said, and then proceeded to describe her in considerable detail. She was nice looking, quite intelligent, and had a great sense of humor. She was twenty-six at the time of my birth and a college graduate. Julie was certain that my birth father, also twenty-six, had visited Denver at one point and had contributed to the hospital expenses.

Julie went on to say that she had seen Jeanne one more time. She was in Cincinnati on business for the *Register*. She called Jeanne, who was still living at home. She was invited out to dinner with Jeanne and her parents. According to Julie they went to a very fancy country club. During dinner, Julie learned that Jeanne's father had been born in Kentucky in the late 1800s. As a young man he made his way to Cincinnati and eventually worked his way through college. He got into the insurance business and had been so successful that he then owned his own agency. After dinner, Mr. Fischer thanked Julie for all she had done for Jeanne but then said, "We need to put this unfortunate episode behind us," and asked Julie not to contact Jeanne again. Julie related to me that she never spoke with Jeanne or her family again but learned from a priest friend in Cincinnati that Jeanne had subsequently married and had children.

Julie was intrigued by our conversation and said she would try to learn more about what had happened to the Fischers by contacting a priest she knew in Cincinnati. She called me a few days later to say the priest was in a nursing home suffering from Alzheimer's and had no recollection of the Fischer family. Julie and I agreed to get together sometime when I was in Denver. I regret that we were never able to successfully schedule such a meeting before I read in the paper several months later that she had died suddenly of a heart attack.

Another month passed after my remarkable conversation with Julie Boggs in which I learned the identity of my birth mother. I was uncertain where to go from there. On June 4, 1991, I was giving a speech in the Penrose Public Library in Colorado Springs. As I was leaving, I walked by a room where people were looking at phone books on microfiche. On impulse I decided to check the Cincinnati phone book. There was no listing for Jeanne Fischer or a Fischer Insurance Agency. But as I was leaving, I spied a physician's reference book. Recalling that Jeanne Fischer had a brother who had graduated from medical school in 1951, I checked the book to determine if there were any Dr. Fischers in Cincinnati. There were six, but only one who graduated from medical school in 1951. Dr. Donald C. Fischer had graduated from St. Louis University Medical School and was the medical director of Good Samaritan Catholic Hospital in Cincinnati. That night, after yet another long discussion with Janet, in which she once again used the word *destiny*, I decided to call Dr. Fischer.

On June 5, 1991, I called Dr. Fischer's office. He was in a meeting, and I spoke to his secretary. I told her it was a personal matter, and I would call back. She persisted in questioning me about the purpose of my call. She kept asking me if I was a vendor. Eventually, I identified myself as the district attorney (DA) in Colorado Springs. That quickly stopped the cross-examination. "I'll have him call you," she said.

About an hour later Dr. Fischer returned my call. I took a deep breath before picking up the phone. He was polite but obviously curious why a DA in Colorado would be calling him. I told him I did not know how to begin other than to ask him if he had a sister named Jeanne. He replied, "Yes, I do. Is there a problem?" I drew another deep breath and said I needed to tell him a story. Again, I started with facts of my birth and detailed what had transpired in the last several months. He was polite but somewhat impatient during most of my story. I'm certain he was saying to himself, *What does this have to do with me?* That changed dramatically when I told him Julie Boggs had identified my birth mother as Jeanne Fischer from Cincinnati, Ohio and told him of Julie's meeting with Jeanne and her parents. I also detailed the information I had about the Fischer family. He acknowledged its accuracy and then fell silent. I told him I sensed this was not something he was aware of. He said he was very close to his sister Jeanne but had no knowledge that she had a child out of wedlock. He reflected for a while and then said that he and his siblings thought their sister was traveling in Europe in the summer and fall of 1951. He continued, "I assure you Mr. Suthers, that this information went to the grave with my parents. My siblings and I had no knowledge of it."

I felt compelled to explain to Dr. Fischer what had motivated me to call him. I was not obsessed about finding my natural parents, but rather was simply following up on information that had fallen into my lap. Perhaps my birth mother would like to know things worked out very well for me. After some discussion we agreed that I would write Dr. Fischer a letter explaining all that had occurred as well as my motivations. He would then have a conversation with his sister.

On June 7th I wrote a heartfelt four-page letter to Dr. Fischer. A few of the pertinent paragraphs were as follows:

> I must begin by thanking you for the manner in which you handled our phone conversation of June 5. To receive a call of that nature out of the blue and to act with the kindness you displayed says a lot about you. Despite the uncomfortable position I put you in, I felt assured that my choice to approach this

matter through you was an appropriate one. I suspect that as a physician you are accustomed to sensitive situations and to real life human drama, although this situation may be outside your job description...

Throughout my life I have never felt any real compulsion to seek out my birth parents. I have always attributed this restrained curiosity to the extremely healthy attitude of my adoptive parents. They told me I was adopted as soon as I was old enough to understand the concept and they constantly reiterated to my sister and me that our adoption was the best thing that ever happened to them...

As I explained to you on the phone, I chose to call you because I am absolutely committed not to contact Jeanne unless and until she indicates she wants to communicate with me. I will absolutely respect her wishes in this regard. My motivation in contacting you was simply this. Your sister made a decision forty years ago that worked out tremendously well for me and I would like her to know that. While it was a decision that was consistent with the times, in light of what's taken place in society since, I am extremely thankful to her and to all those who supported her. I want her to know that also. Needless to say, for the sake of myself and my children, I would like to know more about my genealogy (I'd love to know where the dimple in the chin comes from) and if Jeanne deemed it appropriate, I would love to have her meet me, my wife, and my children. But if she chooses to leave it at this you can be absolutely assured, I will not make any further efforts to locate her. I am blessed with a strength of character which will allow me to live comfortably with any decision that she makes…

Again, I apologize to you for the position I have placed you in. Acquiring knowledge of this nature at this point in your life is, I suspect, somewhat burdensome. It will no doubt be awkward for you, but I will trust your good judgment and I will welcome your reply, regardless of what it entails.

Janet and I returned from a trip to Europe on July 6 to find a four-page handwritten letter from Dr. Fischer. He related that after reading my letter several times he determined to meet with his sister Jeanne and discuss it with her. He said the meeting "took some doing." He said Jeanne was "extremely distressed" when she first read the letter. She had built her entire life around assurances that no one would ever learn of what had occurred in 1951. After some time, she settled down and acknowledged to her brother that I was in her nightly prayers and that she was content to know that things had worked out so well for me. She was particularly glad to learn that I was "a good Catholic boy." But Dr. Fischer indicated Jeanne was adamant that "there is no way she could cope with you coming back into her life… Many people's lives would be seriously disrupted by any contact." While never stated expressly, it was clear from Dr. Fischer's letter that Jeanne was in fact married with children and that neither her husband nor her children had any knowledge of my existence. Dr. Fischer said he had assured Jeanne that I was a trustworthy person who would honor her wishes not to contact the Fischer family. Finally, he wrote that the Fischer family were German Catholics who had gradually migrated to the Republican Party and that good health and longevity were common among family members.

All This I Saw, and Part of It I Was

I wrote Dr. Fischer a short note thanking him for playing the difficult role of intermediary and assured him and Jeanne that I would initiate no further contact with the Fischer family.

With the advent of the internet in the late 1990s, I would periodically do a search for Dr. Donald C. Fischer to see if I could learn the married name of Jeanne Fischer and whether she was still living. In August of 2011 such a search led to the obituary of Jeanne Fischer Splain. Jeanne was born October 25, 1925, and died April 26, 2010, at the age of eighty-four. She was married for over fifty years and had six children (other than me) and fourteen grandchildren. A further search revealed my six siblings were quite successful and included a doctor and lawyer. While it was disconcerting to me to accept the fact that they did not know I existed, I resolved to honor my commitment to Jeanne and made no effort to contact them.

On July 20, 2013, Janet and I visited Gate of Heaven Cemetery in Cincinnati. We put flowers on the grave of Jeanne Fischer Splain and said a prayer thanking her for giving me the gift of life. On November 1, 2016, Dr. Donald Fischer died at eighty-eight and, to my knowledge, any awareness in the Fischer family that I existed died with him. But, as it turned out, that was not the end of the remarkable story.

For Christmas in 2016 I bought Janet an AncestryDNA kit. She could send in a saliva sample and confirm her ancestral roots. But about the same time her identical twin sister got back DNA results and Janet, knowing her results would be the same, suggested I use the kit. I sent in a saliva sample, curious what it would reveal about my biological ancestry beyond the German heritage through the Fischer family. The results indicated I was half German, one-quarter Irish and one-quarter English. But I had not read the fine print on the form I sent in. The results also included DNA matches, the names of other people whose DNA sample had been analyzed and who were related to me. Three people were listed as having a very high probability of being closely related to me. All three were children of Jeanne Fischer Splain!

I probably could have gotten my name removed from the Ancestry database. But I now understood that if my birth father or a child of his submitted a DNA sample their name would appear on my DNA matches. So I would infrequently check the Ancestry website to see if other names appeared as closely related. When I checked the site on July 31, 2019, I noticed that the name Luke Homan appeared as a close relative. When I clicked on his family tree, I noted that his father, Joseph Luke Homan, was born September 8, 1925, and died February 24, 2004, at seventy-eight. An online search revealed his obituary and an accompanying photo. I knew instantly I had discovered the identity of my birth father. The picture showed him as a young ensign in the Navy and his facial features, including a pronounced dimple in the chin, were very similar to mine. The obituary indicated Joseph L. Homan had married in September of 1952 (eleven months after I was born) and was married for fifty-one years until his wife died in 2003, a year before he died. Joseph had five children (other than me) and five grandchildren.

Further online research revealed my birth father was one of several children in an Irish Catholic family. His father, Joseph H. Homan, started a scrap metal business in Cincinnati. After serving in the Navy and attending college for some time, my birth father joined the scrap metal business sometime around 1950 and took it over in 1973 when his father died. After 1973 there was both a Homan Metals and a Joseph H. Homan Metals at different addresses in Cincinnati, perhaps evidencing a family split. When my birth father died in 2004, his son Timothy took over the business until he died of Lou Gehrig's disease in 2016. My other half siblings on the Homan side include a retired investment adviser, an assistant in an eye clinic, and a homemaker.

Between Jeanne Fischer and Joseph Homan, I have eleven half brothers and sisters and nineteen nieces and nephews. But I still viewed my commitment to Jeanne Fischer to preclude reaching out to any of them. I had some trepidation as to what I would do if one of my half siblings listed as closely related on Ancestry reached out to me.

On Valentine's Day in 2021, the inevitable happened. Suzanne Bens, listed on ancestry as a close relative, and who I knew from Jeanne Fischer's obituary to be the youngest of Jeanne's two daughters, sent me an email through Ancestry. "I note that we are shown by Ancestry to be closely related," she said. "Do you know how we're related? I would appreciate hearing from you." The issue was no longer hypothetical. I faced a very real dilemma. I could not respond and see if Suzanne made any further efforts to determine our relationship, or I could, in essence, violate my thirty-year-old commitment to Jeanne Fischer. I discussed the matter at length with Janet. After much thought, I decided to make a very carefully worded response. In a letter I told Suzanne that we were closely related but it may be better if she and her siblings did not know the details. "It was intended that you never have such knowledge," I said. I told her that she could not respond and we "could leave things as they are," or, if she wanted to pursue the matter, "given the passage of time and the circumstances we find ourselves in," I would be willing to share the information with her. "I have no desire to disrupt anyone's lives," I said, thinking back to Jeanne Fischer's reasons for not wanting any contact to occur.

The ensuing communication with Suzanne Bens made me feel much better about the decision I made. She told me she found me on Wikipedia and when she saw that I was born in Denver in October of 1951, and adopted soon thereafter, she was pretty certain we were half siblings. Jeanne had apparently told her children that she worked in Denver for a year before she got married. Suzanne's older siblings found that very curious given her attachment to Cincinnati. When pressed by one older sibling about it, Jeanne said her father sent her to Denver "to get away from a man." That caused the oldest child, Sara, to believe their mother had a child out of wedlock in Denver and she shared that belief with her siblings.

The upshot of the communication with Suzanne was an hour and a half Zoom conference in March of 2021. She was joined on the conference by her two older siblings, Sara and Jim. Janet joined me. We agreed it was a surreal experience to meet siblings for the first time under such circumstances, particularly given our ages. They explained that they had not yet informed their three brothers about the situation because of "family dynamics." They were not close to two of the brothers and were unsure as to how all three would react.

The vast majority of the conversation was taken up by my detailed explanation of the remarkable circumstances that led me to learning the identity of my birth mother. I related my conversations with Julie Boggs, my communication with their uncle, Donald Fischer, and his message from their mother that she wanted no contact with the Fischer family because "many lives would be seriously disrupted." They confirmed my belief that Jeanne probably never informed her husband, their father, of my existence. They also said they had never heard of Joseph L. Homan and could not speculate as to why Jeanne did not marry him, other than to suggest he may have not been viewed favorably by her parents.

When we asked them to tell us about Jeanne, there was a notable pause. Then Jim explained that the three of them had a phone call beforehand to discuss how they would respond to that question. "We decided to tell the truth," he said. They described Jeanne as being physically attractive, very intelligent and having a dynamic "public persona." Her husband adored her. "He always felt like he won the lottery," Jim explained. But they all agreed Jeanne was a difficult person and had challenges as a mother. She was very critical of her children, particularly the two girls. She was a very anxious person and was rarely without a cigarette in her hand. She drank two bourbon and waters between 4 and 6 p.m. every day, which helped her relax. She suffered from dramatic mood swings.

"You never knew what to expect when you got home from school," Jim said. It appeared to them she never felt self-fulfilled. "She tried hard," Suzanne explained, but even with her grandchildren she did not have a particularly loving relationship.

I have continued to communicate fairly regularly with four of my Fischer family siblings, including the youngest child, Michael, who has a great sense of humor. I typically sign the written communications "the oldest." We've learned a lot about each other, and the relationship is developing. They've sent me several pictures of Jeanne that confirm she was quite attractive. I have not received any inquiry from the Homan family and have thus far determined not to reach out to them.

As I reflect on everything that has occurred in regard to the discovery of my birth parents, I can never forget what Jeanne Fischer's oldest daughter, Sara, said to me at the conclusion of the initial Zoom conference. Having described Jeanne Fischer as a mother in some detail and having listened to me describe the loving relationship I had with my adoptive parents before their premature deaths, Sara matter-of-factly stated, "John, you drew the long straw."

Chapter III
"I Wasn't Expected, I Was Selected"

William Dupont Suthers and Marguerite Ann Ryan were married in Detroit, Michigan on the morning of August 1, 1936, more than fifteen years before they would adopt me from Denver Catholic Charities. My mother, who always went by her childhood nickname of Pat, was a twenty-two-year-old secretary who worked in the same building as my father, a twenty-nine-year-old dentist. They met a year earlier. Both were the products of families who had immigrated to America in the middle of the nineteenth century.

The first Suthers to come to America was an Englishman. Jeremiah Suthers was born in Ipswich, a town northeast of London on the English Channel, on February 15, 1840. He was the youngest of at least nine children. His father, William, was born in 1798. According to genealogic records, William's occupation was "hardwareman." However, he was described as an "outdoor pauper" in the census of 1871, at which time he was seventy-three years old. An outdoor pauper was a person who received public assistance from the local government but was not required to live in a workhouse or poorhouse. Jeremiah's mother, Ann Orrell, was born in 1800 in Liverpool and died in July of 1862 at the age of sixty-two.

Jeremiah joined the English Navy and at the age of nineteen went AWOL while his ship was docked in a Canadian port. He made his way to Lockport, New York where he got a job working on the Erie Canal. The Erie Canal was the engineering marvel of the nineteenth century. Linking New York City to the Great Lakes, it spurred the first great westward movement in America. First completed in 1825, it is probable that Jeremiah Suthers worked on a major expansion of the canal that was not completed until 1862.

Jeremiah lived above a pub owned by an immigrant family named Waple. The Waples were Catholics who had recently arrived from Belfast, Northern Ireland, having escaped Protestant persecution. Jeremiah fell in love with the Waple's eighteen-year-old daughter, Mary Ellen, and married her. Whether he enlisted or was drafted is unclear, but it is clear he served in the signal corps on a Union frigate in the Civil War. Family legend stated that he was tasked with signaling to other boats in the Union fleet the news of Lincoln's assassination in April of 1865. After the war, he returned to Lockport and became a tinsmith. Jeremiah and Mary Ellen had five children, the third of which was my grandfather, William Terrance Suthers, born about 1871. William stayed in Lockport where he met and married Amy Esther Feeney. Amy was the second of six children of Michael Charles Feeney and Sarah Elizabeth Dupont. The Feeneys had also come to Lockport from Northern Ireland to escape religious persecution. When Michael Feeney, a Catholic, married Sarah, a French Canadian Protestant, she was banished from her family. Michael operated a grocery store in Lockport.

Amy Feeney and William Terrance Suthers lived on Erie St. in Lockport. They had three children, the youngest of which was my father, William Dupont Suthers, born in November of 1907. Ninety-six years later, in October of 2003, I visited the two-story wood frame house where he was born and raised. My grandfather, William Terrance Suthers, and his brother Harry operated Suthers Brothers, a men's clothing store in Lockport, until it failed in the depression of 1929. He died of a sudden heart attack shortly thereafter at the age of fifty-nine. My grandmother, Amy, lived to be eighty-six.

My father was born forty-two years after Lee's surrender to Grant. The divisions of the Civil War were largely healed, and the

Industrial Revolution was rapidly urbanizing America. Henry Ford would produce the first Model T the following year. The first ten years of my father's life was a time of American optimism. The next four were dominated by World War I. He went to high school during the Roaring Twenties and to college during the Great Depression. By his own admission, all these things impacted him. He was a cautious optimist.

Both sides of my mother's family were Irish immigrants. Her father's family had immigrated from Tipperary, Ireland to New York City, where my grandfather, Cornelius John Ryan, was born in 1874. His father was a policeman in Brooklyn, and he would become an Irish cop in Detroit. He was among the first members of the department's motorcycle squad. In Detroit, he met and married Mary Blanche Holland. The Hollands had made their way from Ireland to Detroit via Ontario, Canada. Cornelius Ryan and Blanche Holland lived on Jefferson Ave. in Detroit. They had nine children, the fourth of which was my mother, Marguerite Ann.

Those who know me well will not be surprised to learn that I'm 50 percent German, 25 percent English, and 25 percent Irish by birth and Irish and English by adoption. Even I have recognized the ethnic characteristics and the ethnic tensions within me over the years. In oratory I occasionally display the passion and spark of an Irishman. And I can display an Irish temper, although the very quick temper of my youth has subsided with age. I have also been known to shed tears quite readily when the topic turns to my deceased parents, my pride in my children, or my love of country. But my subordinates and my loved ones will all say they have no trouble identifying my English/German demeanor. My family and friends have long chided me about my less-than-compassionate attitude toward any type of miscreant behavior, let alone full-fledged criminality. My daughters readily acknowledge that their mother was the nurturer and when they turned to me for advice in the face of adversity my most common response was "suck it up."

I regard that advice as the German-influenced version of my Irish Catholic grandmother's advice to "offer it up."

My father, Bill Suthers, attended Lockport public schools. He played hockey at Lockport High School. A good student, he was admitted to the University of Michigan. Because of his family's financial problems, exacerbated by his father's business failure and early death, he earned his way through college as a drummer in a traveling band. A handsome guy, he also had time to be a varsity cheerleader at Michigan. After three years as an undergraduate, he was admitted to the University of Michigan Dental School from which he graduated in 1933.

My mother attended Northern High School in Detroit, where she participated on the women's swimming team. She attended a Catholic women's college in Michigan for a year, but the family's financial constraints caused her to quit, attend secretarial school, and take a job.

Soon after my parents were married in 1936, my mother had health problems that necessitated a complete hysterectomy and resulted in her inability to have children. They remained in Detroit and applied to various agencies to adopt a child. Those applications were still pending on December 7, 1941, when the Japanese bombed Pearl Harbor. I remember my father telling me that he and two of my uncles were building a bar in a basement at an uncle's house when a radio news flash informed them that the world had changed. Evidencing a love of country and a sense of duty characteristic of his generation, my father, thirty-four, enlisted in the US Army the following day.

In February of 1942 my father was sent to Camp Carson (now Fort Carson) near Colorado Springs, Colorado to join a dental unit that was being formed. It was the first time he'd ever been west of the Mississippi River. My mother came to Colorado Springs to join him for a portion of the basic training period before he was sent overseas in the fall of 1942. It was an important development in my eventual fate. They lived in the Buffalo Lodge in Manitou Springs and in a rental property on Ridgeway Street near the entrance of North Cheyenne Canyon. During this stay of a couple of months, they developed a strong affinity for the Pikes Peak region. They decided that if my father survived the war they would move to Colorado Springs.

When my father was shipped overseas, my mother returned to Detroit to be with her family. My father was part of the allied invasion of North Africa under General George S. Patton. He spent considerable time in the bustling city of Algiers. While there, he provided dental services for various officers in the French Liberation Forces, including Charles de Gaulle himself. He then joined the Seventh Army's invasion of Sicily, again under Patton. As a young child, I recall viewing home movies and photographs that indicated he spent most of his time behind the battle lines treating soldiers with dental injuries. He remained in the European theater until he contracted tuberculosis and was sent home in 1945. While in recovery in Fitzsimmons Army Hospital in Denver, he and my mother reconfirmed their commitment to move from Detroit to Colorado Springs. They did so in 1946 and my father became one of eight dentists in a community of about 40,000 people.

Soon after relocating to Colorado Springs, they were contacted by an adoption agency in Detroit to which they had submitted an application years earlier. The agency asked if they were still interested in adopting. They related their desire to do so, and my sister Sharon was adopted in December of 1946 when she was one month old. My parents drove to Chicago to meet the caseworker and pick her up. Other than the fact that she was born in Michigan City, Indiana and that her birth name was Mary Ann Collins, my sister knows nothing about the circumstances of her birth.

In 1950, my parents began the construction of a home in the North Cheyenne Canyon area in the southwest part of Colorado Springs. The address at 1854 Arroya Street was a very short distance from the cottage they had rented when they moved to town in 1946. The three-bedroom house was completed in the summer of 1951 at a cost of $17,000.

My parents joined a small Catholic parish. Pauline Chapel had been built in 1919 by Mrs. Spencer Penrose, whose husband had founded the adjacent Broadmoor Hotel. It was named after her granddaughter. My parents quickly befriended the parish priest, Fr. Michael Harrington, who had emigrated from Ireland because he suffered from tuberculosis, attended seminary in Denver, and had been placed at Pauline years earlier. Fr. Harrington became a close friend of Mrs. Penrose and was instrumental in her generosity to several Catholic causes. As a result, the Archbishop of Denver made sure that Fr. Harrington remained at the parish for the rest of his life. It would become St. Paul's Parish when a new church was built in 1959. Harrington would baptize me and preside at our wedding. He would bury both my parents. We would visit his relatives in his birthplace of Glengarriff, Ireland on two different trips to the Emerald Isle.

With the assistance of Fr. Harrington, my parents applied to adopt another child from Catholic Charities of the Archdiocese of Denver. Although my father was then forty-four and my mother thirty-seven, the agency at the time had no age limitation for parents seeking to adopt. On the morning of November 14, 1951, at 9 a.m., my mother got a call from Denver Catholic Charities indicating that a one-month-old boy was available for adoption and could be picked up that day from Mercy Hospital in Denver. My father canceled the rest of his patients for the day. My parents picked up my five-year-old sister Sharon from kindergarten and drove to Denver. Family folklore has it that my sister stood the whole way to Denver in the back seat of the car and upon leaving the hospital carrying me in laundry basket blurted out to the nun in charge of the nursery, "Thank you Sister, for making me a little brother."

A group of my parents' best friends were having a party that night and they dropped by the gathering to show off the new arrival. For the next fifty years of my life, I would encounter people who claimed they vividly remembered the night my parents brought me home. Within the next two weeks, my parents sent out a birth announcement indicating that John William Suthers had become part of their family. Indicative of my good fortune, the front of the announcement read simply, *I wasn't expected, I was selected.*

My parents decided to name me after my grandfathers, Cornelius John Ryan and William Terrance Suthers. My mother very much wanted Cornelius to be by first name. I am eternally grateful for the fact that my father strongly resisted, insisting I would suffer through life as "Corny." John William was the resulting compromise. But my mother didn't give up. When I was asked to choose a confirmation name at the age of thirteen, she again insisted on Cornelius. When I initially balked at the notion, she resorted to tears. Assured by my father that no one would ever know my confirmation name unless I wanted them to, I relented. I'm relieved to report he was right. To this day, Archbishop Urban J. Vehr, who presided over the confirmation ceremony, is the only person that ever called me John William Cornelius Suthers.

Chapter IV
I Lived with Ozzie and Harriet

I have extremely fond memories of my childhood. Our house on Arroya Street bordered on more than three hundred acres of pastureland that remains undeveloped to this day. The land was part of the estate of Winfield Scott Stratton, a Pikes Peak area pioneer who became extremely wealthy mining gold in Cripple Creek. In the late 1990s, it became a city park, Stratton Open Space, where I would frequently take a sentimental walk. It contains two large water storage reservoirs. This presented a virtual paradise for a curious young boy and his neighborhood friends. We spent many idle summer days and afterschool hours roaming through the pasture, building hideouts, hunting for fossils, and playing soldier. As was typical of the day, our parents gave us considerable freedom, and our play was not without risks. A neighbor kid once shot me with a BB gun. The pellet hit me less than one inch from my right eye. After he received a severe spanking from his father, we quickly renewed our friendship.

My father typically owned two horses at a time. One, a white horse named Bard, was apparently too old for much riding. He was more of a family pet. In addition, we had a series of Palominos—at least one of which I recall was named Nugget—that my father would ride as a charter member of the Pikes Peak Range Riders, a group of local business and professional men who annually rode around Pikes Peak to promote the local Pikes Peak or Bust Rodeo. One of my favorite childhood photos shows my father washing a Palomino and me, about four years old, standing alongside washing a rocking horse.

The horses also attracted lots of birds which ate their grain, and that led to another story that became famous in Suthers family folklore. When I was a toddler, my mother used to put me outside in a playpen. Apparently, magpies would occasionally torment me, sometimes even landing on my head. My mother, being a feisty and persistent guardian, would take a shotgun and deal effectively with the feathered perpetrators. Although it was not acknowledged in the storytelling, I assume I was taken inside before the carnage began.

Our home was good sized by the standards of the day, probably about 1,800 square feet of living space. It had three bedrooms, two bathrooms, a combined living room and dining room, a kitchen, and a small one-car garage. As a kid I thought my bedroom was pretty big, but when I was invited by the current owner to tour the house in 2002, I was chagrined to find it was being used as a storage closet. The home's greatest feature was its views. To the front, through picture windows, you could see Cheyenne Mountain. To the rear, from a covered patio, you could look down on the city of Colorado Springs. My father loved to sit on the patio at night and watch electrical storms over the city's lights. Because I also came to love the views from my childhood home, it's not surprising that every house I subsequently owned would have a view of the city as well as the mountains.

The neighborhood I grew up in had a typical array of characters of whom I have vivid memories. Next door to us lived two unmarried sisters, the Millards. They were elderly and very kind to us young children. Across the street from them were the Tedescos. They were recent immigrants from Italy; he, an accomplished pianist. The Tedescos were not friendly to us kids, and we were certainly not very culturally sensitive. They would frequently yell at us to get us off their property. As a consequence, they became the Boo Radley of the neighborhood. We tested our courage by venturing close to the Tedescos' house and tempting our fate. As a small child my most frequent babysitters were two maiden sisters, Bertha and Genevieve Wolfe. They lived in a very small house down the street. Being in their sixties, they babysat neighborhood kids for a living. If our parents left town, they stayed at the house with us.

Linda Carlson was my childhood girlfriend who lived across the street. By the time I was four or five I was having frequent arguments with another childhood friend, Gary Megel, as to which of us was going to marry Linda. We spent our preschool days riding around on stick horses. I was Monty Montana, the great rodeo cowboy. We also hitched rides around the neighborhood in the truck of Martin the Milkman. The fact that he and the postman were among the very few who drove our isolated street each day did not deter us from sometimes spending the whole day tending a lemonade stand. The five to ten cents in daily revenues were deemed well worth the effort. Years later Gary Megel would become a jeweler and I would be a longtime customer. Linda Carlson would become a veterinarian.

The biggest difference between my childhood and what I observe about children today was the amount of time we spent creatively entertaining ourselves. Almost all the activity took place outdoors. We could spend hours or even days playing in a space capsule constructed from cardboard boxes. While we had some structured time playing little league baseball or taking swimming lessons, we also spent many hours lying in the grass and staring at the clouds passing by. I now believe such childhood "boredom" is necessary to a full appreciation of the wonders of the universe and to the cultivation of poets and artists. It is also mind boggling to think about all the modern conveniences we take for granted today that did not exist during my childhood. My parents did not have credit cards. My grade school did not have a copying machine (we used mimeographs). We had no calculators (we used slide rules), no microwaves, no cell phones, no pagers, no faxes, no cable or satellite TV, no home computers and, of course, no internet, email, or videogames. We didn't get a colored television until I was in high school. No one I knew had air-conditioning in their house or car. When I was very young, I remember having to wait until our neighbors got off the telephone so that we could use the party line that we shared with them. Describing a party line phone to my children made my childhood sound quite primitive. I understood how my parents felt trying to explain to us what life was like before automobiles, television, or refrigerators.

When I was four or five an incident occurred that I remember vividly and which, although traumatic at the time, probably had a very positive impact on me. My mother bought her groceries at a small store on Nevada Avenue called Hoyle's. (Only some years later would a Safeway locate in our vicinity.) Hoyle's was incredibly small in comparison to today's grocery chain stores. On one occasion when my mom refused to buy me a candy bar, I took one off a stand and surreptitiously put it in my pocket, without telling my mom. When I got home, I took it out to eat, but instead I was overcome by incredible guilt. I went to my mother and confessed my misdeed, probably believing, on the basis of early indoctrination, that it was the only way to avoid the fires of hell. My mother immediately drove me back to the store and I went with her to the store owner and used my ten cents per week allowance to pay for the candy bar. I can honestly say that for the rest of my life I have not been tempted to pilfer anything else. I believe that incidents of that nature, and how they are handled by parents, are incredibly important in the process of raising children. They are the means by which values are imparted from parent to child. Aristotle opined over 3,000 years ago that teaching children "habits of the heart" was the only way to ensure they would grow up to be virtuous citizens. My parents were very good role models in that regard. Janet and I would assume a similar no-tolerance policy in the upbringing of our own children.

I am fairly certain I was six when my parents told me I was adopted and explained what that meant. They said it was such a great event for them that they wanted to celebrate my adoption day as well as my birthday. And we did for several years thereafter, usually by going out to a fancy place for dinner. Presents were reserved for the birthday party.

I was eight when my father found it necessary to sit me down and tell me about the birds and the bees. My sister had been making fun of me because of my sexual ignorance. I was initially disgusted at the notion that people did such things, but the disgust dissipated quickly when I became a teenager.

My mother was a housewife as long as my father was alive, although she was an avid volunteer for a variety of causes and for several years worked part-time for several hours a week to help out a very good friend, Miriam Loo. Miriam had started a note card business in her basement and my mom was her only part-time employee for the first few years. I recall playing on the floor of the Loos' basement, or following one of the Loos' sons around, while my mom stacked cards and packaged them for nonprofit groups who re-sold them as a fundraising project. Miriam's business, named Current Inc., grew tremendously through the years and two of her sons, Dusty and Gary, became actively involved. The Loo family sold the business in the mid-1980s for a reported $115 million. Over the years the Loos became local philanthropists and faithful political supporters of mine. They financially supported the Scholar-in-Residence position I held at the University of Colorado Colorado Springs.

I walked to and from school each day, approximately a mile each way. Typically, two or three of us from the neighborhood walked together to the parish grade school. In what was almost Huck Finn-like fashion, in the spring we would often stop on the way home and fish in Cheyenne Creek for brook trout. My classmate Peter Granger had an uncanny ability to catch fish with his bare hands. My mother was typically at home when I arrived after school. She would often prepare a snack for me before I went out to play or sat down in the basement to watch my favorite TV show, *The Three Stooges.* The television we watched was dramatically different from today. You could watch an entire week of prime-time TV without a hint of violence or sexual innuendo. By the time my daughters were teenagers you couldn't watch thirty minutes without a heavy dose of both.

I often hear people speak with ridicule about the *Ozzie and Harriet* and *Leave It to Beaver* lifestyle of the 1950s and early 60s. They suggest it was unrealistic and demeaning to women. Some suggest it was hypocritical. I believe I can say with great confidence that my mother had no qualms about her life as a homemaker and mother and did not find it the least bit demeaning. She viewed nurturing her children as her job. It also worked well for us kids.

In addition to Miriam Loo and her husband Orin, my parents had many other close friends that contributed to the warm and nurturing environment that I experienced as a child. Close friends in the neighborhood included Marge and Payson Gregory, who moved from Michigan to Colorado Springs about the same time as my parents and wound up living a very short distance away. They were present at nearly every significant event of my childhood. Two other close friends that lived nearby were Kay and Horton Johnson. The Johnsons' oldest son married the Gregorys' daughter. Kay Johnson was my kindergarten teacher at Cheyenne Canyon Elementary School. Both Marge Gregory and Kay Johnson would long outlive my parents, and Janet and I would make sure to visit them periodically throughout their lives.

My parents entertained their friends quite a bit. The parties were modest but lively. I especially recall barbeques on our back patio. Kids were both seen and heard at most of the get-togethers.

I also recall with some amusement that my parents had a cocktail hour virtually every night when my dad got home from work. It was a ritual for them and for most couples of their generation. It is one tradition I am glad we did not carry on. My parents, like so many of their contemporaries, also smoked cigarettes. My father successfully kicked the habit at forty-five after I was adopted. My mother smoked until the day she died, despite my attempts to discourage it. It was another habit I am glad I did not acquire.

My mother cooked dinner almost every night. The entire meal was home cooked. There was no fast food until McDonald's came to Colorado Springs in about 1963, when I was twelve years old. TV dinners were available beginning in the 1950s, but they had a "tinny" taste to them that my parents detested. We rarely went out to a restaurant except to celebrate a special occasion. All our dinners were at the kitchen table and family discussions were encouraged. On Saturday and Sunday nights, our family often watched television together. As I recall, we always watched *Gunsmoke* on Saturdays and *The Ed Sullivan Show* on Sunday. I vividly remember the Beatles' first appearance on *The Ed Sullivan Show* in February of 1964 and my bewilderment at what my sister was so excited about. I also remember asking my mom why Marshall Dillon and Miss Kitty didn't get married. Our favorite game shows to watch were *To Tell the Truth* and *What's My Line?*

My father worked incredibly hard, and I believe he was instrumental in my development of a good work ethic at an early age. Dentistry was a much different profession in the 1950s and 60s than it is today. My father cleaned his patients' teeth himself. Unlike today, he did not have multiple hygienists cleaning teeth and generating income while he was performing other dental services. He also arrived at the office at 6:30 a.m. to do lab work before he started seeing patients. Dentists today send virtually all their lab work out to a commercial lab. He also frequently worked on Saturdays, at least in the winter. When he opened his first dental office in Colorado Springs his assistant, Liz Parish, would answer the phone with the greeting, "No others but Suthers." It would become a family slogan of sorts. Eventually, in 1961, my father was joined in the dental practice by my uncle Jim Ryan, my mother's youngest brother. Only then did he start to take off a bit more time. Years later, in 1975, when I was cleaning out our family home on Arroya Street in order to sell it, I ran across my parents' tax returns.

In 1966, my father's last full year of dental practice before his death, his taxable income was $6,700. While it seems like a paltry amount today, I've since discovered it was fairly typical of professional compensation at the time.

When I was about twelve, I remember overhearing a conversation involving my father that has much greater significance for me today than it did at the time. He was speaking to his good friend Al Cheney. Al and Helen Cheney had an African American housekeeper named Ruth. Ruth needed dental attention and Al asked my father to care for her. He agreed to do so, but only on a Saturday morning. That's apparently when he saw Black patients. On the one hand, I now view my father's unwillingness to let his other patients know that he had Black patients as cowardly. On the other hand, I credit him for his willingness to make sure they were cared for. Given the tenor of the times, the early sixties before the civil rights legislation of 1964, I am slow to condemn him for it. But it is something I thought of frequently when we raised our children. Janet and I were always careful not to tolerate any racial or ethnic bias in the presence of our daughters and to encourage them to judge people based on their personal interactions.

Our family income was sufficient to allow us to take occasional automobile vacations that were a significant part of my childhood education. A lot of family bonding took place when all four of us were in the car together for ten hours a day. I was intellectually very curious and absorbed a tremendous amount of information on trips to California, Niagara Falls, Mesa Verde, the Grand Canyon, Yellowstone, and other places. My lifelong love of history was at least partially inspired by these adventures. Our trip to Yellowstone in August of 1959 was particularly eventful for a youngster. I got briefly chased by a bear, and we were awakened just before midnight on August 17th when the trailer we were staying in shook somewhat violently. It turned out we were a short distance from the epicenter of one of the largest earthquakes ever to occur on the

North American continent. Around thirty people were killed before the park was evacuated.

We didn't travel in luxury. My father often rented a small sixteen-foot motor home from U-Haul and pulled it behind our white Rambler station wagon. All four of us slept in the motor home and it was a bit crowded. I also recall it was not unusual for the car to overheat and for us to stop for periodic repairs.

We also took two trips to Detroit during my childhood to visit relatives, particularly my mother's many siblings. For the most part, the Ryan clan got along famously, and I have fond memories of my aunts and uncles. They all had a good sense of humor. One family prank that dragged out over a decade involved my parents and my mother's siblings passing back and forth two urns containing the ashes of Jack and Laura McKinney, old family friends who had died childless and apparently with no plans for disposing of their remains. When one couple visited the other, the host typically found the McKinneys' urns on their mantle after the guests had left. I also viewed my aunts and uncles through the naïveté of childhood. My uncle George Kurzava, for example, who was my godfather, was the one I liked the most because he was always so playful with the kids. Only years later did I learn he was an incorrigible alcoholic, apparently stemming from traumatic combat experiences in World War II.

It was in Detroit that I got to attend my first Major League Baseball games. I've often said that one of the best days of my life was a Saturday in July of 1961 when, as a nine-year-old, my Uncle Vince DeCorte took me to a doubleheader between the Detroit Tigers and the New York Yankees. Frank Larry, who was known as the "Yankee Killer," pitched Detroit to victory in the first game. Norm Cash was having a career season for the Tigers. Al Kaline was typically excellent. But the Tigers, despite a great start that year, could not keep pace with the likes of Whitey Ford, Mickey Mantle, and Roger Maris, who would wind up breaking Babe Ruth's home run record in the 1961 season. Until the Colorado

Rockies were formed in 1993, the Detroit Tigers remained my favorite team. One of my most prized possessions is a baseball sent to me by Uncle Vince which was signed by the Tigers' 1968 World Series Championship team. I was an avid young baseball player myself and experiences of that nature would make me a lifetime fan of the game and an avid collector of baseball cards and memorabilia.

In fact, from the age of about seven to about thirteen, I was obsessed with baseball. I would spend hours at a time throwing a baseball against a cement wall in our front driveway and making spectacular diving catches of the rebounds. I would constantly oil my glove, put a ball in its pocket, wrap a belt around it and put it under my pillow at night. I could name the starting lineup for virtually every team in Major League Baseball.

Among the fondest memories of my childhood were the times I spent with my father attending sporting events and going fishing. He was a great sports fan. He particularly liked hockey, having played it in his youth, and would take me to Colorado College games. Though a small liberal arts college in Colorado Springs, CC played big-time college hockey. Many of the games were on weeknights and I would hurry home from school and do my homework in order to earn the privilege of attending the game and staying out late. We also went to numerous high school and Air Force Academy football games. We also went fishing frequently in the summer. We belonged to a fishing club on the Tarryall River near Lake George. In 1964 my father and I went fishing with my schoolmate Steve Lusk and his father to Taylor Reservoir near Gunnison, Colorado. We caught lots of fish. Such adventures in the Colorado mountains were all it took to give me a lifelong love of fishing and the incredible beauty of Colorado. From the age of sixteen on, I would return to Taylor Reservoir and the Taylor River virtually every summer for the next thirty-five years. There is nothing quite as inspiring as time spent in solitude fishing a river or stream. I agree with Herbert Hoover when he said, "I'm quite certain God won't subtract from your life the time you spend fishing."

In the winter, we frequently went sledding or skiing. When I was a child, skiing was much less popular and much less expensive than it has since become. The glorious beauty of Colorado was as apparent to me on the ski slopes in the winter as it was on a trout stream in the summer. I've never stopped thanking God that fate brought Jeanne Fischer (and me) to Colorado.

In the 1950s and '60s, Colorado Springs was a city of fewer than 100,000 people and it had a small-town feel to it. My mother dropped us off on Saturday mornings at the Chief Theater in downtown Colorado Springs. For ten cents we watched cartoons and children's movies for several hours. The crime rate was extremely low, and safety was not a big concern. The circus came to town each year and the annual Pikes Peak or Bust Rodeo was a must-see event. All in all, it was a great place to grow up.

My father did not live long enough for me to acquire a realistic sense of his strengths and weaknesses as a man. I have only the perspective of a young boy. I think he was pretty intelligent, and I know he had a great sense of humor. In fact, I frequently use a few of his musings that made a significant impression on me. I can still hear him referring sarcastically to someone or something as being as "useless as a one-legged guy in an ass-kicking contest." And he would often sum up the fruits of his day's labor by saying, "another day, another dollar." I also remember him frequently referring to me as "Honest Abe." In a few short years he did a remarkable job of imparting to me philosophical underpinnings that would be the basis of my views as an adult. In hindsight, I believe the amount of quality time we spent together during my adolescence was to some extent a reflection of the fact he suspected, because of his genetics, that he might not be around during my high school and college years.

My parents were devout Catholics. They prayed together on their knees every night. Often, they said the Rosary together. They attended Novenas to the Mother of Perpetual Help on Monday nights. We never ate meat on Fridays. We fasted on every Holy Day. We went to Mass every Sunday and often to daily Mass during the week. The preparation of my sister and me for the sacraments of Holy Communion, Reconciliation, and Confirmation was taken very seriously. We dutifully participated in the May Crowning celebration at church every year. I can still remember the words to the song "Daily, Daily Sing to Mary." There was a crucifix on the wall of each bedroom in our house. It was a forgone conclusion that Sharon and I would go to Catholic school. While their inspiration was enough to ensure I would actively practice the Catholic faith throughout my life, I admit I have fallen short of the standard they set.

Our family's Irish heritage was evident in a number of ways. St. Patrick's Day was a big event. My mother always attended a St. Patrick's Day card party at our church. We kids always dressed in green and were typically adorned with a shamrock. We always had codfish on Friday nights and roast beef and potatoes on Sunday night. An Irish blessing hung on the wall in our kitchen. My father affectionately referred to my mother as Mother McCree. My wife and I, and our children, have always remained proud of our Irish heritage.

Like most people of their generation, my parents were driven by a sense of duty and responsibility. Unlike so many in my generation, they did not view their personal happiness as their ultimate purpose in life. Happiness was the biproduct of a virtuous life. I believe they genuinely enjoyed life, but they also understood it was short and often brutish and sorrow filled. Their strong faith in God sustained them. They also wanted very much for their children to succeed. My father in particular took great pride in my school and sports accomplishments. When I was quite young, I remember telling my father I wanted to be a garbage man. He responded, "I don't care if you become a garbage man, as long as you are the best darn garbage man that ever lived." But I knew better. Even as a young boy I had a sense that my parents had high expectations for me.

Chapter V
I Survived Catholic School

In 1958 I entered first grade at our local parish elementary school. Pauline Memorial School had been constructed a few years earlier as yet another gift to the parish by Julie Penrose, the wife of mining magnate Spencer Penrose.

I vividly remember every teacher I had during my eight years at Pauline School. As is typical of the aging process, my long-term memory has remained very good despite a marked decrease in short-term memory. My first-grade teacher, Sister John William, was a stern disciplinarian who managed to teach forty-eight first graders how to read proficiently. My second-grade teacher, Miss Walz, had moved from Chicago and was a Chicago White Sox fan. We talked about baseball every day. She convinced me to start collecting baseball cards. I still had an allowance of a dime a week. I would often stop at the small neighborhood grocery store on my way home from school and buy five baseball cards and a stick of bubble gum for a nickel. Between 1959 and 1966, I bought about 1,000 baseball cards for a total of about $10. Little did I know they would someday be worth over $10,000.

In the fifth grade, Sister Anne Pauline made me memorize Latin so efficiently that I was the first in the class to be chosen to serve Mass as an altar boy. It was a big deal. I had a huge crush on my sixth-grade teacher, Miss Holmberg. She was probably twenty-three or twenty-four and I was jealous of the boyfriend who picked her up after school each day. My seventh-grade teacher, George Ulrich, was very encouraging of my intellectual curiosity and predicted that I would get into politics. I remember him saying,

"You're going to be governor, or mayor, or attorney general, or someone important like that." He was a member of our parish and would closely follow my career for the rest of his life until his death in 2009. He often reminded me of his accurate prognostication.

Catholic schools of bygone days are often the subject of humorous depictions—if not ridicule—even by those of us who experienced them firsthand. The image of Sister Mary Ignatius, in full habit, breaking a ruler over the knuckles of a hapless first grader who committed some minor infraction, or lecturing young students on the purpose of limbo, is part of today's folklore and literary satire. I have seen people sport buttons that read, "I survived Catholic school." In fact, a friend gave me one. For my part, I not only survived Catholic education, but I thrived on it. It may not have been for everyone, but I believe the very traditional Catholic grade school education I received at Pauline was instrumental in my personal formation and in the formation of the value system that I have carried throughout my life. Sure, we memorized the Baltimore Catechism, recited prayers daily, and dutifully attended Mass every Friday. But our daily routine was also permeated with discussion about fundamental moral values. My lifelong intolerance for lying, stealing, and cheating began at Pauline, as well as at home. I believe the Catholic guilt I acquired was the formation of my lifelong circumspection about the purpose and meaning of life and the role of character in becoming a virtuous citizen.

And there was no question whether our teachers cared about us. They dedicated their lives to teach us, with little or no compensation. I developed excellent verbal, reading, and writing skills largely because of the encouragement I received from teachers at Pauline. We diagrammed sentences *ad nauseum* and participated in frequent spelling bees. The first prize was typically... you guessed it, a holy card. In schoolwide competitions you might even win a Rosary or a St. Christopher medal! The parish priest, Fr. Harrington, who became a monsignor while I was in grade school, would personally pass out the report cards each quarter and express his pleasure that Johnny Suthers had achieved straight A's.

The nuns at Pauline were also blunt about a student's shortcomings. There wasn't the obsession with self-esteem found in schools today. In third or fourth grade, they had us all sing a few notes and divided the class into the red birds, the blue birds, and a third unnamed group that was instructed to silently mouth the words. I was in the third group, which the other students nicknamed the crows.

At Pauline I learned to love reading. By fifth and sixth grade I was reading a Hardy Boys mystery for fun almost every week. By seventh and eighth grade I had begun to read about the lives of accomplished people. It was the beginning of a lifelong habit. No matter how busy my life would become, I would always spend a few minutes before bedtime each night reading something I was not required to read. I came to enjoy non-fiction more than fiction, particularly biographies, but I liked just about anything other than science fiction.

It was at Pauline that I got my first taste of politics, serving as elected class president in the sixth and seventh grade then being elected student council president my eighth grade year. My campaign slogan was, "No others but Suthers."

My sixth-grade year in 1963-64 was particularly significant in a couple of respects. On November 22, 1963, I was gleefully playing kickball on the playground during noon recess when we were called into our classroom and told by our teacher that the president of the United States, John F. Kennedy, had been killed by an assassin in Dallas, Texas. I can still point to the exact spot I was sitting in the classroom when I heard the news. I suspect the fact that Kennedy was the first Catholic president contributed to the grief we all felt. I became very absorbed in the events of the following days, sensing the historic significance of the times, and I believe it further helped to foster my growing fascination with American history.

In the spring of 1964, a team of three sixth graders, including myself, debated a team of seventh graders in the school auditorium. The debate was attended by the fifth, sixth, seventh, and eighth grade classes, Monsignor Harrington, the school principal, and interested parents. Frankly, I do not remember the precise topic, although it had something to do with the merits of private versus public education. Given the audience, my team had the enviable task of promoting private education. I do remember that when it came time to rebut the opponent's arguments, I pulled out a copy of *US News and World Report* which contained information that devastatingly undermined one of their principal contentions. I had made a strategic decision not to expose the information in my opening remarks, believing it would be much more effective in rebuttal. I took a chance and was right. The opposition was speechless and demoralized. I betrayed no emotion. It was a Perry Mason-like performance. After the sixth-grade team was awarded a decisive victory by the judges, the school principal, Sister John Catherine, came up to me and resolutely said, "John, you ought to be a lawyer." I didn't know how to respond. No one I knew at the time was a lawyer, and I had never thought about the prospect. That night, I asked my parents what lawyers did exactly. As it turned out, Sister John Catherine had not only planted a seed, but had also applied a very heavy dose of fertilizer. I began to think about law as a possible career. In fact, as I reflect on it, it was the only career counseling I ever received.

Sister John Catherine was also the first to tell me I should think about going to Notre Dame. She spent a summer there and brought back brochures about the campus, but her strong encouragement was probably less of an influence than the Notre Dame football team.

In the fall of 1964, when I was in seventh grade, I got a call late one Friday evening from Monsignor Harrington. He was calling his favorite altar boy to see if I could serve Mass at 8 a.m. the next morning for the Notre Dame football team, which was staying at the adjacent Broadmoor Hotel before a Saturday afternoon game against the Air Force Academy. It was Notre Dame's first trip to Colorado Springs. At the Mass I met Ara Parseghian (Notre Dame's first-year coach), quarterback John Huarte (who would win the Heisman Trophy that year), star receiver Jack Snow, and future NFL star Alan Page. (Many years later I would play golf with John Huarte at a local Notre Dame Club tournament and Alan Page, by then a Minnesota Supreme Court Justice, would be the commencement speaker at my daughter Kate's graduation from Notre Dame.) Over the next several years, Monsignor Harrington took every opportunity to encourage me to attend Notre Dame. From his perspective, for a good Catholic boy who wanted to go to a good college, there was no alternative.

It was at Pauline that I began to develop a modicum of athletic talent and a lifelong competitive spirit. Fr. Daniel Kelleher, the assistant pastor of the parish, was the athletic director at the school and strongly encouraged participation in sports. I played baseball every summer in a park and recreation league. I typically made the all-star team. My mother learned to keep a baseball scorebook, and I can still hear her rooting loudly from the stands. A victory, or even a good effort, always earned a trip to A&W Root Beer after the game. I also fared well in summertime golf tournaments, winning several trophies. In hindsight, I wish I had taken the game much more seriously. It would be the only sport I'd still be playing fifty years later. Pauline participated in a Catholic School League in track, basketball, and baseball. From the first through eighth grade, I was the fastest runner in my class and consistently won the 100-yard dash in the Catholic all-city track meets. I was a hustling point guard in basketball. In eighth grade our team was undefeated in the local Catholic league and had a 12-1 record against the city's much larger public junior high schools. Pauline had only twenty boys in the seventh and eighth grade! The season culminated with the

Catholic state championship game in which we lost to St. Francis of Denver 42-41 in double overtime. I consider that team my first great lesson in the benefits of effective teamwork. We had one terrific player, Jeff Holmes, and four competent players who accepted assigned roles, which led to success far beyond what we thought we were capable of. Our coach, Bev Godec, drilled us on fundamentals and impressed on us the fact that you can't be the best unless you take on the best. Our baseball team that year, also coached by Godec, was even more successful. I played shortstop on a team that went undefeated and hosted St. Theresa's of Denver in the state championship game. I came to bat in the bottom of the seventh and last inning with Pauline trailing 2-1. There were two outs and one man on base. I drove a high fast ball over the centerfield's head for a home run and was carried off the field on the shoulders of my teammates. It was a euphoria I have obviously never forgotten. Further, the David versus Goliath aura of our success helped my confidence in future years when I encountered situations in which I felt somewhat intimidated by the apparent superiority of the competition.

A lot has been said and written about the pros and cons of exposing young children to too much competition and on the issue of whether such competition helps build character. Because of my own experience, I think competition, in proper doses, is quite healthy for children. The world is competitive, and kids need to learn that early on. People also need to learn how to win and how to lose. And that they can learn a lot from the competition itself that makes them better prepared for future challenges. I know my wife and kids think I've been overly competitive throughout my life, but I would counter that competition can make most activities, including a recreational round of golf, more interesting.

It was during the summers after seventh and eighth grade that I became an entrepreneur. My grade school chum Tom Kane and I started a lawn mowing business. We both lived on the outskirts of the wealthy Broadmoor area of town and our parents had many friends that were susceptible to our solicitations. We had all the business we could handle and learned valuable lessons about economics and customer service. Hard physical labor in the Colorado sunshine was an ideal way for young men to spend a summer. (My only regret is that sunscreen hadn't been invented yet. It may have saved me from a constant battle with minor forms of skin cancer after the age of forty.) Many decades later, after I had been district attorney, US attorney, attorney general, and mayor of Colorado Springs, I would still overhear some elderly former customers remark to others, "He was the best lawn boy we ever had." Some of my old lawn business customers in the Broadmoor would also be the ones who nominated me, by then a successful young lawyer, for membership in the prestigious and exclusive Cheyenne Mountain Country Club.

As valedictorian of my graduating class from Pauline in June of 1966, I gave a speech, the content of which I have no recollection whatsoever. I was also awarded a full-tuition academic and athletic scholarship to St. Mary's High School, the city's only Catholic high school.

Chapter VI
Sic Transit Gloria Mundi

St. Mary's High School was located in downtown Colorado Springs. It was originally built as part of St. Mary's Parish, the oldest in the city. The high school was started in 1885 by the Sisters of Loretto and the order still ran the school when I enrolled in September of 1966. In about 1960, an adjacent parish grade school had closed, and the high school occupied that space as well as the original building. The original building was not only seventy-five years old, but it was also painted a rather unsightly green. While I was there, school athletic teams on bus trips would sing, "We go to school in a dirty green latrine" to the tune of the Beatles' song "We All Live in a Yellow Submarine." In the fall of 1966, the school had an enrollment of over 500. Our freshman class was around 140. The school had great esprit de corps which tended to revolve around its sports teams. My father's dental practice was less than a mile from the school and he dropped me off in the morning during my freshman year. If I did not have sports after school, I would take the bus home. If I did have sports practice, I would catch a ride home with my father.

On the basis of an entrance exam, I was put in a group of the best students. I excelled, managing to get straight A's my freshman year, except for gym class in the fall semester, in which I got a B. That was curious because I was a model student and quite athletic and I had been chosen captain of the freshman basketball team. But the gym teacher was an assistant football coach that refused to give any boy an A who did not go out for football. In fact, I would wind up going out for track my freshman year, rather than baseball, my first love, because the football and track coach, Ed Kintz, essentially challenged the manhood of male students who did not go out for either football or track. In the fall each year he put a sign over the front entrance of the school that read, "In the fall the leaves turn yellow. Do you? See you at the first football practice." Kintz was one of those overzealous high school coaches that his players never forget. They're the topic of conversation even at the fiftieth high school reunion.

My social life at St. Mary's also got off to a good start. I took Rosie Sayers, one of the most popular girls in the class, to homecoming. On the last day of school my freshman year, I was elected president of the next year's sophomore class. As far as I was concerned, life was almost perfect. But two days later I changed my mind.

On Sunday morning June 4, 1967, I awoke about 7 a.m. and went out to the living room in my pajamas. I retrieved the morning paper from the driveway and, as I always did, started with the sports page. The night before my parents had discussed attending 8:30 a.m. Mass and then playing golf. I was starting to get pretty good at the game and liked to play with my parents. The day before my parents had attended a wedding and my father had gone to bed early because he did not feel well. He said we would play golf if he felt better in the morning.

About 7:30 I was startled when I heard my mother scream from my parents' bedroom. As I started down the hallway to their room my mother ran past me sobbing and saying something I could not comprehend. As I heard her pick up the phone in the kitchen and start dialing, I looked in the door of my parents' bedroom. I did not need to get any closer. I saw my father's rigid, lifeless body, lying in the bed, eyes open, staring at the ceiling. I do not remember anything that transpired from that point until the mortician removed the body from the house an hour or so later. I suspect I was in shock.

My father had died of a massive heart attack at the age of fifty-nine. His premature death seemed inconceivable to me because he was so active and careful about diet and exercise. But he was doomed by genetics, especially in the era before bypasses and other preventive surgical procedures. Both his father and grandfather had died of a heart attack at the same age. It was yet another reason to feel fortunate that I was adopted.

My mom's brother, Jim Ryan, who practiced dentistry with my dad, and his wife, my Aunt Jo, were our only relatives in Colorado Springs and, along with the Gregorys and the Johnsons, who lived in the neighborhood, were among the first to arrive at the house that morning. I recall Horton Johnson, who was dying of cancer, walking in the house with a look of grief on his face and saying to us, "I was sure I would be the first to go." I also have a very vivid recollection of my uncle Jim and me standing in the backyard of our home later that afternoon. I was crying. I remember saying repeatedly, "I was going to make him so proud of me." And I remember his response. "You still can," he said. I took his words to heart. He told me that because my sister Sharon was in college now, I would shoulder more responsibility for my mother's well-being.

My father's picture appeared on the front page of the local newspaper, the *Gazette-Telegraph*, the next day with an article captioned, "Prominent Local Dentist Dies." Over 800 people attended his funeral, including his two older sisters, many friends and patients, and several relatives from around the country.

My father's sudden death was clearly the most traumatic event of my life, and I am now convinced it had a profound impact on the course of it. In fact, in hindsight, it was *the* defining event of my life. To this day, I cannot think about it without tears welling in my eyes. I believe it was an event that caused me to grow up much faster than I otherwise would have and made me much more focused at a young age. I became resolutely centered on the meaning and purpose of life and the desire to live a consequential one. Further, while I am generally not into psychoanalysis, especially of myself, I suspect that much of the ambition I have manifested in my life stems from a largely subconscious obsession to make my adoptive parents, particularly my father, proud of me and perhaps even to prove my worth to the biological parents who gave me up. I wasn't willing to acknowledge that possibility until much later in life.

Over the next few years, I would frequently lie in bed at night listening to my mother crying. She was a strong and determined woman but had been traumatized by the suddenness of her loss. While I felt relatively helpless to assuage her grief, I did work hard to help her lead an active life. My father left a paid-for house, a $25,000 life insurance policy and about $20,000 in other liquid assets. Because my sister was in college and I was approaching college, and because her social security survivor benefit was fairly minimal, my mom went back to work full time for the first time since she had been married thirty years earlier. After brushing up on her secretarial skills, she went to work for the American Numismatic Association (ANA), a national coin collectors' organization based in Colorado Springs. She soon became the secretary to the executive director of the ANA. The ANA was not far from St. Mary's High School, and I would frequently stop by to visit her during the day. One of her responsibilities was organizing the annual national convention held each August, and I accompanied her to such meetings in New Orleans, Boston, and Washington, DC.

The trip to Washington, DC was my first, and we stayed several extra days to see the sites. We toured the White House, the Supreme Court, the Capitol, the Smithsonian, and all the monuments. Neither my mother nor I could have envisioned that over the next sixty years I would return to DC well over 200 times to meet with presidents, cabinet members, to testify before Congress, to argue in the Supreme Court, and to be a plaintiff in one of the most high-profile Supreme Court cases in history.

Although my mother was only fifty-two when my father died, and she was asked out by several men over the next several years, she never accepted. My sister and I were her only focus. It also would have been very understandable if my mother had used my father's death as a reason to suggest that I downgrade my ambitions regarding college and graduate school. It would have been in her interest that I go to a state school close to home. But she never once suggested to me that I do so. Only years later did I fully appreciate her sacrifice.

In both my freshman and sophomore years in high school, I was required to take Latin. My teacher was an elderly nun named Sister Georgetta. She was close to eighty and stood no more than five feet tall. She took her vow of humility so seriously that she never allowed herself to be photographed. She was one of several nuns at St. Mary's who came over to our house the day after my father died to assure me they would assist me in an attempt to get a college scholarship. They had all been pro bono patients of his.

Despite her size and her age, Sister Georgetta was a stern disciplinarian who had absolute control over her classroom. To compensate for her height, she sat at a desk on a foot-high platform situated in the front of the classroom. But the key to maintaining control was putting each student's name on an index card, the boys by their last name and the girls by their first name. She would constantly shuffle the deck of index cards. When she would ask a question, as she did constantly, she would draw a card and call upon the named student. If the student did not correctly respond in a few seconds, she would draw the next card. Because the deck of index cards was constantly being shuffled, a student who had just been called upon could not relax, lest he or she be called upon again in short order. The resulting tension was the key to a very quiet classroom.

Sister Georgetta was a recognized Latin scholar who periodically spent summers analyzing ancient documents at the Vatican. She was also a student of Roman history. She would frequently interject stories about the Roman Empire into our Latin class, particularly during my sophomore year. One day she described the typical scene when Roman conquerors would return to Rome from foreign conquests. The ceremony was called a triumph. Thousands of Roman citizens would line the Appian Way, exalting as the campaign's heroes paraded by, each on their own horse-drawn chariot. Positioned behind each hero on his chariot was a slave whose job it was to continuously whisper into the hero's ear, "*Sic transit gloria mundi*," which means, "thus passes the glory of the world." The admonition was to serve as a reminder that life is short and uncertain, fame is fleeting, a good soldier puts service above self, and that character is all that endures. The admonition was also used in subsequent centuries at the investiture of a new Pope as the Bishop of Rome. Perhaps it was because it came soon after my father's death, my first dramatic confrontation with mortality, or perhaps it was because she told the story in such a captivating fashion, or perhaps both, that the story Sister Georgetta told that day made such a great impression on me.

In May of 1970, at my high school graduation, I received several honors, and it was announced that I had received a scholarship to the University of Notre Dame. After the ceremony, as I was leaving in a hurry to play in the city all-star baseball game, I had a brief conversation with Sister Georgetta. In her parting words she looked me straight in the eye and said, "Remember John, *sic transit gloria mundi*." It was the last time I saw her. She died a few years later. But I would never forget her parting admonition, and I would relate the story of Sister Georgetta to friends, family, and selected groups for the rest of my life.

On the day I was sworn in as the elected District Attorney of the Fourth Judicial District of Colorado in January of 1989, I took my family to look at my new office after the swearing-in ceremony. My sister Sharon then presented me with a small needlepoint banner, about ten inches high, that read, "*Sic transit gloria mundi*." I put it on the wall next to the door of my office. It has been similarly situated in every office I have occupied since, serving as a constant reminder of where I came from and cautioning me to be less concerned about what headlines might result from the decisions

I make and more concerned about the integrity of those decisions. Just as it was to ancient Romans, it is also a reminder to me that character is all that endures.

I believe Sister Georgetta's admonition to me, particularly at a time when I was searching for meaning in life, is at least partly responsible for my decision to spend so much of my career in public service. Many years later, I established a scholarship fund at St. Mary's High School in honor of Sister Georgetta.

Chapter VII
Even the "Goose" Couldn't Strike Me Out

High school proved to be a great experience for me. People make their closest friendships at varying stages of life. Many of mine are ones I made in high school. I met Bob Schneebeck when he was assigned as my locker mate in the middle of my freshman year. He had just transferred from a high school seminary. We've been lifelong friends and fishing buddies ever since. We went to Notre Dame together and he has been my stockbroker since 1976. Tom Kane, who had been a classmate at Pauline and a partner in the lawn mowing business, also went to St. Mary's and we were involved in student government together. We went to law school together and he also became a lawyer and eventually a judge. I have greatly valued his friendship. Ed Rivera, a high school buddy, was in my wedding. Mike and Betty Faricy were also St. Mary's classmates who became lifelong friends. My lifelong friendship with Jack Wiepking began in high school when we played for opposing baseball teams.

At St. Mary's, I dated several girls and learned a lot about what was important to me in such relationships. I tended to date very intelligent girls who were the best students in school. Some guys felt intimidated by smart girls. Not me. I found them the most interesting and I knew early on that I would eventually marry one.

As you might suspect at a Catholic high school in the late 1960s, illicit drug use was virtually non-existent. I was told of people who smoked pot, but never witnessed it myself. None of my close friends ever drank alcohol until we reached the age of eighteen and were able to lawfully imbibe 3.2 percent (alcohol) beer. Years later, when I would have to disqualify otherwise well-qualified people from sensitive government jobs because of illicit drug use in their youth, I would occasionally be challenged by them as to whether I had ever used drugs as a youth. I could honestly answer that I was never even tempted to do so.

In the fall of my sophomore year, I was required to do a science project. Inspired by a Time Life book about mathematics that my parents bought me, I did a project in which a laboratory mouse would choose between three doors, each alternately marked with one, two, or three geometric shapes. The food was placed at the end of the maze behind the door with two geometric shapes. The experiment was meant to determine whether the mouse could distinguish the number of geometric symbols. My conclusion was that the mouse, after considerable training, could eventually distinguish two symbols from one and three and I posed the question whether this ability to distinguish multiplicity exhibited some fundamental level of mathematical understanding. As the winner of the school science fair, I was required by my teacher to enter the project in the National Aeronautics and Space Administration's Annual Youth Science Contest. While my project earned an A for me in my science class, I frankly had no other ambitions for it. But in the spring of 1968, I received a letter from NASA inviting me to attend a Youth Science Congress and exhibit my project to a panel of scientists and other contest winners. I excitedly accepted the invitation, having little idea what I was in for. When I arrived at the NASA conference, I immediately determined that I was the only sophomore present. There were two juniors, and the rest were seniors. The fact I had shaved my head for the track season exacerbated my immature appearance. I also quickly noticed something else. I was intellectually out of my league. While I was among the smartest students at St. Mary's High School, these kids were virtual geniuses. Their projects were infinitely more complex than mine and their scientific and mathematical knowledge base was greatly superior. After each presentation the panel of scientists as well as other students asked questions. As the time approached to make my presentation, I became increasingly nervous. The two presenters before me only heightened my anxiety. One was from New Mexico and had constructed a small observatory in his backyard from which he tracked the orbital degeneration of satellites. He was so proficient at it that NASA paid him $1,000 a month to share his findings with them! The other presenter had a cryogenic experiment. He had developed a method to suddenly freeze small animals in such a way that they could subsequently be quickly thawed and shocked back to life! The lack of sophistication of my project was comical in comparison. After my twenty-minute presentation, I was subjected to a brutalizing cross-examination from the other students, who readily detected my inferior scientific intellect. But a funny thing happened in the process. Instead of wilting under the onslaught, I aggressively countered the attacks, continuously gaining strength as I attempted to appear calm, professional, and resolute in my convictions. At the conclusion of the conference, two scientists who organized it told me they were impressed by my verbal acumen, if not by my scientific knowledge. It proved to be an incredible learning experience. It made me tougher and probably reinforced in me the growing notion that my talents might lie in the art of advocacy.

In a memorable scene from the movie *The Way We Were*, Robert Redford and his old college buddies are sitting around on a small boat drinking beer when he asks them to relate their best Saturday afternoon. Each then details an episode of once in a lifetime athletic perfection. Unfortunately, mine came in my sophomore year in high school in a junior varsity basketball game against Air Academy High School. I envy those athletes who peaked later in life and in front of larger crowds. I played point guard and made the first ten shots I took, some from considerable distance. (There was no three-point line in those days.) Before I was benched at the end of the third quarter because we were so far ahead, I had made fifteen of eighteen field goal attempts and was six for six from the free throw line. My thirty-six points were two-thirds of the team's total. I had the sense I was in a trance. I could not miss. While I had good days on various other athletic fields, none was quite like that.

I played enough varsity basketball my sophomore year to earn a letter and was expected to play a lot my junior year. However, in the summer, while jumping on a trampoline, I suffered a severe ankle fracture and dislocation that had to be surgically repaired. It took almost a year to heal and spelled the end of my high school basketball career. All total, I would earn four varsity letters; one each in basketball and track and two in baseball. Every year the high school had an athletic awards banquet for lettermen and their fathers. I was very appreciative that my uncle, Jim Ryan, consented to go as my surrogate father.

As you might suspect from my previous observations about sports and competition, I view my high school athletic successes and failures as good character builders. A summer league American Legion baseball team I played on finished 0-14. Talk about a character builder. It was very difficult to lose with dignity fourteen consecutive times.

If pressed to identify the best year of my life, I would have to seriously consider my senior year in high school. It was probably the first year that I was significantly recovered from the trauma of my father's death. I had been elected student body president the previous May. Four very good candidates competed for the job, but I was elected by a vote of the entire student body, largely on the basis of a speech that was well delivered and well received. I handled the responsibility well. Mr. Tom McCeney, a veteran history teacher who served as the faculty student council advisor, wrote an incredibly flattering recommendation letter for me to colleges and scholarship committees.

In July of 1969 before the start of my senior year, a group of my classmates and I watched live on television as an American walked on the moon, and there was a sense of anticipation among us that our generation was in for an era of incredible technological advancement. We would not be disappointed.

I also had a steady girlfriend. Jean Bonham was smart, pretty, and fun to be around. We dated throughout my senior year and for several years thereafter. My mother let me drive a 1963 Rambler American that my father had driven and having "wheels" provided a great sense of freedom. In short, I was a big man on campus. Despite my heavy extracurricular activity, I managed to finish third in my graduating class of one hundred and win admission to Notre Dame. It was a great year indeed.

Throughout my life I have been a great fan of rock and roll music from the '60s and 70s. It became a joke among family and friends that my car radio was always tuned to golden oldies stations. I think my nostalgia for the music stems in part from the fact that I have such fond memories of my high school experience, and in part from the fact that it was great music, as evidenced by its long-term survivability on the American landscape. Nothing can make you young again, but a great pop tune can make the memory of your youth a more tangible thing.

I've had a few experiences in life where I felt I had performed poorly, but in hindsight my performance was better than originally perceived. One such experience occurred on the night of my high school graduation. When Ed Kintz, the fanatic coach who had intimidated me into going out for track, left St. Mary's after my sophomore year, I returned to baseball for my junior and senior year. The coach, Dick Fanning, was a former minor league player who loved the game and made it fun to play. I was the starting second baseman both years and captain of the team my senior year. I batted .330, played good defense, and was among the league leaders in stolen bases. Although we had a mediocre team, I had played well enough my senior year to make the all-city team. That resulted in an invitation to play in the annual city all-star game at the end of the season. The best graduating seniors in the Pikes Peak region were invited to play. The game was scheduled on the same night as my high school graduation ceremony. As a result, I arrived late, after the third inning of the seven-inning game. In the bottom of the fifth, I was inserted into the lineup as a pinch hitter. We were behind by three runs and there was a runner on base. The pitcher for the opposing team was a tall, skinny fastballer from Wasson High School named Richard. He blew two strikes by me before I knew what was happening. I awkwardly swung at the third pitch and popped it up in foul territory for the third out. I felt badly that I had let the team down. But the pitcher went on to be inducted into the Baseball Hall of Fame in Cooperstown, and twenty-five years later, when I was trying to impress my daughters with tales of my youthful athletic prowess, I did not hesitate to brag that even Richard "Goose" Gossage, one of the most feared relief pitchers in the history of Major League Baseball, could not strike me out. It is amazing how time changes your perspective on things.

Chapter VIII
God, Country, Notre Dame

In addition to Notre Dame, I applied to and was accepted at Santa Clara University and the University of Colorado. My mother could not afford to send me to Notre Dame or Santa Clara, so I applied for scholarships. By the first of April in my senior year, one month before I had to select a college, I had received a sizable scholarship to Santa Clara, but had received nothing from Notre Dame. It seemed unlikely that dream would materialize. But then my mother had a phone conversation with an old family friend, Hilyard Hicks, a Detroit dentist who served with my father in World War II. When he inquired about how I was doing, my mother explained my situation. Dr. Hicks indicated he had a patient, George Herbert Zimmerman, who had a foundation that awarded college scholarships. He said he would talk to him. A few days later we received a scholarship application from the Zimmerman Foundation in the mail. I applied and just two days before I had to choose a college, I received notice that I had been awarded a $5,000 scholarship to Notre Dame. The cost of four years at Notre Dame at the time was about $16,000. I was also invited to interview with the foundation scholarship committee during Thanksgiving break of my freshman year and they would consider increasing the award. With that understanding, and my mother's acquiescence, I accepted admission to Notre Dame.

When I went to Detroit in November 1970, I met with the foundation board and spent the day with George Zimmerman. He was about seventy-five years old. He had worked his way from night janitor to CEO of Commercial Credit Corporation. He took me to lunch at the Detroit Athletic Club, where we sat at a table with the chairman of General Motors. Afterward he dropped me off at my aunt and uncle's house in a chauffeur-driven limousine. My middle class relatives were very impressed! As I got out of the limo, Mr. Zimmerman informed me that, as long as I made the dean's list each semester, the foundation would pay my full tuition, room, and board for four years at Notre Dame.

I was not a confident young man when I arrived on the Notre Dame campus in September 1970. I had been a big fish in a small pond in high school. Now I was a small fish in a big pond. I knew that St. Mary's High School had not been a top-notch academic environment, particularly in the math and sciences. All Notre Dame freshmen, regardless of their anticipated field of study, were required to take calculus and either chemistry or physics. I learned on the first day of class that, in a calculus class of almost 100 students, only four of us had not taken calculus in high school. St. Mary's did not even offer it. In light of my scholarship situation, I felt a great deal of pressure. I studied an incredible amount. I would frequently study on Friday and Saturday nights. I appropriated a study carrel on the twelfth floor of the Notre Dame library and claimed ownership of it throughout my undergraduate career. I would frequently stay until the library closed at midnight. The fact that the only money I had for living expenses was a $42 per month social security check (due to my father's early death) also limited my social options.

The weather in South Bend, Indiana is conducive to study. In between some nice days in the fall and the spring is a long, wet, cold, and grey winter. A wind chill factor of below zero is the norm. The joke on campus was that the French missionaries that founded Notre Dame were floating down the St. Joseph's River and stopped to let the weather clear. They have been there ever since. The city of South Bend had seen better days than when I was there. It had once been a thriving manufacturing center that was home to the Studebaker car company and had several affluent neighborhoods.

In fact, Knute Rockne had been the spokesman for Studebaker before his death in 1931. But Studebaker had shut down in 1958 and the economy of South Bend had still not recovered. By 1970 the university was the city's largest employer.

The only leisure time I permitted myself was to regularly attend football, basketball, and hockey games. Watching Joe Theismann as quarterback, or Austin Carr or Adrian Dantley on the basketball court was a great diversion. The football team, still coached by Ara Parseghian, was 38-6 during my four years, losing only two games at home. Notre Dame won the National Championship in football my senior year by beating Alabama 24-23 in the Sugar Bowl. I was also in attendance on January 19, 1974, when the Irish snapped UCLA's record eighty-eight-game winning streak in basketball by scoring the last twelve points of the game. It was the most exciting sports event I ever personally witnessed. Occasionally I would play in a pickup game of basketball or flag football. Notre Dame was full of accomplished high school jocks and the competition in such informal events was keen. On Sunday nights I would phone or write my mom and/or my girlfriend. Otherwise, I studied.

Notre Dame prides itself as a residential university. Ninety-five percent of the undergraduate students live on campus. There are no sororities or fraternities. Social and, to some extent, academic life revolves around the dormitory. Students usually stay in the same dorm for all four years. Dorms sponsor parties and dances. All intramural sports are organized by dorms. Many of the best colleges and universities in the country have retained or adopted this residential system to enhance their academic environment. I was asked my preference as to the dorm I wanted to live in during the summer before my freshman year. Many freshmen chose older dorms on campus because they had family members that had lived there, or they were otherwise aware of a dorm's unique history. Without such sentiment to guide me, I applied other criteria. I chose a new dorm with air-conditioning! I lived in Grace Hall, an eleven-story high-rise named for shipping magnate J. Peter Grace, for all four years. We called it the "State of Grace." About twenty years after I graduated, Grace Hall was converted to a faculty office building.

My obsession to study led to a memorable incident during September of my freshman year. It was the day of Notre Dame's first home football game. I had gotten up very early that Saturday morning to study for a few hours before going to the game. At about 6:30 a.m. I was taking a shower in the shower room at the center of our dormitory floor. I heard someone enter the shower stall next to me. Suddenly the person in the adjacent shower started singing. I was paralyzed. It was either a Vienna choir boy or a girl! I was at that point too naive to realize that hometown girlfriends were occasionally snuck into our all-male dorm. I decided to try and wait her out. I would get out of the shower after she left. But after about ten more minutes, my skin was starting to wrinkle. So, I got out of the shower and started to dry off. Within seconds, the other shower turned off, and out stepped a very attractive and very naked young lady. She did not skip a beat. "Hi," she said, "my name's Debbie. I came to visit my boyfriend this weekend for the football game." I tried to be cool. I meant to say, "Nice to meet you," but it came out, "Nice to see you." After an exchange of further pleasantries and a very quick dry off, I quickly departed. I told the story to my mother when I came home for Christmas. She laughed uproariously and made me repeat the story for many of her friends.

Despite my Herculean effort I got a C in calculus the first semester. I had all A's and an A- in my other courses and finished with a 3.3 grade point average. Making the dean's list required a 3.25. It was a close call. The second semester I had a 3.8 grade point average, and my scholarship was never again in jeopardy. I would end up graduating *magna cum laude* with a 3.749 grade point average. But if I had been graded on my social life, I probably would have flunked.

Notre Dame was a great intellectual environment. While the student body was 85 percent Catholic and the minority population was relatively small, it was a liberal environment in the sense that social justice issues were fiercely debated. The anti-Vietnam war movement was very active on campus, and virtually every Catholic dissident in America seemed to choose Notre Dame as their forum to air grievances against the church. Every Notre Dame freshman was required to take a demanding core curriculum known as the Freshman Year of Studies. The school has maintained the program through the years, and it has been one of the keys to its annual rankings among the elite undergraduate colleges in the country. During my freshman year, in addition to calculus and physics, I took a "great-books" course from an English professor who had been a Rhodes Scholar. We read a book a week and wrote an essay about it. I found it intellectually stimulating in a way I had never previously experienced. I also took two philosophy courses at Notre Dame that involved more abstract thinking than I had ever been exposed to. A course on world religions also greatly broadened my world view. In hindsight, I believe it was a high quality liberal arts education at Notre Dame that became the foundation of a lifelong intellectual curiosity. At Notre Dame I learned the importance of "a life of the mind" and I have continued to be a voracious reader of books, primarily history and biographies, and to enjoy intellectual oratory and debate. My college experience greatly enhanced my intellectual confidence. I also credit the intellectual environment at Notre Dame for reinforcing my desire to lead a life with meaning and purpose.

The great-books seminar also taught me that there really was such a thing as a student athlete. While very few athletes were among the most intellectual students I encountered at Notre Dame, there were exceptions. Dave Casper, who starred as a football player at Notre Dame and as an all-pro tight end for the Oakland Raiders, and who was subsequently inducted into the Pro Football Hall of Fame, was in my small seminar section. He was conscientious—never missing a class when not traveling—hardworking, creative, and articulate.

In terms of piquing my social conscience, an incident that occurred during the Christmas break after the first semester of my freshman year was instructive. Notre Dame was playing Texas in the Cotton Bowl. My friend, Bob Schneebeck, and I drove to the game in Dallas, Texas with two of his roommates. One, named Jeff Jackson, was Black. On the day of the game, we took a bus from our hotel to the Texas State Fairgrounds where the Cotton Bowl was located. I sat next to a Texas fan, a man about sixty years old. I was not wearing any clothing that betrayed my allegiance. Bob and Jeff were several rows in front of me on the opposite side of the aisle. Jeff was wearing a jacket with Notre Dame written across the back. The man I was sitting next to tapped me on the thigh and inconspicuously pointed to Jeff. He whispered to me, "That's why this game is so important. We need to prove that southern white boys can beat northern teams with coloreds. This is the civil war all over again," he said. I was speechless. I was shocked to realize that such sentiment still existed in 1970 and that I had led such a sheltered life in terms of the state of race relations in America. Ironically, our seats at the game were only about twenty rows behind former president Lyndon Johnson, a Texan who had done so much to advance the status of African Americans. When I returned to campus in January, I signed up to be a reading tutor at a predominantly Black grade school in South Bend.

When it came time to choose a major at the end of my sophomore year, I chose government and international studies. It was Notre Dame's political science department. It was an area I was interested in and a fairly typical liberal arts major for Notre Dame students thinking about law school. The only downside to the major, according to upperclassmen I knew, was the fact that one of the required courses, Constitutional Law, was taught by a legendary professor, Paul "Black Bart" Bartholomew. Bartholomew was a man in his mid-sixties who had a well-earned reputation as being very demanding. Students were required to read several notable court opinions, one each night from a casebook Bartholomew had authored and be prepared to succinctly summarize the facts and holding of the case when called upon in class the next day. Class participation counted for a lot. Frequent tests were also important.

As it turned out, my obsessive study habits were perfectly suited for the course. I loved the subject matter and eventually became Bartholomew's "go-to guy" when other students faltered. The experience strengthened my resolve to be a lawyer. I wound up taking two other elective courses from "Black Bart" and became a star pupil of his. He personally invited me to a small reception he was having for a friend, William Rehnquist, who had recently been appointed to the US Supreme Court by President Nixon. In my senior year, Bartholomew agreed to write a letter of recommendation to each of the law schools to which I applied. I remember a conversation in his office in which I expressed some concern about whether my law school admission test score was good enough to get into my first choice, the University of Colorado. He quite matter-of-factly said to me, "Not to worry Mr. Suthers. When I recommend a student, law schools pay attention." I think he was right.

In hindsight, I credit some of my government courses at Notre Dame, including my introductory political theory class, taught by a well-known conservative, Gerhart Niemeyer, for planting the seeds of my conservative political philosophy. Niemeyer has come to be regarded as one of the foremost conservative political thinkers of the twentieth century. He was a German socialist who barely escaped the Nazi takeover and fled to America. He eventually became a strident anti-communist and frequently appeared on the television show *Firing Line* as William F. Buckley's expert on the evils of communism. For the rest of my life, I would tend to view the law as a social contract, as Niemeyer did, and evaluate crime and punishment issues, including the death penalty, on that basis. Under the social contract theory, people in a free society, through their elected representatives, enact laws which constitute a social contract between them. They also proscribe punishments for violation of the laws which they deem necessary to ensure compliance with the contract. Without widespread adherence to the social contract, anarchy will ensue. Frankly, the handful of political conservatives I encountered at Notre Dame seemed more disciplined and consistent in their thinking than the more numerous political liberals I encountered.

I emerged from my political science studies with a view of a conservative as a constructive critic. A conservative recognizes that when certain ideas and institutions have triumphed and endured over time as a source of good, those ideas or institutions should not be lightly abandoned. To do so may well do more mischief than good, under the doctrine of unintended consequences. A conservative seeks wisdom from human history and human nature. While liberalism sports the shine of whatever is currently regarded as ideal, conservatism lacks the shine of newness because it has stood the test of time. A conservative is likewise skeptical about government's ability to solve problems other than those inherent in its charter, such as public safety. Yet a conservative will advocate change when institutions or governments do not stand the test of moral or intellectual scrutiny. Englishman Edmund Burke, the source of much modern conservative political thought, opposed slavery, opposed the English subjugation of Ireland, and defended the American Revolution. A conservative can be a revolutionary but comes to the role very slowly. Because of my college experience, for the rest of my life I would admire intellectual conservative thinkers and detest the rant of "redneck" conservatives who had no ability to rationally articulate why they believed as they did.

A humorous episode in the late spring of my sophomore year seemed to suggest that politics would not be a part of my future. One of my roommates (there were six of us in a three-room suite), Floyd Kezele from Gallup, New Mexico, was campaigning to be the student government president the next year. I was in charge of delivering the vote in our dormitory, Grace Hall. My friend Bob Schneebeck, whose roommate was the vice-presidential candidate on the same ticket, was in charge of the adjacent dorm, Flanner Hall. With two weeks to go we thought we had a pretty good chance to win. Then suddenly a last-minute candidate emerged. R. Calhoun Kersten, a.k.a. "King Kersten," a flamboyant pre-med major from Iowa, ran a most unusual campaign. He campaigned in the dormitories between midnight and 4 a.m. so as not to interfere with his studies. He wore a paper crown from Burger King on his head. The school newspaper featured a front-page picture of King Kersten, crown and all, walking on the waters of St. Joseph Lake. He promised, if elected, to force a "marriage of state" between Father Ted Hesburgh, Notre Dame's high-profile president, and the nun who was president of the nearby Catholic women's college, St. Mary's. Their progeny would govern the combined campuses for future generations. Finally, and most significantly, the King told the student body that he would be too busy to run student government himself and promised to turn over power to his vice-presidential running mate, which was a cat.

No serious candidate stood a chance against the King. He won a landslide victory. Living up to his campaign promise, he quickly abdicated in favor of the cat. Student government didn't miss a beat. Ever since, I have lived with the fact that in my first experience as a political campaign operative, my candidate lost the election to a cat. The election became part of Notre Dame lore. The invitation I received to my thirtieth college reunion featured a picture of King Kersten with the cat on his shoulder. Thirty-five years after my graduation I met the King, who had become a plastic surgeon, at an alumni event in Denver. He was still quite a character.

Notre Dame took the momentous step of going coed during my junior year. Despite the protests of old-time alumni, it was a great move for the university's academic standing and campus social life. However, it had virtually no impact on my social life. I was still an obsessive studier. But despite my lack of a social life, I loved my experience at Notre Dame. In addition to the educational opportunity, the tradition and mystique of Notre Dame is hard to beat. The beautiful campus goes a long way to make up for the oppressive mid-west winters. The campus is full of landmarks. A replica of the original building on campus, a log chapel, still overlooks St. Mary's Lake. Near it is a plaque with a copy of a letter Notre Dame's founder, Father Edward Sorin, a French missionary priest, wrote to his superior in France in 1842. In it he relates his vision of founding "a great Catholic university to rival the great universities of Europe" and predicted it would be "a source of great good" for the country. The Main Building with its golden dome is the most photographed structure in Indiana. The Basilica of the Sacred Heart and Hesburgh Library are also beautiful landmarks. And Notre Dame Stadium is the final destination on the pilgrimage of legions of Fighting Irish fans, whether alumni or not. There is nothing quite like a football weekend at Notre Dame.

Rarely does someone attend the school for four years without becoming a full-fledged member of the Notre Dame family. It happened to me, and I watched in some amazement as it happened to my daughter Kate thirty years later. Notre Dame students walk under an arch on campus that lists their priorities, "God, Country, Notre Dame." Membership in the "family" is for life and Notre Dame alumni clubs in almost every major city in the world make continued participation in the family the rule rather than the exception. "Domers" seem to seek each other out in various areas of endeavor. My Notre Dame education has helped open up a few doors during my career.

My graduation from Notre Dame was a big event for my mother, who had sacrificed a lot to make it happen. I am sure she was very lonely during those four years when I was in college. Her siblings and friends came to South Bend for the event, more to support her than to honor me. When Notre Dame president Theodore Hesburgh asked parents to extend their arms and join him in blessing their graduating children, she wept for several minutes.

Every summer during high school and college, I worked in the landscaping business. Tom Kane, my partner in the lawn mowing business in the summers of 1965 and 1966, had gone to work at a motel. So I got a job at Cumming Landscaping, which worked primarily in the affluent Broadmoor area of Colorado Springs. I spent the first two summers on the lawn mowing crew. What an experience that was! The owner, Gordon Cummings, a kindly man in his sixties who loved flowers and getting his hands dirty, had few business skills. He hired many older laborers simply because he felt sorry for them. Frankly, he relied on the college kids working for him to keep the older guys sober and in line. Observing the antics of the fifty- to sixty-five-year-old men who were hourly laborers was enough to inspire any teenage boy to stay in school. One memorable character on the mow crew was named Bill. He had a depressingly negative attitude toward life and could be heard constantly muttering, "What a life without a wife." But my years on the mow crew left me with a lifelong appreciation for those who do hard labor for an hourly wage.

At the beginning of the third summer, I was assigned to work full time in the yard of a wealthy couple, Cady and Jeanette Daniels. Mrs. Daniels's maiden name was Peet, and her grandfather, who had emigrated from England to Kansas City, started a soap business that eventually became the Colgate-Palmolive Company. She was the largest individual shareholder. They moved from Kansas City to Colorado Springs in 1924 because of her health problems. She had tuberculosis. The dry Colorado air quickly cured her. Cady then started Daniels Chevrolet, which still operates in Colorado Springs under the direction of their descendants. They purchased a large house on Pourtales Road in the Broadmoor and became very active in the social scene. They counted Spencer and Julie Penrose, Colorado Springs's most prominent citizens, among their close friends. Now in her eighties, Jeanette Daniels was obsessed with her lawn and gardens and spent large sums of money to care for them. She insisted that Mr. Cummings send only college students to work in her yard during the summer. She took an immediate liking to me, and I worked there for each of the next six summers.

I greatly enjoyed listening to her tales of parties with the Penroses and of political corruption in Kansas City under the Thomas Pendergast machine. She enjoyed my stories about college life. I was paid a nominal amount by Mr. Cummings, from $2.25 to $3.50 per hour. But Mrs. Daniels would pay me a few thousand dollars extra each summer to make sure I could pay all my personal expenses in college. I have always been very grateful for her generosity as well as that of the Zimmerman Foundation. Mrs. Daniels is also the source of some wisdom I have often repeated in my life. Each morning when she came out to survey her elegant grounds she would say, "It's a great life, if you don't weaken." It ranks among the best pieces of advice I ever received.

Chapter IX
The Paper Chase

I was ecstatic to be accepted into the University of Colorado (CU) Law School. While I had also been accepted to other law schools including Georgetown, CU was the logical choice for me. I knew I wanted to live in Colorado. In-state tuition was very reasonable, and given my mother's very limited resources, that was a big factor. CU was a fairly small law school with only 150 students per class and was ranked in the top forty law schools in the country. To celebrate my good fortune my mother bought me a 1974 American Motors Gremlin. It cost about $2,400. I loved it, despite the fact Gremlins have gone down in history as perhaps the ugliest automobile ever made.

It never occurred to me *not* to go to law school right after college. Lack of money ruled out any extensive travel and no other interesting proposition presented itself. It was not until I arrived at CU Law School and discovered the average age of my entering class was twenty-five that I realized I might have worked for a few years before starting law school. In hindsight, I have some regret that I did not join the military for two years after college. I believe I would have benefited from such an experience. However, that is easy to say now. At the time I graduated from college in May of 1974, the United States was still embroiled in a rapidly deteriorating war in Vietnam. In fact, all US troops were being withdrawn and South Vietnam would fall to North Vietnam forces less than a year later. I had a draft lottery number of 361 and stood no possibility of being drafted. I did not even require a college deferment. While I never protested against the war, I did not volunteer to go either. Like so many men my age, I have some ambivalence about that. I didn't believe the Vietnam War was our country's finest hour. It was more a war about a country's self-determination than it was a war about the spread of communism. But I firmly believe that the young Americans who answered their country's call to fight—and in some cases die—deserve our respect and honor every bit as much as those who fought and died in causes that history, in hindsight, views as more noble. Like many people my age, I am very moved when I visit the Vietnam Veterans Memorial on the mall in Washington, DC and see the names of 58,000 Americans who died.

My first year of law school I lived in a house in Boulder with my longtime friend, Tom Kane. We had attended grade school and high school together. He and several of his siblings went to undergraduate school at CU and his parents had the foresight to purchase a house to save on room and board expenses and take advantage of the rapidly appreciating real estate market in Boulder. Sharing the misery of first-year law school with Tom made the experience more tolerable. The first year is an exhausting intellectual challenge that is seen as somewhat of a game by students and faculty alike. It is an atmosphere not unlike that portrayed in the movie *Paper Chase* about the first year at Harvard Law School. Learning to "think like a lawyer" is the stated purpose of this process, but it is also an initiation process of sorts. Most law professors are political and philosophical liberals and, from my perspective, at least part of their goal was to get you to view the world in the same light they did. Frankly, although I did well in law school, I cannot say I enjoyed the law school experience very much. Many of my older classmates seemed overly serious, to the point of unfriendliness. I didn't frequent the offices of law professors after class as many of my classmates did. And I certainly was not a part of the "in crowd" that formed study groups to help each other prepare for exams. It was in the criminal law courses in particular that the liberal bias of faculty members was most evident. The defense function was exalted as a noble undertaking while the prosecution was viewed as a necessary evil at best and as politically ambitious zealots at worst. In fairness to CU, my experience was at the end of the Vietnam War era, a high point for anti-establishment thinking, and the liberal bias I describe was present at virtually all of the most respected law schools in America. I also have to confess that my feeling about my law school experience improved considerably when CU awarded me their distinguished alumnus award in 2004.

Many lawyers I know who say they enjoyed their law school experience cite the inspiration of one or more professors. Unfortunately, I cannot point to any one of my law school teachers as having left a lifelong impression on me. In fact, the professor I've told the most stories about was a neurosurgeon turned law professor who taught my first-year contracts class. He was so comically detached from the real world that it was clear he couldn't do well with real patients or real clients. It was only after I had left the law school and became a prosecutor that I came to admire Professors Bill Pizzi and Bob Nagel. Pizzi had been an assistant US attorney for a few years and wrote several pro-prosecution articles about high-profile decisions of the Colorado Supreme Court. Nagel was a very lonely conservative voice on the faculty. I interacted with Pizzi and Nagel through the years (and they contributed to my political campaigns).

In November of my first semester in law school, two weeks before examinations began, I got a call late one night from my uncle, Jim Ryan. My sixty-year-old mother had a brain aneurysm as she left work that day. Over the course of the next several hours she lost various faculties and lapsed into a coma. She was then in intensive care. He told me that minutes before she had gone into a coma, she had instructed him not to call me and disturb my studies. She also made him help her write checks for two unpaid bills "in case she couldn't get to it later." This concern for others before herself was typical of my mother. My uncle told me that things did not look good and that I should come to the hospital immediately. I drove the 100 miles from Boulder to Colorado Springs in the middle of the night, crying most of the way. I couldn't believe the sudden premature loss of a parent was happening once again.

When I arrived, I learned my mother was being kept alive by machinery with very little chance for survival. My sister Sharon flew in from New Jersey the next day. Jointly we authorized a long-shot surgery on the brain. It was unsuccessful. We then authorized physicians to disconnect the life support systems. She died within minutes. Several of my mother's siblings came to Colorado Springs, and we held the funeral and burial two days after Thanksgiving in 1974. She was buried next to my father at Evergreen Cemetery in Colorado Springs. At a relatively young age, I was parentless. The two people who had adopted me as an infant, given me a warm and loving childhood and taught me all the values I needed to succeed would not be there to see how their efforts would influence my adulthood.

My sister had been married for almost three years when my mother died. She and her husband, Tim Stelzner, had been trying to conceive for some time. My mother, who was a regular attendee at Monday night Novenas to the Mother of Perpetual Help, had been fervently praying for my sister to have a child. A few months before her death, my sister announced she was pregnant and the exuberant grandmother-to-be had begun to knit a baby blanket. It was uncompleted when she died, never to see any of her five grandchildren. It is my greatest regret in life that neither of my parents ever met my wife, Janet, or our two wonderful daughters.

I returned to law school three days before final exams started. I never seriously considered not taking the exams. Although they had all been informed of the nature of my absence, only one of my professors offered condolences and acknowledged my plight. Because of the nature of law school, with only one exam and no homework, there was no real makeup work to be done. Despite the difficult circumstances, I finished the first semester ranked high in the class and won an award for being the best first-year student in Civil Procedure.

The second and third years of law school were much easier than the first. It is not that the academic rigor of the courses is less; in fact, some are more difficult. It's simply that there is a sense of acceptance after the first year that you belong in law school, and you will make it through. It's purely psychological. My coursework pretty well convinced me I did not want to be a business lawyer. I could not see practicing law without going to court. I signed up for the Legal Aid and Defender Program in which I defended several indigent individuals against misdemeanor charges. I enthusiastically advocated my clients' causes, but the experience probably had a lot to do with my inclinations toward prosecution. I was particularly disgusted by one client who sold marijuana to junior high school kids.

During the third year I took a seminar on corrections. As part of the seminar, our class visited a state prison in Cañon City, Colorado. It was my first time to visit a prison and it was a sobering experience. Little did I know that twenty-two years later I would be running the Colorado prison system.

During the summer before my first year in law school and the summer afterward, I had a job as a legal editor for Shepard's Citations, a legal publisher located in Colorado Springs. I got the job through the editor-in-chief, Ed Kirches, who lived across the street from our family home on Arroya Street. While I appreciated having a law related job, the work was somewhat tedious, and I wanted to get an internship that got me closer to courtroom drama. In December of 1975, during Christmas break of my second year of law school, I interviewed for an internship with the Fourth Judicial District Attorney's Office in Colorado Springs. CU Law School had a program where I could get credit for working in a public law office a few hours a week during the school year and reporting on my projects to a supervising law professor. Robert Russel, who was in his third term as DA, and his assistant, Ron

Rowan, were receptive to the idea, and I began working as a research intern during the second semester and continued through the summer of 1976 and throughout the following school year.

Two of the cases I did research for were very high profile. One was the murder of a nurse who was staying at a ski lodge in Aspen. The DA's office in Colorado Springs had been appointed to prosecute the case because the Aspen DA's office lacked the necessary experience to do a death penalty case. During preparation for the trial the defendant had been identified as a suspect in the murder of several young women in Washington, Oregon, and Utah. It appeared he may well be a serial killer. Just weeks before the trial in Aspen was to begin, the defendant made a daring escape from the county jail. Two weeks later he killed three more women in Florida before being arrested, tried, convicted, and eventually executed for the murders in Florida. By the time of his execution, the name of serial killer Ted Bundy had become familiar to most Americans.

I was also assigned to do research on a series of notorious local murder cases. A group of young Army soldiers at Fort Carson, recently returned from Vietnam, had formed a robbery gang and actually gathered together on certain designated nights of the week to perpetrate their crimes. Unfortunately, they also made a pact among themselves that they would kill any victim whom they believed could recognize them. Over the course of two months, they murdered at least five people. Each of the crimes was heinous in nature. A cook at a local hotel was abducted on the way to his car in the parking lot, taken to the edge of a nearby stream, and shot point-blank in the head. The robbery netted $1.50. Another soldier was stabbed to death for a marijuana cigarette. At a party after that killing, the perpetrator, a young GI named Michael Corbett, displayed the bloody knife he had used, reenacted the killing, and explained how thrilling it had felt to turn the knife in the victim's chest and listen to his bones crack.

But undoubtedly the most heinous case in the soldiers' murder spree was that of Karen Grammer, the younger sister of Kelsey Grammer, who over the ensuing years would become a major television star. Karen was a waitress at a local Red Lobster restaurant. The restaurant had closed at 9 p.m. on a Sunday evening and she was waiting outside for a friend to pick her up. The gang of soldiers drove up for the purpose of robbing the restaurant. Finding it closed, they changed their plans and kidnapped Karen Grammer. They took her to the apartment of one of the soldiers and took turns raping her. They then drove around discussing in her presence what to do with her. Upon concluding that they could not risk releasing her, a nineteen-year-old GI named Freddie Glenn took her out of the car, slit her throat, and stabbed her up to 100 times. They then left her for dead in an alley. But she was not dead yet. She crawled about sixty yards to a trailer in a nearby trailer park. She attempted unsuccessfully to reach the doorbell, leaving bloody handprints on the side of the trailer. She died in that position, to be found some hours later by the trailer's owner, a man named Ray Hudson, the next morning. Fourteen years later, when I became district attorney, Ray Hudson was a volunteer in my office.

The District Attorney's Office asked for the death penalty for Michael Corbett and Freddie Glenn, perceiving them to be the ringleaders of the murderous gang. Several other defendants pled guilty or were convicted at trial of murder charges. In highly sensational trials both Glenn and Corbett were convicted of multiple counts of first-degree murder and sentenced to death.

I was commended for the work I did researching the many legal issues arising in the murder trials and death sentencing hearings. Perhaps as a sign that I had earned the respect of the lawyers in the DA's office, they invited me to play basketball with them on Saturday mornings, a ritual that would continue for a dozen years. By working part-time for the office during my third year of law school, I positioned myself well for permanent employment upon graduation.

But the Corbett and Glenn cases had an even more far-reaching effect on me. I had never previously been personally exposed to such evil. It was inconceivable to me that anyone would treat another human being as they did. As a small part of the prosecution team, I felt the incredible satisfaction that prosecutors feel when they represent the public in an attempt to hold a defendant responsible for a reprehensible act against an innocent victim. Prosecutors bear the very heavy burden of vindicating the interests of victims and the public as a whole. I found the work incredibly fascinating and meaningful, and I was certain I wanted to begin my legal career as a prosecutor.

Prior to witnessing the Corbett and Glenn trials I had been somewhat ambivalent about the death penalty. I had written a paper in college in defense of the death penalty but had no personal exposure to the issue and lacked strong conviction about it. But after sitting through major portions of the Corbett and Glenn cases, seeing the frightening lack of remorse of cold-blooded killers and the incredible trauma of the survivors, I would no longer hesitate to advocate the death penalty as an appropriate punishment for particularly heinous murders. In my mind, any punishment short of death for Corbett and Glenn depreciated the value of their victim's lives and constituted an inadequate societal response to their depraved deeds. No tale about the harsh circumstances of their childhoods could cause me to view their case differently. In future years, I would often cite the case in speeches I gave about the evolution of my views on the death penalty.

The death penalty law under which Corbett and Glenn were convicted was subsequently held unconstitutional by an increasingly liberal Colorado Supreme Court. All the death sentences they received were reduced to consecutive life sentences. Unfortunately, under "life sentences" then in effect in Colorado, a defendant was eligible for parole after serving only ten years. But the crimes of Corbett and Glenn were regarded as so heinous that twenty-five years later, when I resigned as Executive Director of

Corrections, the Colorado Parole Board had still not seen fit to release them. Kelsey Grammer testified at several of the parole hearings.

When I reported back to my supervising law professor about the nature of the work I was involved in as an intern at the DA's office, he seemed somewhat shocked. When I showed him crime scene photos, he almost became ill. I do not believe he or any of my other criminal law or criminal procedure professors had ever actually been involved in a murder trial. Such is often the divide between academia and the real world.

Chapter X
The Straight Arrow Takes a Bride

During the summer after my first year in law school, I had the unenviable job of selling off the furnishings in my family home and putting it up for sale. My sister Sharon was living on the East Coast, and I certainly could not afford to maintain the house, let alone purchase her 50 percent interest in it. I cleaned out twenty-five years of accumulated belongings. I held a couple of large garage sales. It was a depressing experience. The previous March, I had ended a five-year dating relationship and a four-month engagement to Jean Bonham, and that added somewhat to a certain sense of isolation as I confronted the task of selling the Suthers family household.

Apparently my aunt, Jo Ryan, felt sorry for me. One evening in early June of 1975, she called and said she had been talking to an old friend, Mary Nittman, who was a nurse at the Hewlett-Packard facility in Colorado Springs. In the course of their conversation, my aunt had updated Mary on my situation. Mary called her back a few days later to give her the names of three young women at HP who Mary thought would be appropriate for me to call for a date. According to her, all three were under twenty-five, never married, nice looking, played tennis, and were Catholics. Frankly, I was a bit perturbed at my Aunt Jo and Mary Nittman for this unsolicited matchmaking project. I suspected some privacy law had been violated to obtain such information. I reminded my aunt that I was not exactly the type who would blindly call women I had never met and ask them out for a date. She told me to just take down the names in case I ever had a need for a doubles partner in tennis. Reluctantly I did.

About two weeks later I was mowing the lawn on a Friday evening and wishing I had someone to play tennis with that weekend. Two friends I had contacted were unavailable. When I went into the house, I saw the list of three possible blind dates lying by the telephone. In an act of extroversion that was uncharacteristic of me then or throughout my life, I decided to call one of them.

The first one on the list had a long Italian name that I was not confident I could correctly pronounce, so I moved on to the second. Her name was Janet Gill. I called her. She indicated Mary Nittman told her I might call but thought it unlikely I would actually do so. I told her it *was* unlikely and explained what had changed my mind. We talked for almost an hour. It was somewhat amazing our paths had not crossed previously. She had lived in Colorado Springs for almost fifteen years, had graduated from Wasson High School a year before I graduated from St. Mary's, and her family had belonged to the Colorado Springs Country Club, as had mine before my father died. We had even played in some of the same youth golf tournaments at the club. Janet had graduated from the CU in 1973 and worked for Hewlett-Packard since then. She was an active Democrat, having recently worked on the campaign of Colorado Governor Dick Lamm. I acknowledged an interest in politics but craftily concealed the fact that I had registered as a Republican upon returning to Colorado Springs after college and that I had strong conservative leanings. She would learn soon enough. The conversation was interesting and fun. I asked Ms. Gill if she would like to go out for dinner on Saturday night and perhaps play tennis on Sunday. She agreed.

Janet was living in a basement apartment in a residential section of town not far from where her parents lived. A sixty-year-old single woman, Dottie Hull, owned the house and lived upstairs. On our first date we went to the Sunbird Restaurant, which was located on a bluff overlooking the city. She was quite sophisticated, and I was quite captivated. We talked for hours about numerous topics. Afterward, we went back to her apartment and talked until 1 a.m. When I left, I found a car had crashed into the curb in front of a nearby house with an unconscious and apparently very drunk driver at the wheel. I returned to her apartment to call the police. We then sat on the curb talking for another half an hour while waiting for the police to arrive. It was after 2 a.m. before I left for good. It was a great first date. Forever after when I told people Janet and I met on a "blind date," I would suggest that she was the one who was blind.

Our tennis game the next day was humorous in the sense that it was indicative of our personalities and indicative of what lay ahead. Janet was playing regularly at a local racquet club and was clearly the superior player. I was an ex-high school jock who had never taken a tennis lesson but who had an obsessively strong competitive drive. I wound up winning by a small margin. My manhood intact, we agreed to see each other again.

A week later, on July 4, 1975, Janet and most of her five siblings were going over to her parents' house for a picnic to celebrate her youngest brother Ben's nineteenth birthday. It was my first opportunity to meet the Gill clan. In what has become the focus of much family humor in ensuing decades, I wore Bermuda shorts and a T-shirt that simply had an arrow on the front, signifying the wearer was a "straight arrow." It had recently been given to me as a gift by my friend and law school classmate Tom Kane and little did I know it would be viewed so significantly in hindsight. Ben Gill was the emcee at a dinner given in my honor twenty-five years later and produced a replica of the T-shirt as part of his comedic monologue. He's repeated the performance at roasts of me several times since.

My introduction to the Gill family was warm and gracious. For a guy with very little family around, it was a radical change. I could tell I connected well with her parents. Her dad, Bud Gill, liked me because I had short hair and was a law student with apparently good prospects. Her mother Anne, whose maiden name was McGrath, liked me because I was an Irish Catholic who went to Notre Dame.

Bud and Anne Gill were an interesting combination. Bud grew up in rural New Mexico during the Great Depression. His mother died when he was a boy. His father was a hardscrabble farmer and rancher, and the family lived in a small rustic farmhouse. His high school class consisted of a handful of students. After two years in college and about to be drafted into the Army, he enlisted in the US Navy, became a pilot, and made it a career. His last assignment was the North American Air Defense Command (NORAD) in Colorado Springs, where he retired as a commander. Despite his military career, he never lost the aura of his rural New Mexico upbringing. Anne, in contrast, was born and raised in New England, in the town of Manchester, New Hampshire. Her father died when she was a baby. She became a nurse and eventually a pioneer flight attendant for American Airlines. She had a gentility about her that was in marked contrast to her husband. Anne and Bud met on a flight from Washington to Los Angeles during World War II. Anne had a car and Bud had gas rations, so they got together for a date. They were married four months later in September 1943. It sounds very impulsive, but they were married for fifty-six years before Anne died in 1999 at the age of eighty-three.

Janet and I dated on weekends during my second year of law school. When I came to Colorado Springs, I would stay with Jim and Jo Ryan and my cousins Pat and Terri. They became my surrogate family. Janet and I became engaged at Christmas in 1975 and were married May 21, 1976, two days after the last final exam of my second year of law school.

Growing up, I had always assumed I would marry and have a family, but like most young people, I never seriously contemplated the enormity of the decision one makes in choosing a mate. Most everyone I knew, my parents, my many aunts and uncles, and my parents' friends all had long-standing marriages. How hard a decision can it be? Only with the benefit of many years of hindsight do I now recognize that the choice of a mate is typically the most critical one you make in terms of your future happiness. It shapes your future and that of any children you have, just as the choices of others helped shape your life. Marriage impacts all your values, some obviously and some subtly. You choose an individual as a mate, but in doing so you also choose their environment, their ancestry, and their values. On May 21, 1976, I'm sure I didn't fully comprehend that. As I nervously said, "I do," I had little inkling of just how brilliant a choice I'd made. Over the ensuing decades I learned that the keys to happiness are someone to love and something meaningful to do. In a very real sense, Janet has been responsible for all my success in life.

A remarkable number of my aunts and uncles and out of town friends came to Colorado Springs for our wedding. We had a large rehearsal dinner and a wedding with approximately 200 guests. Janet's sisters were bridesmaids with her twin sister, Jane, as the maid of honor. My lifetime friends Tom Kane, Bob Schneebeck, and Ed Rivera were the groomsmen, with Bob Schneebeck serving as best man. Janet's brothers were ushers. We got married at Janet's parish, Holy Trinity. It was a Friday evening wedding, and the Gills did a great job of enhancing the venue with the help of candlelight and flowers. My parish priest Monsignor Harrington performed the ceremony with the assistance of Janet's pastor, Father Madden. Harrington's closing blessing, in his marked Irish brogue, was, "May the Lord take a liking to you, but none too soon." The reception was held at the nearby Colorado Springs Country Club, where the Ryans were members.

Our choice of where to go for a honeymoon was also indicative of what our future life together might be like. In 1976 America was celebrating the 200th anniversary of the Declaration of Independence. Both of us were history buffs and political science majors. So instead of going to a honeymoon resort or on a Caribbean cruise, we chose to take a bicentennial honeymoon. Over a two-week period, we went to Boston, Philadelphia, New York, and Washington, DC, using my sister Sharon's and her husband Tim's home in Matawan, New Jersey as a staging point of sorts. They let us use their Volkswagen Beetle to get around and helped us pick up Broadway play tickets. It was a great trip and a great start to our married life.

In the fall of 1976, we moved to Boulder for my third year of law school, living in the same apartment complex, Eden East, which I had lived in the year before. We had a two-bedroom second-floor unit with a balcony for which we paid $227 a month. I used the second bedroom as my study room. Janet was able to transfer to the Loveland division of Hewlett-Packard, which was about a forty-five-minute commute from Boulder. She quickly found a carpool. The third year of law school was definitely more relaxed than the previous two and we had a fun first year of marriage. I would study very hard during the week, and we would recreate on weekends by going to cheap movies on campus, CU football games, and finding other diversions. One afternoon each week I would drive to Colorado Springs and back to continue working as an intern in the Colorado Springs DA's office. Tom Kane and I teamed up in the third year moot court competition, trying a civil personal injury case to a jury of undergraduate students. Janet played the role of witness to the accident. Despite all the distractions, I was able to graduate in the top 25 percent of my law school class in May of 1977.

Janet and I stayed in Boulder for the summer after graduation while I studied for the bar exam, which was held over three days during the last week in July. I took a bar refresher course which I found very helpful in preparation. I scored well on the practice tests and had a fair degree of confidence going into the exam. Nevertheless, I was nervous. The night before the exam started, we saw the movie *Rocky*, starring Sylvester Stallone, and I marched into the exam humming the inspirational theme song. Janet cooked breakfast for me each morning during the three-day exams. I still remember driving back from Denver to Boulder after the last day of the exam and physically feeling the adrenaline dissipate in my body.

After taking the bar exam, we took a two-week trip to California, taking in San Francisco, Lake Tahoe, Hearst Castle, Highway 1, Disneyland, and Marine World. It was a great trip. When we returned, Janet transferred back to Hewlett-Packard in Colorado Springs, and I secured an employment offer from the DA's office, dependent upon passing the bar exam. On the first Sunday in October, I picked up the morning newspaper only to read a blurb that said, "Bar exam results page B-5." Contrary to representations, I had not yet received any notice in the mail. I shook like a leaf while trying to find my name in incredibly small print. It was there! I was sworn in as a member of the Colorado Bar on October 17, 1977. The following day, my twenty-sixth birthday, I went to court for the first time as a deputy district attorney in Colorado Springs at the whopping salary of $750 per month.

Chapter XI
The Prosecution Never Rests

Trial by fire was the training program at the Fourth Judicial District Attorney's Office when I started as a deputy. You were essentially handed a pile of misdemeanor and petty offense cases and told to handle them. The first day on the job I tried two cases and plea bargained many others. My first trial was a shoplifting case. A man went into a department store and proceeded directly to the shoe department. While being observed by an overhead camera, he took off his shoes, tried on a new pair, put his old shoes in the new shoebox, put it back on the shelf, and proceeded to walk out of the store wearing the new shoes without going near the cash register. He was stopped by store security in the parking lot, offered no explanation, and was charged with shoplifting. It seemed like a straightforward case to me. The evidence was strong, and the witnesses did well. But the trial judge, Dick Webster, a former head of the Public Defender's Office, acquitted the defendant, who did not testify, speculating that he may have forgotten to pay for the shoes and that there was insufficient proof of "intent to permanently deprive." I was stunned. I was not informed until after the trial that Judge Webster routinely acquitted obviously guilty defendants as his way of dispensing equity to the downtrodden. The second trial went much better. A jury of six quickly convicted a man who had several large marijuana plants growing in his garden, despite his contention that he did not know they were there. "We weren't born yesterday," the foreman of the jury told me after the verdict. I successfully managed to establish a proper chain of custody for the evidence and for the lab testing of the marijuana, a somewhat difficult task for a new attorney.

My first day on the job would prove to be a good lesson. For the rest of my legal career, I would tend to trust the judgment of most juries and distrust the motives of some judges. Years later as a district attorney, as my office bore the brunt of an occasional bizarre jury verdict, and the nation suffered through spectacles like the O. J. Simpson murder trial, I would still give speeches on criminal justice reform that were supportive of the uniquely American constitutional right to trial by jury.

Every new prosecutor—and every new peace officer for that matter—needs to quickly learn the true role of a jury in order to maintain their mental health. Contrary to what the media often reports, juries do not find people innocent. They are not asked to determine that the accused didn't do the crime. They find defendants "guilty" or "not guilty." "Not guilty" means that this particular group of jurors was not convinced beyond a reasonable doubt that the prosecution had proved its case. It does not mean *they* concluded he didn't do it. While it is certainly possible for a jury to be affirmatively convinced that a defendant didn't do it, I never had a jury tell me that after a case that I tried.

The nine months I spent in El Paso County Court handling traffic and misdemeanor cases was a great introduction to trial lawyering. I was often responsible for disposing of fifty to sixty cases a day. I typically tried one or two trials to the court each day and three or four jury trials a month. I also learned valuable people skills balancing the demands of judges, witnesses, and defense counsel in the high-volume court. I remember one case where a man was charged with indecent exposure on a complaint taken from two elderly women. He was parked in a grocery store parking lot waiting for his wife to return from shopping. Having a bladder problem related to recent surgery, he relieved himself behind a Salvation Army donation box. Unbeknownst to him the two ladies saw him and summoned a nearby policeman who issued the complaint. The defendant had no sexual motive, and clearly, I could not prove indecent exposure. Yet the elderly ladies were vehement when they came to court that his conduct was unacceptable and should be sanctioned. Paging through the statute book, I came up with an ingenious solution. The parties agreed to a disposition whereby the defendant pleaded guilty to "littering," for failing to put "a foreign substance in an appropriate container." The judge complimented my creativity, and the local paper ran a humorous blurb about the disposition of the case.

The fact I was a lifelong resident of Colorado Springs also created some interesting situations in court. In early 1978 I was choosing a jury in a drunk driving case in front of Judge Matt Railey. A longtime family friend, Louise Fritchle, was in the jury panel. The judge asked the potential jurors if they knew the defendant or either of the lawyers. Louise raised her hand and announced to all present that, "I've known little Johnny Suthers since the day his parents brought him home." The judge then asked Mrs. Fritchle if she could objectively assess the evidence despite the fact that she knew me. She quickly responded that, "I couldn't disbelieve anything that little Johnny Suthers told me." She was quickly dispatched from the jury panel, but I am sure the other jurors were impressed by her endorsement of my character. For years thereafter Judge Railey's staff would jokingly call me "Little Johnny Suthers." Judge Railey would also relate the story to the FBI twenty-three years later when they interviewed him as part of my background investigation to be the US attorney. I would also relate the story at Louise Fritchle's funeral in April of 2003, when she died at the age of ninety-three.

I worked extremely hard as a deputy district attorney. I typically arrived at work each day about 7 a.m. and was in court from 8 a.m. until 5 p.m. During lunch and after work for an hour or two, I would make phone calls and line up witnesses for the next day's cases. Each night, while watching TV at home, I would review fifty to 100 files and fill out witness subpoena sheets. This work ethic earned me respect from my superiors, my peers, and the judges I appeared before. I was promoted to district court and to felony cases as soon as possible. The experience also made me more empathetic with my daughter Alison when she became a deputy DA in Denver thirty-five years later.

Over the next thirty months, I tried almost two dozen felony trials ranging from burglary to rape to first-degree murder, winning all but three cases. My first solo felony trial involved the kidnapping and robbery of a prominent restaurant owner. He was abducted from his home in the middle of the night, taken to the restaurant to open the safe, and left there bound and gagged to be found by the cleaning crew the next morning. The police arrested two career criminals for the crime, who in turn identified a former disgruntled employee of the restaurant as the mastermind of the plot. The defendant, Ricky Ricardo Mateos, was a highly intelligent young man from a close-knit, middle class family who attempted to provide him an alibi. It was a very contentious trial, but the jury found the defendant guilty after two days of deliberation. With the victory, I had begun to make a name for myself at the courthouse and with the local police department.

One case I lost during my tenure in district court was also particularly memorable. An Air Force Captain, Ron Ball, was accused of murdering his ex-girlfriend's new boyfriend. The captain had dated the girlfriend, Laurie, for several years. They had met at The Pentagon, and she followed him to Colorado Springs when he was appointed assistant to the general in charge of NORAD. He had a doctorate, had been promoted rapidly, and was considered by all his superiors to be general officer material. Unfortunately, Captain Ball began to take his girlfriend for granted. She desperately wanted to get married. He was in no hurry to do so. Eventually tiring of his complacency, she began to see another man. That got the captain's attention. He unsuccessfully tried to get her back. One day he parked his Corvette across the street from the apartment complex where Laurie lived, suspecting the new boyfriend might appear. In fact, he eventually did come to pick up Laurie for a date. Laurie testified at trial that they were sitting in the cab of the new boyfriend's pickup when Captain Ball drove up next to them. He calmly got out of his Corvette, wearing his Air Force uniform, and walked up to the driver side window of the pickup. He asked the new boyfriend, Mike, to get out of the vehicle so they could talk about things. Mike said there was nothing to talk about. After another request by Ball to discuss the situation was rejected, the captain pulled out his Vietnam-issue revolver and shot Mike in the side of the head from point-blank range. Laurie testified that Ball then calmly walked away, got in his car, and drove away at a normal speed.

Captain Ron Ball was arrested about four hours later in the washroom of a Mexican restaurant about ten miles from the crime scene. He claimed to the police to have no knowledge of what had transpired. No weapon was ever found. But any chance of beating the murder charge was undermined by the fact that two witnesses had seen him hiding out across the street from Laurie's apartment and microscopic blood splatter was found on his Air Force uniform. The captain's attorney, a high-priced, high-profile local defense counsel, got permission from the court to plead not guilty by reason of insanity, allegedly over the objection of his client, who vehemently protested his innocence.

I tried the case with District Attorney Bob Russel. Russel had been a great trial lawyer but was well past his courtroom prime and was, frankly, not well prepared for the case. He did not tell me what the division of labor would be until the morning of the trial. So, I had to prepare as though I was trying the case alone. The defense hired two high-priced psychiatrists, both of whom testified that Ball suffered from a psychiatric disorder called hysterical neurosis, dissociative type. It was described by the psychiatrists as a form of temporary insanity suffered by a highly rigid personality who snapped due to a stressful event and then had no recollection of his antisocial actions, which appeared to others as being very deliberate.

The prosecution's court-appointed psychiatrists were not nearly as flashy as the defense's hired guns. The jury of nine women and three men apparently wanted an explanation other than jealousy for Ball's despicable deed. They found him not guilty by reason of insanity. The defendant spent two years in the state mental hospital before another jury released him, finding that he was "no longer a danger to himself or others." He became a dance instructor and collects a lifelong military pension due to his discharge from the military for a mental disability. Six months after the case was tried, the American Psychiatric Association voted to remove the diagnosis of hysterical neurosis, dissociative type from the Diagnostic and Statistical Manual, having been discredited as a genuine mental affliction.

Another memorable case I tried had a mixed result. A Colorado Springs lawyer named Orville Kenelly and his client, Kyle Jarret, were charged with soliciting a bribe and obstructing justice. Jarret had been shot by a fellow drug dealer in a deal gone bad. After recovering, Jarret and Kenelly allegedly told the shooter and his defense attorney that Jarret wouldn't show up to testify in the shooter's criminal case, despite having been subpoenaed, if he was paid $50,000. If proven, that was both illegal and unethical. The shooter's attorney informed the DA's office of the alleged bribe, and an undercover operation was set up, including taped phone calls and body mikes. The trial judge, who was from Denver because all the local judges had recused themselves, severed the defendants for trial. At the first trial Jarret was convicted. At the second trial, Kenelly was acquitted. We left the wife of an attorney on the jury, and it proved to be a big mistake. The Colorado Supreme Court took a different view of Kenelly's conduct than the jury and, despite the acquittal, disbarred him from practicing law.

During 1978 and most of 1979, I was the on-call deputy DA for vehicular homicide investigations. I would get called at all hours of the day or night by police agencies seeking legal advice on such cases and would frequently respond to crime scenes to help direct evidence-gathering efforts. I still have a vivid recollection of helping gather body parts at a multi-fatality crash scene about 2 a.m. on a cold winter night. A particularly grisly aspect of the scene was the fact that a woman's head had been decapitated from her body and laid along the roadside. I eventually became able to cope with such blood and guts in an astonishingly detached manner. Such efforts also helped me develop a close working relationship with many police officers in El Paso and Teller Counties, and those relationships would be very beneficial in the coming years.

In 1978 and 1979, I was asked to teach criminal law and procedure in the Police Science Department at El Paso Community College (now Pikes Peak State College). I enjoyed it greatly. My students ranged from semi-literates who should never have graduated from high school to people who would have done well at Harvard. Student evaluations gave me consistently high marks as a teacher. Throughout my legal career I would accept invitations to speak to classes at all levels. I also taught at police academies and I taught prosecutors courses. In 1994 I was given the Outstanding Faculty Member award by the Colorado District Attorney's Council. Years later, I would take on the mantle of distinguished adjunct professor at the University of Denver Law School and scholar in residence at the University of Colorado, Colorado Springs.

In August of 1979, District Attorney Bob Russel called me into his office and informed me he was promoting me to chief deputy district attorney in charge of the Economic Crime Division. It was a pleasant surprise. I had been in the office as a deputy less than two years and there were more than two dozen lawyers that had more seniority than I did. His decision reflected a high level of confidence in me.

Eight months later, in April of 1980, Bob Russel's opinion of me took a dramatic but temporary change. The DA's office bookkeeper came into my office and closed the door behind her. She started to cry and said she wanted to talk to me because she was sure I would do the right thing. She proceeded to tell me that Russel was taking advances on his salary. He had recently remarried, and his new wife was making demands which caused him to live beyond his means. After brief research that made it clear elected officials could not take advances on their salaries, I knew I had to do something. I met with a distinguished local attorney, Alan Spurgeon. Spurgeon was a former chief deputy district attorney, assistant US attorney, and friend of Russel. He agreed I needed to report the matter to authorities. We met with the chief judge of the Fourth Judicial District, Bob Johnson, and we collectively reported the matter to the Colorado attorney general, J. D. McFarlane.

When the three of us informed Russel of what we'd done, he was livid. When investigators from the attorney general's (AG) office seized the office books the next day, I was certain I'd be fired. But things turned out for the best. The attorney general sent Russel a letter of admonition and made him refund the advances with interest but did not charge him criminally. Russel divorced his new wife, who had serious mental health issues, after less than a year.

Amazingly, the press never learned of the investigation, or if they did, chose not to report it, and Russel was reelected in November of 1980. Russel subsequently thanked me for "saving him" from himself. For the next thirty years Russel and I would be close. After he retired, he would frequently call me when I was US attorney or attorney general and offer unsolicited advice. He closed every such conversation by telling me he loved me. I was a pall bearer at his funeral in January of 2012.

My fifteen-month tenure as head of the Economic Crime Division was perhaps the most fun I ever had as a lawyer. The other attorney assigned to the division was a former newspaper reporter, Gary Shupp. We had a very close-knit group of investigators and paralegals. We were extremely aggressive in investigating all sorts of consumer fraud schemes and white-collar crimes. We would review complaints from the public and determine which consumer fraud perpetrators to target. We uncovered scams in pre-need funeral plans, going-out-of-business sales, and many other promotions. With the help of a whistleblower, we caught a high-end department store that was going out of business taking its high quality merchandise off the shelf and substituting junk for the clearance sale. That generated headlines for several weeks. We used the grand jury to secure testimony of reluctant witnesses. We made the front page of the *Wall Street Journal* for prosecuting a silver-tongued disbarred lawyer who conned several hundred high-profile victims, including high-ranking officials at the Air Force Academy, into investing in a non-existent "gasohol" manufacturing plant in North Dakota. We persuaded Aamco Transmissions to invest $50,000 to assist us in an undercover operation to expose the fraudulent practices of a rogue franchisee. Dozens of our division's investigations received newspaper coverage and my standard consumer fraud speech became quite popular among service clubs and senior citizens groups. I always ended with the caveat, "If it sounds too good to be true, it is." As a result of such publicity, I began to develop a higher community profile.

In 1980 Gary Shupp and I wrote a book describing in detail almost sixty fraud schemes we had learned about in our investigations. *Fraud and Deceit: How to Stop Being Ripped Off* was published by Arco Publishing in New York and was syndicated in the *Los Angeles Times* and other newspapers. We did radio talk show interviews throughout the country. The book sold about 30,000 copies and we each made about $4,000. While we did not get rich, it was a fun and worthwhile experience. It was the first of a half dozen books I would author.

Decades after my stint as a line prosecutor in county and district court I realized that my days as a trial lawyer proved to be great experience that helped me succeed in the art of politics. Good trial lawyers are quick on their feet; they're skilled in debate; and they can explain complicated matters to a jury in a way that most people can understand. Those were some of the important skills I brought to the various public service positions I subsequently undertook.

Chapter XII
"I Love You, Daddy"

In July of 1978, Janet and I purchased our first house in an area of Colorado Springs called Upper Skyway, not far from where I had grown up in the southwest part of the city. We had spent the previous nine months living in an apartment in a nice complex known as Glen Pond, also in the southwest area of the city. Because we had done a good job saving money, we made a sizable down payment on the purchase price. It was a great bi-level house with four bedrooms. It was situated in the foothills of the mountains and had a tremendous view of Colorado Springs from the front picture window. The only drawback, which we would not discover until the next winter, was that the snow never melted on our steep north facing driveway. I was constantly shoveling snow. The house had a small, secluded backyard in the midst of scrub oak and a terrific back patio. It was a serene and tranquil setting, and we were then ready to start a family and to begin to learn what would make our lives so meaningful and be the source of so much happiness.

On June 29, 1979, three years after Janet and I were married, our first child, Alison Marie, was born. Three years later on May 30, 1982, Catherine Patricia was born. I was present in the delivery room on both occasions and can honestly say that I noted they both had dimples in their chin like their father before I noticed their gender. When Janet and I married, we knew we wanted to have children. I had given some thought to what fatherhood would be like, but as all parents know, it is an experience which is difficult to conceptualize. I had no real comprehension of how meaningful and rewarding the experience would be. My family life has been the source of the greatest joy in my life and our daughters are the source of tremendous pride. They were great kids. As adults, they are both intelligent, articulate, caring, and responsible citizens of their communities.

It did not take long to figure out that Alison was a very bright child. She memorized the poem "The Night Before Christmas" at the age of two-and-a-half. One day when she was three, she and I were out running an errand. She was in a car seat on the front passenger side, and I was driving. The Kingston Trio song "Charlie on the MTA" was playing on the radio. It is about a poor chap named Charlie who is stuck on a Boston subway train because he does not have a nickel to get off the train. I was singing along, Alison was listening. There is a line in the song that describes how Charlie's wife "goes down to the Scollay Square Station every day at quarter past two and through the open window hands Charlie a sandwich as the train comes rumbling through." At the end of the song Alison was silent for a moment, then turned to me with a puzzled look on her face and said, "Daddy, why doesn't Charlie's wife just hand him a nickel instead of a sandwich?" It was indicative of the analytical mind that would lead her to be valedictorian of her class at Cheyenne Mountain High School and admitted to Harvard and Stanford. She would choose to attend Stanford and go on to Georgetown Law School. It was not until we watched Alison in the state mock trial championship her senior year in high school that we had an inkling that she would follow her father into the law.

From the time of her birth, we started calling Catherine "Katie," after her maternal grandmother. But one day she came home from preschool and announced to us that henceforth she would be called Kate. It was indicative that, in many respects, she would be the most unique and creative of the Suthers family. She is certainly the most plain spoken. She also knew how to handle her father. When she was in the third grade, I was driving the carpool to school one morning. She had gotten in the back seat and left the rear passenger side door open. I backed out of the garage and smashed the car door. I jumped out of the car and furiously stomped around the garage, yelling (yes, cursing), and barely containing my anger. We had a long, silent drive to school. Even the non-family carpoolers were afraid to say anything. When Kate got out of the car she hesitated for a moment and then sheepishly said, "I love you, Daddy." I was totally disarmed and simply said, "I love you too, Kate." I never recall ever losing my temper with her again.

When Kate was seven, she came into a room where I was watching a Notre Dame football game with several other people. No chairs were available, and she sat on my lap. After watching for a while, she said, "Dad, do you think I could go to Notre Dame someday?" I said, "Yes Kate, but you'll have to work very hard." That is exactly what she did. She finished near the top of her high school class and earned a Navy ROTC scholarship to Notre Dame. We are particularly proud of the fact that Kate chose to serve her country in the military after she graduated and as a Navy reservist throughout her career, attaining the rank of commander. She would also earn a Master's in Business Administration from the University of Hawaii.

Both Alison and Kate went to grade school at Pauline Memorial, the same Catholic elementary school that I attended. In fact, they had the same French teacher! After sixth grade they switched to the Cheyenne Mountain Public School System for junior high and high school in order to take advantage of the honors and advanced placement course offerings. I believe the private-public combination of education and social influences worked well for both of them. They were educationally challenged but their values were such that neither of them ever got into the run-with-the-crowd mentality of so many teenage girls. They have always been independent minded and have exercised great judgment throughout their lives.

When the girls were born, I confess that I had a moment of distress at the notion that I would not have a boy to play baseball and other sports with. Was I ever off base. Luckily the world had changed since my boyhood. Title IX, the federal law requiring comparable accessibility to sports for men and women in schools receiving federal funds, is one of a few federal mandates I believe has had a positive societal effect. As it turned out, our house was constantly cluttered with bats, baseballs, soccer balls, volleyballs, and tennis rackets. Only jock straps were missing. Our daughters won fourteen high school varsity letters between them. Almost freezing to death at their soccer games is still one of Janet's and my favorite memories during their childhood. We were true soccer parents, traveling hundreds of miles all over Colorado and Wyoming to various games. Both Alison and Kate played for the Cheyenne Mountain High School team that won a state soccer championship in 1997. We felt like storming the field ourselves.

When the girls were small, I built them a log cabin that they promptly named the Little House in the Scrub Oak. They loved it and spent many hours in it. At their mother's direction, they gave me a plaque for high achievement in architecture, construction, and fatherhood. Along with a small rubber "Best Dad" statue they gave me for Father's Day, it is one of my most cherished possessions.

Parenting is part luck and part hard work. I do believe that one of the keys to our children's success is that we kept them incredibly busy, while still allowing them time to play like kids are supposed to. We exposed them to a broad range of activities as small children, including sports, music, dance, and art, and then let them choose the pursuits they most enjoyed to concentrate on as they got older. They really had very little time for mischief of any kind.

In 1989, we moved farther up the mountainside to a newly developed area called Top of Skyway. Once again, because we had done a good job of saving money and had experienced considerable appreciation in the value of our previous house, we were able to make a very sizable down payment on our new house. The three-level, six-bedroom home on Electra Drive would prove a great place to raise the kids through their adolescence. Its greatest feature was that it backed up against Bear Creek Park, a 1,250 acre county park with hiking trails and numerous varieties of wildlife.

The house had a three-level deck on the backside from which you could view the park, the grandeur of nature, and the bustling city beyond. Deer, fox, raccoons, coyotes, and even mountain lions and bears roam the park. It would not be unusual to see six to ten deer roaming through our yard at a time. It was an idyllic setting and Janet and I often commented how lucky we were to live in such a beautiful place.

In 2004, with both our daughters pursuing careers, Janet and I decided to downsize to a ranch style house. But we could not leave Bear Creek Park and the incredible views from Top of Skyway. So we wound up moving a very short distance away. Our home is a perfect empty nest house. Our first improvement was an expansive deck that overlooks Colorado Springs. It's a great house for entertaining.

For over forty-six years, I have tried to walk a few miles in Bear Creek Park at least once or twice a week. I have found it the very best time to reflect on life's events and to take stock in my career. Something inspirational happens when you amble through the world at three miles per hour. Kierkegaard in 1847 described the benefits of perambulations best when he said, "I have walked myself into my best thoughts and I have no thought so burdensome that I cannot walk away from it." Thomas Jefferson viewed walking as the best possible exercise and the key to his health and long life. I made some of the most important decisions of my life while walking in Bear Creek Park. The park is also a great place to intimately experience the miracle of changing seasons. You don't have to be a naturalist to be in awe of the annual transformations that occur to both animal and plant life. When our daughters were small, I often took them on walks in the park, and I was greatly touched when Alison wrote of the meaningfulness of that experience in an essay submitted with her applications to college.

Janet continued to work throughout our marriage for Hewlett-Packard and its spin-off, Agilent Technologies. She retired at age fifty-five after thirty-three years on the job. In the early parenthood years, we were fortunate to have a stable day care situation. From the time they were three months old until they went to school, both Alison and Kate were loved and nurtured by Marty Harvey, whose house was on Janet's way to work. Our greatest asset was Janet's organizational abilities because she's the one that made sure everyone, including our busy daughters, got to every place they were supposed to be when they were supposed to be there. That meant organizing carpools and juggling lots of obligations. She spent a great deal of time doing advanced planning. In an almost comical year long period of our lives in 1988, I was campaigning for district attorney during every spare hour I had, and Janet was getting an MBA at night while working full time. We would actually exchange the kids at designated street corners in Colorado Springs. They handled it well. They always knew who would pick them up and they always felt secure and loved. Janet and I made it a priority that one or both of us would attend every significant event in their childhood and adolescence, even if it meant rescheduling a work-related obligation. I think the kids liked it when I was responsible for feeding them, because it always meant a trip to McDonald's or some other fast food restaurant.

Janet's income, in combination with a very successful savings and investment strategy, resulted in us having a relatively comfortable lifestyle and eventually the ability to send our children to the best colleges and graduate schools in the country. They both had foreign travel opportunities that neither Janet nor I could even contemplate at their age. It was Janet's willingness to work outside the home that made it possible for me to have the career flexibility that I have enjoyed. I have watched many other people engage in politics to the detriment of their marriages and their children and I am thankful I could engage in a public life without doing so.

As the years have passed, I have grown increasingly aware of the fact that my personal happiness stems from a wonderfully fulfilling personal life as well as a meaningful career. Fatherhood has been all it is cracked up to be . . . and more. My marriage has been the source of great love, support, and encouragement. I am a happy man, and for that, Janet deserves most of the credit.

In August of 2008 our daughter Kate married Neil Beckwith. Kate had met Neil in her first week in the Navy after graduating from Notre Dame in May of 2004. They were taking the same class in Jacksonville, Florida to become communications officers. Neil was from Connecticut and graduated from Maine Maritime Academy. Needless to say, he loved ships and set his sights on being a marine engineer. The wedding was at the historic Pauline Chapel that is part of our parish. I had been baptized in the chapel fifty-seven years earlier. After their marriage, Kate and Neil settled in Honolulu, their last active duty station. After leaving active duty they joined the Navy Reserve. Kate went to work for the Department of Defense and Neil has worked as a marine and nuclear engineer for US government agencies. In May of 2016, our first grandchild, Scott Gregory Beckwith was born. Shortly thereafter, Kate and Neil moved to York, Maine where they both work at the Portsmouth Naval Shipyard and are commanders in the Naval Reserve.

Our daughter Alison embarked on a legal career. After graduating from Stanford and Georgetown, she clerked for Judge Tim Timkovich on the Tenth Circuit Court of Appeals. She then spent five years at the Denver-based law firm of Holland and Hart before becoming a deputy district attorney in Denver in 2012. In November of 2013 she married Mark Karla. Mark grew up in Western Pennsylvania, graduated from the University of Pittsburgh Dental School, and did post-graduate work at the University of Colorado Dental School. He stayed in Colorado and built up a solo dental practice. I regretted my father wasn't around to welcome another dentist into the family. Mark and Alison gave us our second grandchild, Isabelle Catherine Karla (Izzy), in August of 2016.

In November of 2018 I joined our son-in-law Mark on a two-week medical mission trip to India. Mark had done it three times before and I had expressed interest in joining him on a future trip. We worked in two different slums in Calcutta and in a village outside of the city. I served as one of Mark's dental assistants. It was hard work. Mark performed tooth extractions almost all day and those who helped him prepped patients, served as interpreters, prepared anesthetics, and sterilized equipment. I gave fluoride treatments to all our patients under fourteen years old.

The trip was a very impactful experience. Being immersed in third world poverty for two weeks can't help but give an American a different perspective. For me, as mayor of a large city, I would never again take for granted sanitation systems, water and sewage infrastructure, and government services in general. I fear the experience made me a bit less sympathetic with my constituents who complained about relatively trivial issues.

The India trip was also a wonderful opportunity to learn more about our son-in-law. Mark showed a compassion toward the poor and a determination to improve their lot one small step at a time. He had a servant's heart to go with his warm and friendly personality. This opportunity to know him better became even more significant to me when, seven months later, he was tragically killed in an automobile accident. He was a passenger in an Uber just four blocks from his home when a parolee, who had just stolen a car, ran a red light going over sixty miles per hour and broadsided the Uber. The Uber driver died instantly. Mark suffered massive brain injuries and was comatose for twenty-one days, dying four hours after life support was removed. Our family was devastated by the loss of Mark. Janet and I resolved to do everything we possibly could to help our daughter Alison, and their three-year-old daughter Izzy, recover from the tragedy. We supported Alison during the trial of the perpetrator. We sat through the entire trial, after which he was convicted of numerous felonies and sentenced to seventy-two years in prison. We tried to help Alison with the burdens and anxieties of single motherhood. We have never overcome the profound sadness the tragedy brought but have worked hard to ensure Mark's legacy lives on in our family and in the community. An annual golf tournament in his name raises funds to continue his work in India. We are so proud of how Alison coped with this tragedy and built a new life for herself and Izzy.

Being a grandparent *is* all it's cracked up to be. Our grandchildren bring us great joy and much of that joy is unburdened by the heavy responsibilities of parenthood. Yet we hope that we'll be successful in passing on our values to our grandchildren. That's certainly part of being a good ancestor.

Next to family and faith in importance is good friends, and Janet and I have been blessed to have many very good friends. Because we have had a high profile in the community, we know literally thousands of people. But it's the much smaller circle of truly good friends that give meaning to your life. Beginning in 1977, we acquired Denver Bronco season tickets with three other young couples and for many years, before kids came along, we made fun social outings out of the games. Early on, perhaps 1983 or so, we also started a tradition of having four or five couples rotate hosting a New Year's Eve dinner. It continued for twenty years. As you might suspect, our children's friendships and school involvements brought about new friendships, many of which have endured long after our children's school days. Politics has also been the source of some close friendships. The fact is you really find out who your loyal friends are in the vicissitudes of politics. When Janet turned fifty, I wanted to invite our closest friends to a surprise birthday party at her favorite restaurant. It was a small French restaurant that could hold only seventy-five people under the fire code. I think it is indicative of our good fortune in life that I had extreme difficulty arriving at a guest list of only six dozen from among our good friends. We had the same issue limiting our guest list for a fortieth anniversary celebration. The older we get, the more we cherish long-standing friendships.

Chapter XIII
The Practice

In the fall of 1980, I got a call from Ken Sparks, the senior partner in a small Colorado Springs law firm named Sparks, Dix, and Enoch. He wanted to talk to me about the possibility of leaving the DA's office and joining the firm. In light of our previous brief but very contentious relationship as legal adversaries, I was quite surprised. My division of the DA's office was responsible for representing the Department of Motor Vehicles in appeals from driver's license suspensions. Two of Sparks's best clients, both prominent citizens of Colorado Springs, had their licenses suspended at hearings after acquiring too many traffic offenses. The firm appealed, hoping to delay the suspensions. They failed to file the opening briefs by the deadline in each appeal and I immediately filed motions to dismiss the appeals. By doing so I got the appeals dismissed and the license suspensions reinstated. One of the clients of the firm got arrested soon thereafter for driving with a suspended license. Sparks was furious and complained to District Attorney Bob Russel that I had not extended him the professional courtesy of giving him more time. His anger only intensified when I told him his client should blame him, not me, for his problems. One of the partners in the firm, Bart Enoch, was an acquaintance of mine. He apparently advised Sparks that "if you can't beat 'em, join 'em." He took the advice to heart.

I loved my work at the DA's office. The job of running the Economic Crime Division was downright fun. But after almost four years as a government attorney, I felt I was ready to try my hand in private practice. I had a notion that to be a "real" lawyer I needed to succeed in both the public and private sector. The firm offered to match my DA salary of about $32,000 and told me I could expect substantial pay increases and bonuses. I committed to join the firm effective January 1, 1981. The day after I committed to Sparks, Dix, and Enoch, Bob Russel offered me the job of assistant district attorney, the number two position in the office. I declined. I knew that if I ever returned to the DA's office, it would be as the district attorney.

I chose to join Sparks, Dix, and Enoch over a few other firms that had approached me because I thought they had a good client base and an opportunity for growth. I also liked the fact they were truly a local firm. I did have some initial reservations about Ken Sparks, however. The first time I met with him for an interview he looked at my resume and asked, "Are you a Catholic?" I answered, "Yes, is that a problem?" "I guess not," he replied. It turns out Ken was an agnostic and not too crazy about religious types. He definitely was *not* politically correct. He was outspoken and opinionated. People tended to like Ken a lot or dislike him strongly. But he was incredibly fair when it came to splitting up the financial pie and he was resolutely loyal to those who were loyal to him. I also think he mellowed a bit over the years. He would be very supportive of me in future years as I moved from the private sector to public service, and I am greatly indebted to him for that support. I was privileged to eulogize him at his funeral in 2007.

On my first day at the law firm, Ken Sparks asked me to begin working on a case that had been languishing in the office for a couple of years. A small group of chiropractors from Wichita, Kansas had retained the firm to sue a Colorado Springs based organization called Clinic Masters. Chiropractors all over the country had responded to a marketing blitz by Clinic Masters and signed contracts with the company in which they agreed to pay $20,000 in exchange for the company revealing to them "the Clinic Masters System." They would pay the $20,000 over time by paying one-half of the amount by which their gross income each month exceeded their average monthly income for the two years prior to joining Clinic Masters. In essence, the plaintiff chiropractors represented by Sparks, Dix alleged in their suit that "the Clinic Masters System" was nothing more than a sophisticated way of saying "raise your fees." The firm had succeeded in having the case certified by the court as a class action, but it had then lost momentum. After starting out with local counsel in Colorado Springs, Clinic Masters had retained the largest firm in Denver to defend the suit. Both sides were beginning to contemplate pretrial motions and Sparks asked me to research possible theories for a summary judgment motion.

After researching the case, I felt there was something fundamentally deficient about the Clinic Masters contract. But I was having trouble articulating a theory that might be the basis of a dispositive motion. Then one night, as I was lying awake in bed, I was thinking back to the first week of law school and I had a sudden inspiration. Recalling the most basic fundamentals of contract law, I developed and refined a theory that the Clinic Masters contract lacked "consideration." In exchange for the payment of $20,000 Clinic Masters promised to reveal "the Clinic Masters System," but the contract failed to give even a basic description of what constituted "the system." Without a general description of what the Clinic Master system was all about, how could a court ever determine whether the company had in fact performed its obligations under the contract? If a court could not enforce the contract, the consideration was illusory. This theory formed the basis of a summary judgment motion that I drafted. In an order that shocked the defendants and their lawyers, the district court judge hearing the case granted the motion. In doing so, he nullified almost three million dollars' worth of contracts involving several hundred chiropractors. Our firm was eventually given a large attorneys' fee award by the court. I had gotten off to a very good start with the firm. My first-year bonus equaled my salary. Only eighteen months after joining the firm I was invited to become a shareholder and the firm became Sparks, Dix, Enoch, and Suthers, P. C.

During my first year with the firm, the wife and baby of one of our best clients, who owned a chain of pizza restaurants, were kidnapped from their home. The client received a ransom call threatening to kill the captives if the police were contacted. Because of my prior experience in law enforcement, I was consulted as to the appropriate strategy. I advised that the police should be immediately contacted, despite the threat. I coordinated with the police during the ordeal, including securing a possible ransom payment. The incident culminated when the police made a dramatic rescue of the victims and arrested the perpetrators at the location where the ransom was to be paid.

Over the next few years, I would have several significant litigation victories that enhanced my reputation as an attorney. I represented the City of Manitou Springs in a high-profile hillside zoning case that was ultimately decided in favor of the City by the Colorado Supreme Court. It was the first of about a dozen cases I would argue to the state's highest court. Our firm represented plaintiffs in cases that eventually helped uncover scandals that led to the demise of the infamous Penn Square Bank in Oklahoma City and the incarceration of Frank Keating, the chairman of Lincoln Savings and Loan in Phoenix. In my most high-profile criminal defense, Ken Sparks and I represented a vice president of a large highway construction firm who was charged with federal antitrust violations for bid-rigging the construction of the famous Eisenhower Tunnel on Interstate 70 in Colorado.

But what I enjoyed most about private practice was helping individuals and small organizations solve their problems. One of my best memories in that regard was an elderly man who came in to see me at the advice of his minister. He felt strongly he had been wronged by a fellow church member he hired to do some work. But he had a religious objection to litigation as a way to solve problems. He told me he was a poorly educated and inarticulate man, and he simply wanted me to draft a letter for his signature to the person who wronged him, explaining his position. I did so, and he was absolutely delighted with the letter. He wrote me a few years later and said it was the best $50 he ever spent.

I was able to bring two very good clients into the firm in the first couple of years I was there. Almost immediately after joining the firm I was able to use my relationships with police officers in Colorado Springs to become counsel for the Colorado Springs Police Protective Association. The firm did all the corporate and tax work for the association, and I personally represented officers facing disciplinary hearings, criminal charges, or seeking disability retirements. In the fall of 1983, I was retained by Richard Hanifen, the newly designated Catholic bishop of the new Diocese of Colorado Springs, which was to be carved out of the Archdiocese of Denver effective January 1, 1984. I would personally perform or supervise the firm's representation of the church. This client produced a great deal of corporate, tax, real estate, employment, and litigation work. Over the next fourteen years, the diocese would be one of the firm's best clients.

Soon after I began representing the diocese, it was sued by an estranged husband and wife alleging that a parish priest they had sought marriage counseling from had ended up having an affair with the wife. The complaint was couched as a clergy malpractice case, the first of its kind in Colorado. Despite the bad facts, I aggressively defended the case in the trial court, asserting that the case was in essence an alienation of affections claim that had long ago been barred in Colorado. I further asserted that the Constitution's First Amendment Free Exercise Clause prevented the court from scrutinizing the quality of counseling services performed by a minister of religion. In other words, the Constitution would not permit a clergy malpractice case. The case of *Destefano v. the Diocese of Colorado Springs* was dismissed by the trial court and that dismissal was affirmed by the Colorado Court of Appeals after spirited oral argument, in a 2-1 decision. It was not until the case reached the Colorado Supreme Court that the bad facts ultimately produced bad law. After another very spirited oral argument, the Supreme Court agreed that there could be no such thing as a clergy malpractice claim under the free exercise clause of the Constitution but found that a claim of breach of fiduciary duty, which had traditionally been limited to financial relationships, could also include a relationship of trust that did not involve financial duties. The case has proven problematic for churches and nonprofits ever since.

As counsel for the Diocese of Colorado Springs I attended the annual meeting of the National Diocesan Attorney's Association. Among the problems discussed extensively were the scandals in various dioceses involving sexual assault on children by pedophile priests. In about 1985 the General Counsel for the U. S. Conference of Catholic Bishops disseminated the latest research on pedophilia indicating it could not be "cured" and instructing that the tendency of bishops to retain afflicted priests after some form of rehabilitation, or to pass them on to another diocese, should be stopped. Such offenders had to be drummed out of the priesthood. There was also clear direction to develop psychological screening of seminarians to attempt to weed out pedophiles. As a consequence, when even more high-profile scandals involving clergy pedophilia ensnared several large dioceses twenty years later, I had very little sympathy for the plight of my church. Several US bishops, with full knowledge of the nature and extent of the problem, had failed to take the necessary action to stop it. At the recommendation of some therapists, they had taken a more compassionate but less effective approach. That was also the conclusion of an independent panel formed to investigate the scandal.

Throughout my tenure in private practice, I was very involved in community and political activities. Because of my prosecution background I was invited to join the board of directors of the local Crime Stoppers Organization. In 1984, the local Community

Corrections Program, which had previously been run by El Paso County, became a nonprofit organization. I joined the board soon thereafter as a director and eventually served two years as president. Com Corr, as it was called, had contracts with the county jail, the State Department of Corrections, and the Federal Bureau of Prisons. They provided housing and programming for offenders sentenced directly by the courts as well as for those transitioning out of state or to federal prisons. During my board service, the nonprofit corporation reached approximately $3 million in annual gross revenues. It has continued to grow ever since.

I continued to be active in St. Paul's Parish, serving my second term on the parish council and a lengthy term on the parish finance committee. From my childhood, the parish was a constant in my life and I looked for ways to give back.

I was also one of four charter members of a Catholic lawyers group, the St. Thomas More Society. More is the patron saint of lawyers and politicians, having risen to the office of Chancellor of England, only to be beheaded by Henry VIII for his refusal to sign an oath in support of the king's divorce from Catherine of Aragon in order to marry Ann Boleyn. I have particular admiration for More as an example of a principled man in a secular world. As a good lawyer, he did not hesitate to use the letter of the law to try to save himself, arguing that his silence on the issue should be construed under English common law as acquiescence in the King's action. But he steadfastly refused to violate the sanctity of an oath and was willing to die for the principle. Over the ensuing decade the local St. Thomas More Society would sponsor some of the most meaningful discussion groups I ever participated in on such subjects as character, the seven deadly sins, and the compelling question of "whether a good Christian can be a good lawyer." Mal Wakin, a retired Air Force Brigadier General and former head of the philosophy department at the Air Force Academy, typically led the very interesting discussions.

Throughout my ensuing political career, I would often be asked what public figures I most admired. Most politicians would play it safe and say Abraham Lincoln. I would answer Thomas More. When asked why, I would respond, "He was a lawyer, a politician, and a saint. The fact that's possible gives me hope." He also provided sage advice I have passed on to many young lawyers: "Never lose your soul to win a point." Given my admiration for More, I was very touched when the University of Notre Dame Law School gave me its St. Thomas More Award in 2017 as "A distinguished public servant exhibiting uncompromising integrity and loyalty to conscience."

In 1982 and 1983 I was invited to join the two most prestigious social clubs in Colorado Springs. In 1982, as soon as I became a shareholder in my law firm, I joined the El Paso Club. The downtown club had been started in 1877 by Colorado Springs's most prominent pioneers, including its founder, General William Palmer. It was a delightful place to have a business lunch or to entertain for dinner, and Janet and I took friends and clients there frequently. My membership at the El Paso Club was sponsored by two of my law partners, Ken Sparks and Tim Dix. In 1983, I was asked to join the even more exclusive Cheyenne Mountain Country Club. Located in the Broadmoor, the club had been founded in 1891 by some members of the El Paso Club looking for outdoor recreational opportunities. Located a block east of the original Broadmoor Casino, the club's early membership was a real Who's Who of Colorado Springs, including General Palmer and Spencer Penrose, and has remained so ever since, with only about 250 resident members. The club had started out primarily as a polo and skeet shooting club but had evolved over the years to provide tennis and swimming in the summer and elegant dining and social functions throughout the year. While the El Paso Club was somewhat of a meritocracy and included many of the city's most successful business people, the Cheyenne Mountain Country Club was a Broadmoor dominated group whose parentage was as important, or even more so, than their performance in life. A number of the members were heirs to fortunes and had no occupation other than to explore creative ways to spend their money. Some were, in the words of my law partner Ken Sparks, "degenerate descendants of virile ancestors." So how did I manage to be invited to join? Ironically, my application was sponsored by Gary Loo and Dr. Richard Vanderhoof, two men whose lawns I had mowed just a dozen years earlier. While I was not really one of them, I was generally liked by the Broadmoor crowd. Membership in these two clubs by the age of thirty-two gave me a clear sense that I was becoming part of the community's influential establishment.

I would remain a member of the El Paso Club until after I was elected district attorney in 1989. At that time a distressing incident caused me to reconsider the propriety of the area's chief prosecutor socializing so closely with the city's most influential people. A junior member, who happened to be a lawyer and the son of a local judge, was charged by my office with selling drugs to an undercover cop. An officer of the El Paso Club suggested to me, in a serious manner, that it would be appropriate to give this fellow member of the club "consideration" because that is what was expected among club members. Stunned, I resigned shortly thereafter. I had no similar experiences at the Cheyenne Mountain Country Club and my family greatly enjoyed our membership there for seventeen years, until a realization of another sort caused me to reconsider that affiliation.

During my service as a deputy and chief deputy DA, I had become a Republican precinct committeeman. In 1982 my law firm's senior partner, Ken Sparks, convinced me to be the county chairman for Natalie Meyer, a candidate for Colorado secretary of state. Meyer started late but gained momentum throughout the campaign and won the office. In the course of the campaign, I met a lot of Republicans in El Paso County and around the state. Natalie Meyer also became a strong political ally, and that would prove to be important in future years. I also served on two occasions in the early and mid-eighties as chair of the local Republican Party's Lincoln Day Dinner.

But the most important political development of my young career occurred in early June 1984. My old boss, Bob Russel, was running for a sixth term as DA. Frankly, most of his former deputies, including myself, hoped he would step down. His assistant DA, the person he hired when I turned down his offer to take the job in late 1980, had recently been arrested for drunk driving and the public's view of the DA's office was at a low ebb. Russel's personal problems, including alcoholism, had been the subject of media attention and he was viewed as politically very vulnerable. It was one of those times in politics when a time-for-a-change slogan by the opposition might carry the day. Yet Russel had been an excellent talent scout. Over a twenty-year period, most of the top-notch trial lawyers in Colorado Springs had worked in his office. His top assistants had included Bob Isaac, a longtime mayor of Colorado Springs, Bill Hybl, chairman of the El Pomar Foundation and president of the US Olympic Committee, and many other community leaders.

I was one of several former deputies who were considering running if Russel did not run again. But Bob had been very loyal to his employees, and none had ever run against him. That changed in 1984. A former chief deputy, Ed Arcuri, took him on in the Republican primary. Two weeks before the nominating convention, Russel called me and asked me to nominate him. Virtually everyone I talked to recommended against it, suggesting it would be contrary to any future political ambitions I might have. Russel was a "goner" one prominent Republican told me. Why jump on to a sinking ship?

Because Bob Russel had been so good to me (despite the episode in which I caused him to be investigated by the state attorney general), I defied the advice and agreed to do the nomination speech. It was a political turning point for me. The less than five-minute speech was not particularly brilliant in content, but it was very well delivered and gave the crowd a valid reason to support the embattled incumbent. I had a great opportunity to display my oratory skills to about 800 of the area's most prominent Republicans. For several weeks thereafter I had Republicans calling me or sending me notes to compliment my speech. Several asked, "Why don't you run for DA?" Russel got top line on the primary ballot by just a few votes and won the primary by only 150 votes. He lost the general election to Barney Iuppa, a former public defender, by 12,000 votes. Russel had defeated Iuppa by the same margin four years earlier. The Republicans had lost the DA's office for the first time since 1960, but largely because of my speech at the nominating convention in 1984, I quickly became the "heir apparent" to the party's nomination in 1988.

By 1987, I was thriving in private practice. I was thirty-five years old and making over $130,000 per year. That was a good income for a young lawyer in Colorado Springs at the time. It was clear I could be making considerably more in the future. I had achieved an "A rating" from Martindale-Hubbell, a publication which rates lawyers based on input from other lawyers in the community. An "A" rating was unusual for someone my age. Because of our income, our family was able to afford some nice vacations to places like Ireland, Bermuda, Jamaica, Hawaii, and Mexico. It was a very comfortable lifestyle. But in the summer of 1987, I had to make a decision whether to run for district attorney in 1988. Barney Iuppa was moderately popular, but El Paso County was predominantly Republican, and I believed the incumbent could be beaten if the Republican candidate could win back the Republican voters who had abandoned Russel in 1984. Despite the fact the DA's salary was only $60,000 at the time, I had Janet's support. She had become convinced over the last four years it was something I would regret for the rest of my life if I did not at least give it a try.

Chapter XIV
The District Attorney

In mid-January of 1988, at a press conference attended by my law partners, Republican stalwarts, family, and many friends, I announced my candidacy for District Attorney of the Fourth Judicial District. Largely because of the party networking and campaign planning that had already occurred, no other Republican entered the race. I was able to use the party nominating convention to prepare the party faithful for the hard-fought campaign ahead. The incumbent, Barney Iuppa, also had no competition in the Democratic Party. 1988 was a relatively quiet political year in El Paso and Teller Counties. The two counties, consisting of approximately 500,000 people combined, comprised the Fourth Judicial District. The DA's race quickly became the premier local race of the election year.

It did not take me long to ascertain the very real benefits of incumbency. I remember one particularly hard day on the campaign trail that really drove home the reality. I started the day at 6:30 a.m. speaking to an Optimist Club in Fountain, Colorado south of Colorado Springs. Only fourteen people showed up and I soon learned that least ten of them were Yellow Dog Democrats. At 9 a.m. I spoke to a class of seventh graders. I did it with the naive notion that they might take my campaign brochure home to their parents, who were at least old enough to vote. That notion was shattered when the brochures started flying back towards me as paper airplanes. At noon I spoke at a tea for ten elderly Republican women. I spent a whole hour convincing them to vote for me before I realized they would vote for me even if I was the Boston Strangler or endorsed euthanasia. In the afternoon and evening I spoke to three other small groups, spending an inordinate time trying to earn very few votes. I dragged myself home at 9:30 p.m. only to pick up the newspaper and find my opponent, the incumbent, pictured on the front page next to a flattering article. I figured 200,000 people would read the article. I then fell into bed in time to watch the ten o'clock news. There was my opponent cutting the ribbon at a new Child Advocacy Center. I figured at least 100,000 people were watching. I was extremely discouraged but vowed to press on.

Several local political observers commented afterward that we ran an almost textbook campaign. We had a tremendous grassroots effort. An El Paso County political activist, Ken Ball, who had lost a primary race for county commissioner in 1986, asked me if he could be the campaign chair. I declined because I had a high-profile local lawyer to play that role, but I offered to let him organize the precinct level campaign. He did a masterful job. He analyzed the 1984 DA's race precinct by precinct to determine where the largest Republican defections had occurred. We targeted those precincts. Over a six-month period, we walked more than eighty precincts and rang almost 20,000 doorbells. What a slice of life that revealed. I was once attacked by a German Shepherd. At another house a lady answered the door with only a bra and panties on. It was a real art to make sure that you didn't spend more than thirty seconds at any one house. We had a sign in the yard of just about every person who had ever heard of John Suthers. During the last two weeks we drove an antique fire truck loaded with campaign signs through all the local shopping malls.

Our campaign headquarters was an abandoned gas station at the corner of Nevada and Pikes Peak Avenues, in the heart of downtown Colorado Springs. The building was in such bad shape that campaign workers had to go across the street to City Hall to use the restrooms. But we attracted lots of volunteers to the energetic campaign. I remember one lady named Elvira, who drove

120 miles round trip each day to volunteer and answer telephones at the headquarters. I suspect we had over 100 volunteers.

We also raised almost $100,000, an almost unheard of amount in a local race at the time. Several prominent businessmen who were clients of my law firm and several prominent local lawyers helped greatly by soliciting their colleagues. Gil Johnson, who owned a large construction company our firm represented, was particularly helpful in raising funds. We also got some help from the state Republican Party and its chairman, Bruce Benson. We were able to buy a significant amount of TV time between the middle of September and Election Day. I could tell that the TV ads were having an effect because people answering the doorbell started saying, "I saw you on TV." I was also helped by an endorsement by the Police Protective Association, which represented a large number of Colorado Springs police officers. I expected the endorsement because of my close association with the group as their legal counsel, but it was problematic for the incumbent DA who had to explain why the police supported his opponent.

The incumbent's campaign also made a strategic mistake that was costly in terms of allowing us to gain attention and momentum. A longtime friend of mine, Mike Faricy, was a new car dealer. I asked him to raise funds for the campaign. He got donations ranging from $100 to $500 from several dealers in town, a total of about $4,000. When Barney Iuppa's campaign learned of the donations from disclosure forms, he wrote a letter to all the same dealers saying that his father, a car dealer, had told him that business and politics don't mix and their contributions to my campaign could be bad for business. He suggested they "make things right" by contributing to his campaign. A few of the car dealers were offended by the tone of the letter and we "leaked" it to the city newspaper. *The Gazette* ran a copy of it on the front of the Metro section along with quotes from some of the dealers accusing the incumbent DA of extortion. To add injury to insult, the "shakedown" was the subject of a widely viewed political cartoon in the Sunday paper.

A month before the election, the state Republican Party paid for a telephone poll. The results were mixed. It appeared I had won back the majority of the Republican vote, but I remained way behind among unaffiliated voters. Only 20 percent of unaffiliated voters said they supported me, 40 percent were undecided. I needed 40-45 percent of the unaffiliated vote to win. My law partner, Ken Sparks, called a friend, Walt Klein, who was a political consultant for US Senator Bill Armstrong and others. As a favor, Walt helped design a mailing targeted to unaffiliated voters. During the last week of the campaign, Armstrong appeared at a rally on my behalf. It was an effort to offset the fact that Colorado Governor Roy Romer had just done the same for Barney Iuppa. Presidential candidate George H. W. Bush came to Colorado Springs two days before the election, and I was given the privilege of introducing him to the crowd at a large rally at a local hotel. I was in a room with the vice president waiting to go on stage when an aide handed him some poll results. He smiled at me and said, "I think you're about to introduce the next president of the United States."

The DA campaign also included more than fifteen head-to-head encounters. They were covered heavily in the newspaper, and one was shown on prime-time television. Another was live on drive-time radio. It was a clean but hard-fought campaign. The criticism directed at me was tougher for Janet to handle than for me. During the campaign she cut a quote from Thomas Jefferson out of the newspaper and put it on our refrigerator. It read: "Politics is such a torment that I would advise everyone I love not to mix with it." It would still be on our refrigerator thirty-five years later.

My campaign team felt strongly we were peaking in the last two weeks. They were right. On November 8, 1988, I was elected District Attorney of the Fourth Judicial District by a margin of 12,000 votes. I would be the district's twenty-second DA since Colorado became a state in 1876. Barney Iuppa gave a gracious concession speech after which I gave a victory speech to an excited group of campaign workers, friends, family, and party loyalists. I tearfully alluded to my parents' influence and their premature death that prevented them from sharing the moment. I thanked Aunt Jo and Uncle Jim and many others that supported me through the years

As Janet and I left the hotel to go home well after midnight, she said something to the effect of "You did it, John." Before I could think about it, I remember muttering, "Yes, not bad for a bastard." As soon as I said it, I recognized it was a bizarre thing to say and was probably loaded with significance for any psychoanalyst who might attempt to analyze my motives for seeking public office. The next day I felt compelled to visit my parents' graves at the local cemetery. That also caused considerable introspection.

My campaign for DA in 1988 would be only the first of seven campaigns for public office. My three statewide campaigns would be more difficult, more taxing, more complex, and a lot more expensive. But in this first campaign, I had learned how to be a good lawyer running for a public service position. It worked and I would keep to the script in years to come.

Between the election on November 8 and taking office on the second Tuesday in January, I interviewed every deputy DA in the office. The office at the time consisted of about forty-two attorneys and a total staff of 150. I also talked to law enforcement officials and judges about possible choices for my assistant district attorney, the number two job in the office. I chose Jeanne Smith, who had been in the office for about six years, having been hired by Bob Russel and promoted to chief deputy by Barney Iuppa. The choice would prove to be a terrific one. I also made a good decision to elevate Linda McMahon to be chief trial deputy. She was a stern taskmaster and produced good results for the criminal division.

The first several months as district attorney was a time of adjustment for my family. District attorneys are covered heavily in the local print and electronic media, and I quickly became a high-profile public figure in Colorado Springs. Even on the local level, public life has its challenges. Alison was nine and Kate was six when I was elected. We quickly discovered that whether we were at the grocery store, at the kids' school and sporting events, or in a restaurant, people wanted to talk to the DA. We took our first vacation after the election to Manzanillo, Mexico in March of 1989. The four of us were sitting at a small restaurant and my wife commented how nice it was not to have our dinner interrupted by people who recognized me. It could not have been two minutes later when a man came up to our table and said, "Aren't you the District Attorney in Colorado Springs?" That was a good indication of how hard it would be to escape public surveillance. One of my favorite stories in that regard involved an exchange with a checkout person at Walmart. It occurred after I had been DA for several years. After looking at me for some time the clerk said, "Has anyone ever told you that you look like the district attorney?" My ego was stroked, and I decided to play along. "Yes," I said, "several people have commented on that." She then said, "But I'm sure he is a lot taller." She was entirely serious. That certainly put me in my place, and I simply smiled and walked away. When Janet would use her credit card at a store or otherwise identify herself to a stranger as Janet Suthers, she would sometimes be asked, "Do you know John Suthers?" If she was in a humorous mood she would respond, "I know him in the biblical sense."

I also quickly learned that with a high public profile can come threats to your safety. There are a lot of mentally ill and angry people in our society that threaten public figures. The difficult task is to figure out which threats to take seriously. One situation I took very seriously as DA involved a police raid on a militia compound in the mountains west of Colorado Springs. Among the documents seized was a hit list that had my name on it. I wore a bulletproof vest to public appearances for the next two months.

I believe our family handled the higher public profile pretty well. Janet and I would always be polite but at the same time send a clear message that our family and our children had a life outside

All This I Saw, and Part of It I Was

of politics. I thought we did a particularly good job of insulating Alison and Kate from the trials of politics until they were in high school and could deal with them better. They would participate in parades and other fun things but generally did not attend debates or other functions with hostile audiences. Nor did we talk about the pressures of the job at home. I do remember one compelling experience to the contrary, however. One Saturday morning Kate, who was about nine or ten at the time, was looking at the morning newspaper. She asked, "Dad, what's a racist?" I went to see what she was looking at. It was a headline that read, "Parents call Suthers Racist." My office had just charged five high school students, including two star football players, with kicking and beating a Fort Carson soldier, named Layne Schmidtke, to death on a street corner in downtown Colorado Springs. They did so because he and a companion—contrary to their admonition—had walked into their territory. They were juveniles who had all been charged as adults because of the violent, heinous nature of the crime. All of the defendants were African American or Hispanic. The youths' parents held a protest on the courthouse steps, alleging I was motivated by racism. All the defendants were eventually convicted of charges ranging from criminally negligent homicide to second-degree murder and served prison sentences.

After the election I quickly fulfilled a campaign promise by setting up a specialized unit to prosecute child abuse cases from the charging stage through trial and sentencing. It was called "vertical prosecution." It had the intended effect of vastly improving the results of such cases. Cases of sexual assault on children are particularly difficult to handle and need the attention of deputy DAs who are specially trained and psychologically suited for such cases. Such specialized units are now commonplace in large prosecutor's offices.

My predecessor had started a Child Advocacy Center, where victimized children could be interviewed, examined by doctors, and otherwise assisted in a safe, comfortable, and non-threatening environment. Unfortunately, it did not have sufficient financial and volunteer support from the community. I, along with Rebecca Stocker, a DA's office employee who helped establish the center, embarked on a strategy to establish a community board, hire an executive director, and get the Child Advocacy Center on stable financial footing. I convinced the El Paso County Sheriff and Colorado Springs Police Department to join the DA's office in contributing seed money of $30,000 per year. In 1993 the board hired Janet Buss, a newcomer to Colorado Springs to be the executive director. It was a great decision. Over the next decade, largely through Janet's efforts, the center became a national model. Now called Safe Passage, it continues to do great work.

We also continued to improve on the handling of domestic violence cases. When I started as a prosecutor in 1977, the office had a "drop charges day" every Wednesday afternoon at which victims who wanted to have charges dismissed would meet with a paralegal, explain why they wanted charges to be dropped, and sign a release. In almost every case the request would be honored. Virtually all the people requesting charges to be dismissed were women and many of them still showed bruises or other visible signs of abuse. It was a depressing sight. Thankfully, by the time I became DA much had changed, but there was still a lot of work to be done to help the victims of domestic abuse and still be able to hold the abusers accountable. We never dropped charges if we thought the case could be proved. But in first-offense misdemeanor cases where the victim, after counseling, wanted the abuser to be offered a diversion program that included counseling or treatment, we would offer the defendant that opportunity. We got tremendous assistance from domestic violence support groups. In serious cases they offered shelter to the victims and encouraged them to cooperate in the prosecution of the abuser.

Yet for all our efforts, domestic violence remained a societal scourge. I personally experienced a nightmarish scenario. A woman made an appointment to see me. She was bright and articulate. She had taken every available step to protect herself and her children from her abusive ex-husband, a former Colorado Springs policeman, including securing a restraining order. Despite the court order, he had recently put a hose in her basement window and flooded the basement. He was arrested for the misdemeanor and was pending a bail hearing. She told me that if her ex-husband got out of jail, within a few days either she or he would be dead. I told her we would seek the highest bail possible. In fact, we got a $10,000 cash bond, which was high for the nature of the offense. But he bonded out, and two days later he went over to his ex-wife's house, raped her at gunpoint in front of their young children, and then turned the gun on himself and committed suicide. I actually thanked God he killed himself instead of the others.

We also frequently suffered the frustrations of uncooperative victims. One twenty-four-year-old college educated woman was beaten unconscious with barbells by her cocaine-addicted boyfriend. He fled the scene but was arrested in another state. When the victim came out of a coma after sixty days, she married the guy. She refused to testify at the trial. We proved the case without her by using blood evidence and the defendant was sentenced to prison over the tearful objection of his brain-injured wife. Sadly, domestic violence will remain a serious societal problem for the foreseeable future.

Three months after I took office, in April of 1989, the Colorado Supreme Court issued an opinion which, for the first time in fifteen years, upheld the Colorado legislature's attempt to enact a criminal obscenity statute. They had been attempting to do so ever since the 1973 US Supreme Court decision in *Miller v. California*, which had legally defined *obscenity*. The Colorado court insisted that the state constitution required a higher standard of scrutiny, despite the fact that the language of the Colorado Constitution was identical to that of the US Constitution. I then sent a letter to all the adult entertainment establishments in the judicial district advising them of the case, the standard established by the court, and the fact that they were now subject to criminal prosecution for crossing the line into obscenity. I soon got a glimpse of the tactics of the sex industry. All hell broke loose. Letters began pouring into editorial pages accusing me of censorship and portraying the industry as being in the highest ideals of the First Amendment. I simply responded that the court had ruled that the First Amendment did not protect child pornography, bestiality, and explicit sado-masochistic materials. I was heartened to receive over 1,000 supportive letters from citizens and a public endorsement of my efforts from Colorado US Senator Bill Armstrong. It was a battle many of my prosecution colleagues were unwilling to take on, but I would continue to do so throughout my prosecution career. The vast majority of sexually-explicit material is protected by the First Amendment. But the courts have allowed prosecutors to pursue the worst of the worst, including child pornography, and I was willing to do so.

During my eight years as district attorney, my office was involved in hundreds of fascinating cases. To detail even the most interesting twenty-five would take a manuscript of considerable length. I will allude to a few that have proven to be among the most memorable to the community or to me personally.

In June of 1989, I personally tried my first case as the elected district attorney. Although the job of running a large DA's office was primarily administrative, I was also determined to personally handle a few cases each year. The defendant, Charles Limbrick, was a fifteen-year-old charged as an adult for killing his mother. Limbrick was a bright young man who was well liked by his ninth grade classmates. On the day of the murder, he had given a speech to the class seeking to be class president. But he and his friend, Chris Marrow, had also been plotting for months to run away, and for some reason, decided they needed to kill Limbrick's mother so she would not thwart their plans. Testimony at trial indicated that his mother was a very caring person who was much concerned for her son's welfare. The week before the murder, Limbrick had come home one evening and his mother suspected he had been drinking. When he denied it, she took him to a nearby emergency medical facility for a breathalyzer test, which proved her suspicion. He was angry about the incident and apparently decided to accelerate his plans. Limbrick had been soliciting friends at school to help him get a gun and Chris Marrow had succeeded. On the day in question, they hurried home from school in order to arrive at the Limbrick home shortly before Mrs. Limbrick arrived home from work. Marrow stayed in Charles's room on the lower level of the house while Charles waited for his mother with the gun at the foot of the stairway leading to the lower level. According to the trial testimony of Chris, when Mrs. Limbrick came into the house she called out, "Chuckie, are you home?" Then she came down the stairs. Chris testified he heard a gunshot after which he heard Mrs. Limbrick exclaim, "Chuckie, I love you, but you just shot me." He testified he then heard another gunshot. He came out to find Mrs. Limbrick dead. They first tried to dispose of the body, but then decided to go next door and tell the neighbor they had come home to find Mrs. Limbrick dead. The neighbor called the police and testified at trial that Chuck fell asleep on the couch while they were waiting for the police to arrive.

The coroner testified that the first shot went through Mrs. Limbrick's hand as she held it in a defensive posture in front of her face. The second shot was point-blank to the head.

The defense tried alternative theories. They tried to portray the mother as abusive, but friends and siblings of Limbrick pretty much squelched that effort. They also tried to convince the jury that the killing was not premeditated. So, the first words out of my mouth in the rebuttal closing argument were, "Chuckie, I love you, but you just shot me" and I repeated the phrase three more times in the course of the argument. The jury convicted Limbrick of first-degree murder and he was sentenced to life in prison with parole eligibility after forty years. The police detectives who handled the case gave me a small plaque with the date of the verdict and the words, "Chuckie, I love you." It has hung in my den ever since.

Limbrick performed well in prison and became an accomplished musician. I subsequently recommended to the governor that his sentence be commuted to make him eligible for release much sooner. The commutation was granted, and he was eventually paroled in 2010, after twenty-one years in prison, at the age of thirty-six. In 2012 Chuck Limbrick personally invited me to a concert he was giving at a mega-church in Colorado Springs where he was employed as a music minister. My wife and I joined a thousand others in attendance to watch him sing and play at least four instruments. He was an incredibly talented performer. It was an experience every prosecutor should have in order to impress upon them the reality of redemption. Unfortunately, Charles Limbrick suffered from alcoholism, and died in a one-car accident in 2017.

During my first year as DA my office prosecuted a serial rapist, Gregory Lindsey, for crimes against ten different women. The "East Side Rapist" had terrorized the community for several months. The unusual thing about the case was that all but one of the counts was proven through the use of a new forensic breakthrough called DNA. It was the first time DNA was admitted as evidence in the courts of Colorado and it was eventually sanctioned by the state Supreme Court in the case of *People v. Lindsey*. The use of DNA would become commonplace in the next decade. DNA was an incredible advance in forensics because it not only led to conviction of the guilty but also, as I would subsequently observe, exoneration of the innocent.

In 1990 I was appointed a special prosecutor in a police corruption case in Denver. Two Denver detectives had been dubbed "the super cops" by the Denver media because they made frequent dramatic arrests of armed robbers and burglars, often while the crimes were in progress and sometimes while TV cameras were rolling. Then a career criminal testified at a hearing in one of the cases that the two cops had paid him to convince other fellow criminals to rob a convenience store and that he had driven them to the crime scene and then abandoned them as the cops instructed. The "super cops" made the dramatic bust of the robbers as they entered the store. Other cons started making similar allegations. None of the DAs in the Denver Metro area were able to adequately investigate and prosecute the matter, because some of their previous convictions could be undermined by the allegations. As the Colorado Springs DA, I was appointed by the Denver District Court to investigate the case. I did so with the help of Bob Brown, a chief deputy in my office. We found sufficient corroborating evidence to bring charges against the officers. Needless to say, we faced a daunting challenge. There was some significant opposition to the prosecution in the Denver Police Department. Further, the best witness in the case had five previous felony convictions. Many of the witnesses were also drug addicts. Because of their checkered histories, the witnesses were brutalized by defense attorneys at preliminary hearings. Nevertheless, we persevered. Eventually, both officers agreed to plead guilty to official misconduct, and the ringleader, Daryl Cinquanta, who was a very high-profile member of the department, was forced to resign. The other officer was demoted to airport duty. Because of the nature of the case, the proof problems it presented, and the positive impact of the disposition on the Denver Police Department, I considered it a very good plea bargain.

The unsettling consequences that often flow from the difficult decisions prosecutors have to make were exemplified in another case I will never forget. A sixty-eight-year-old, retired Colorado Springs fireman named Daryl Atkinson owned several rental properties. A man that rented one of them was taken to the hospital with carbon monoxide poisoning. The city utility department ordered Atkinson not to re-rent the property until the furnace had been fixed and inspected by the department. Atkinson subsequently re-let the property and an entire family of five people died from carbon monoxide inhalation. Atkinson initially claimed that he had never been informed by the utilities department that the furnace had to be fixed. But a witness from his property management company came forward with a taped phone message from Atkinson in which he asked the company to get the furnace fixed because it had been "red tagged" by the utilities department. The company had a repairmen go out at once, but they were unable to get on to the property because of a threatening dog. Before they could return, Atkinson called and canceled the request. He then re-let the property to the ill-fated family.

I had police and DA investigators procure a warrant for Atkinson's arrest for five counts of involuntary manslaughter. He was arrested by Lou Smit, an investigator in my office, who helped him arrange to post bail. However, that night, apparently overcome with guilt, Atkinson killed himself. Ironically, he did so by carbon monoxide inhalation in his garage. The event received heavy news coverage. The next morning, I received a phone call from Larry Ochs, a former mayor of Colorado Springs who knew Atkinson. In the course of the highly confrontational conversation, he screamed that I had murdered Atkinson. He had no interest in hearing the evidence against him. While I felt bad about what had transpired, upon reflection of the events, there was nothing I would have done differently. Making tough decisions and doing what you believe is right does not insulate you from controversy. In fact, it sometimes generates it. But it does let you sleep well at night. One of my strengths as a public prosecutor was my ability to make a decision and then calmly withstand the ensuing controversy, making an articulate explanation for the decision when it was ethically permissible.

Principled politicians frequently lose friends along the way and principled prosecutors tend to lose a lot. In my tenure as DA, my office sent two contributors to my first campaign to prison, prosecuted several people that I knew for drunk driving and other indiscretions, and prosecuted the children of many prominent citizens as juvenile delinquents. I had similar experiences as US attorney and Colorado attorney general. While I tried to be as professional as possible about such matters, some of them took it very personally. I can name a dozen or so notable citizens of Colorado who don't speak to me. But if you want to be an effective public prosecutor, there is no other way to handle the job.

Another case pitted me against one of the most venerable institutions in Colorado Springs, Penrose Hospital, a Catholic hospital run by the Sisters of Charity of Cincinnati. My office was prosecuting a nurse for stealing drugs off a medical tray to feed her personal addiction to barbiturates. She and her attorney came in to see me, unhappy with the offer that had been made to her by the line prosecutor. She asked me why I did not prosecute drug addicted doctors. "Do you know of any I should prosecute?" I asked. She proceeded to tell me that two weeks earlier the highest volume obstetrician at Penrose had overdosed in a closet in the doctors' lounge while a nurse delivered a patient's baby. While I found it hard to believe, I sent an investigator to check out the story. He called back to say that after much cajoling, two very frightened obstetrics nurses had acknowledged the incident. I could hear one of them crying in the background. They also indicated that the president of the hospital, Sister Myra James, who was an icon in the local community, had personally come to the scene and walked off with the syringe the doctor had used in the pocket of her habit! I immediately called the Colorado Board of Medical Examiners and learned that Penrose had not reported the incident. It turned out the doctor had suffered from a drug problem for at least seven years. I prosecuted the doctor, convicted him of a felony, and he lost his license, despite personal appeals from Sister Myra James and other prominent members of the community. Penrose was the subject of an audit by the Drug Enforcement Administration and a very large fine was levied against it for inadequacies in its drug inventory system. A short time later, Sister Myra James left Penrose Hospital for a new assignment as head of Good Samaritan Hospital in

Cincinnati. To my knowledge, I was the only public official in Colorado Springs not invited to her going away party.

I made another very difficult decision when I charged a Cripple Creek man with assisting in the suicide of his mother. The mother was a seventy-two-year-old Christian Scientist who had been experiencing very severe abdominal pain for some time. Finally, her forty-eight-year-old son convinced her to allow him to take her to the emergency room at a small rural hospital. A doctor told her she could have something as easily curable as a kidney infection or as incurable as pancreatic cancer, but that he needed to do a biopsy to determine the exact nature of the problem. The mother refused to have a biopsy and her son took her home where she lay on the couch immobilized with pain. The next day she asked her son to get a gun and bullets so she could kill herself. He refused at first but eventually relented and brought her a gun. He waited in the next room while she put the gun to her head and pulled the trigger. He called the police and told them he had come home and found his mother dead. Only after a suspicious DA investigator challenged his story did he confess to his role. An autopsy determined the mother suffered from a kidney infection that could have been treated with antibiotics.

As a matter of law and public policy, I felt strongly that I should act to deter assisted suicide. I charged the son with a section of the Colorado manslaughter statute that made it a class four felony to assist a suicide. But I also had sympathy for the obedient son's plight and quickly contacted his attorney to offer a deferred sentence. That meant he would not be jailed, and the case would be dismissed if he succeeded in avoiding any further legal problems during a probationary period. While the offer was imminently reasonable, his attorney had already been contacted by the Hemlock Society, an organization that promotes suicide as a viable option and the legalization of assisted suicide. They were looking to make the tragedy a showcase for their viewpoint. They agreed to supply all the funding necessary for the defense of the case. I had no illusion that a jury would follow the law and convict the defendant. And in fact, they worked hard to find an excuse to acquit him. Once again, I had no regrets.

In 1991, I was again appointed as special prosecutor to handle a high-profile murder case in Walsenburg, Colorado, a small community sixty miles south of Pueblo. After a ten-year feud between two ranchers over property lines, one killed the other. The prosecution contended it was a highly premeditated act after the defendant, Tom Ferrero, had lured the victim, Orville Halsey, to a disputed fence line where the murder occurred. The defendant contended he acted in self-defense, shooting Halsey because he thought he was about to harm family members who were arguing with him. Each day of the trial at the small rural courthouse was very tense. The victim's family and friends filled one side of the courtroom, and the defendant's family and supporters filled the other. One remarkable aspect of the case was the fact that the victim's daughter was taking pictures of the defendant while he was shooting her father. She did not realize he was actually shooting at him at the time. But my most vivid memory of the case was the courtroom disturbance that ensued when the jury returned a verdict of first-degree murder. The defendant and his family went into a rage. While the judge and jury were whisked from the courtroom by sheriff's deputies, I was shielded in a corner of the courtroom by an armed DA investigator, Lou Smit. We got an escort to the county line by the Colorado State Patrol. Ferrero was sentenced to life in prison and died of heart failure in 2001, while I was running the state prison system.

In September of 1991, a thirteen-year-old girl, Heather Dawn Church, was abducted from her home in the Black Forest area, north of Colorado Springs. Heather had been babysitting her younger brother while her parents attended a school function. When they returned, Heather was gone from her bed, but her younger brother was undisturbed in his bedroom. A screen had been removed from her bedroom window to gain entrance. There was no sign of a struggle and the only forensic evidence recovered from the scene was a single fingerprint on the screen. The investigators ran the print through the national fingerprint database, but no match was found.

Two years to the day after the abduction of Heather, a skull was found in the mountains west of Colorado Springs. Dental records showed it to be Heather's. But there was still no match of the fingerprint and no other evidence to go on. Finally, in 1995, investigator Lou Smit, a great detective whose name appears frequently in this book, ran the fingerprint again through a variety of databases. It got a hit. The print matched that of a man named Robert Charles Brown, who lived in Louisiana. Through great investigative work we were able to show that Brown lived in Colorado, just a half mile from the Church residence, when the crime occurred. We had him arrested and extradited to Colorado. We considered seeking the death penalty but there was an issue of whether Colorado had a death penalty on the date of the murder. There was a several day gap in September of 1991 between a Colorado Supreme Court ruling invalidating the death penalty and a legislative fix that occurred within days thereafter. Because of our limited evidence and the thorny legal issue, we wound up accepting an offer from Brown to plead guilty and accept a life sentence without parole.

After going to prison, Brown sought unsuccessfully to withdraw his plea. When all his appeals were exhausted, he started writing strange letters to El Paso County Sheriff's investigators implying he had killed others. One investigator gained his trust and over the ensuing years Brown confessed to forty-eight homicides across the country and while he was overseas in the military. While only a fraction of the murders was fully corroborated, it does appear that Brown was a serial killer. Everyone involved in the Heather Dawn Church case felt some satisfaction that, by finally catching Brown, we had no doubt prevented other murders from occurring.

My office prosecuted gang members for drug dealing, car thefts, assaults, and murders. We were the first District Attorney's Office in Colorado to successfully use the state's organized crime statute to dismantle a gang, the Gangster Disciples. One murder case I personally handled brought about an encounter I'll never forget. A fifteen-year-old boy had been killed in a drive-by shooting near a high school in southeast Colorado Springs. The police determined the shooting was part of an ongoing fight between rival gangs. When I met with the mother of the dead teenager, I explained to her what the investigation had determined and how we would go about proving the case in court. She became very angry at me and denied her son had ever had any involvement with a gang. After almost an hour of trying to calm her down, I finally pulled out an autopsy photo of her son, naked on the table at the coroner's office, with gang tattoos all over his body. She collapsed in my arms in tears.

Three local law enforcement officers died at the hands of criminals while I was DA. A female El Paso County deputy sheriff, Cecilia Benefiel, was found shot to death in her home. While the case remains unsolved, her estranged husband, who was then a state patrol officer, has been the prime suspect. Another El Paso County deputy sheriff, Hugh Martin, was killed by drug dealer Robert Seikich, during a drug raid. Seikich was paralyzed from the waist down from return fire. He was convicted of first-degree murder and died in prison a few years later. A Teller County sheriff's deputy, Brent Holloway, was murdered while he guarded an arson scene during the night. That case was particularly haunting to me because of my personal involvement in its aftermath. A cabin had been intentionally set fire in rural Teller County. After the fire was put out about midnight, Holloway remained at the scene until arson investigators could return at daylight. When they returned, Holloway was found dead in his cruiser, shot at point-blank range in the head.

When I arrived at the scene, I thought it looked like suicide, until we found his service revolver still holstered. As it turned out a paranoid schizophrenic had started the fire in order to attract police to the scene. He watched from an adjacent cabin about a quarter mile away. As he watched, he wrote in his diary how much he wanted to know how it felt to kill a cop. When Holloway was left alone, he snuck up behind him and shot him. He then returned to the cabin and wrote in his diary that he did not feel as "fulfilled" as he thought he would. He also described in detail how easily he could kill the many people who responded to the murder, including "those in suits who were walking around within yards" of where he was hiding out. That included me! I remember looking in a window of the very cabin where he was hiding. When law enforcement officers eventually got in touch with the owner and checked the cabin, the killer shot himself in the head as they entered the bedroom where he was writing in his diary. Within hours I read portions of the chilling diary to the press. The writings were eventually forwarded to psychological profilers at the FBI, who found it some of the best material they had seen in terms of analyzing how a demented criminal mind works.

Nothing outrages a prosecutor more than the torture of an innocent child. Many severe child abuse cases occurred while I was DA, including several that resulted in the death of the child. But no such case left a more lasting impression on me than the murder of Ebony Robinson, an eight-year-old African American girl, by her parents, Jackie and Todd Robinson. The Robinsons had several children but singled out Ebony for outrageous abuse. They starved her, burned her with cigarettes, and left her in a dark closet for days at a time. The child died of malnutrition. Pictures of her emaciated body inspired the efforts of prosecutors in my office who secured first-degree murder convictions and life sentences for both parents. Such evil seemed incomprehensible.

But nothing torments a prosecutor more than an unsolved homicide, especially one where the prosecutor has a strong suspicion as to the culprit. I inherited a few such cases from my predecessor, Barney Iuppa. In one case, which occurred on Valentine's Day in 1985, a young woman named Cassandra Rundle and her two small children were bludgeoned to death in their home. An ex-boyfriend was the chief suspect. Unfortunately, Rundle had dated quite a number of unsavory characters, and our prime suspect had a better alibi than several of the others. Incredibly, the extremely bloody crime scene produced virtually no forensic evidence.

Another extremely frustrating case I inherited involved the murder of Barbara Freyschlag, the wife of the president of the Colorado Springs Chamber of Commerce. In my opinion, the police made a mistake early on in the investigation by not taking Mr. Freyschlag down for questioning on the night his wife's body was found. That gave him time to coordinate an alibi with his mistress and eventual wife. To this day, I am quite certain who committed the murder and why, but there was not sufficient evidence to proceed with a prosecution.

On the other hand, I also inherited two fifteen-year-old cases involving the murder of two wealthy Broadmoor area women, Anne Phillips and Eloise Bonicelli. We strongly suspected their husbands had hired their barber, an ex-con named Delphino Ortega, to do the murders. Grand juries had considered the cases but failed to return indictments. In 2001, when I was director of the state prison system, we got a tip from an inmate that eventually led to my successor as DA, Jeanne Smith, convicting Ortega of both murders. By that time one of the husbands was dead and the other was dying. Nothing is more satisfying than to help a victim's family to find the closure that a successful prosecution of a murder case can sometimes bring.

I was personally involved in another high-profile case that spanned over twenty years. In 1975 someone went into a massage parlor in Colorado Springs and murdered an Asian woman with a gun and left another woman for dead. The survivor's description of the perpetrator's vehicle caused police to focus on a young soldier at Fort Carson named Park Estep, who had recently returned from Vietnam. Estep was convicted by an El Paso County jury after a very tense trial that included a controversial in-court identification of the defendant by the surviving victim. Estep maintained his innocence and had a large group of supporters who championed his cause. In about 1983, two investigators working for Estep's attorneys went to Florida and obtained a taped confession to the crime from Otis Toole, a death row inmate who was confessing to crimes all over the country. *People* magazine ran an article about how Estep had been wrongfully convicted of the crime. My predecessor, Barney Iuppa, handled a new trial motion hearing for Estep in 1985, at which Colorado Springs police detective Lou Smit presented evidence that Toole was in Jacksonville, Florida on the day of the massage parlor murder. In fact, he had reported a vandalism incident to the Jacksonville police. The court denied the new trial motion but, subsequent to my election as DA, an appellate court ordered a new hearing be held, at which Otis Toole should be personally called to testify. By this time, Park Estep had been paroled, having served eighteen years in prison for the murder. After much negotiation with the state of Florida, they let us bring Toole to Colorado in a private plane. By the time he got on the stand Toole was in a foul mood and I got him to admit that Estep's investigators had met with him once and given him all the facts of the case and had come back the next day to tape his so-called confession. He admitted he had never been in Colorado before in his entire life. When the defense attorney tried to question him, Toole launched into a tirade of profanity about how dishonest the defense team had been. He was despicable but convincing. The court denied the new trial motion. Toole died of AIDS a few years later, before Florida could execute him. Had Estep been given a new trial, we were prepared to use some forensic ballistic evidence, not technologically available in 1975, to link him to the shotgun shells used to commit the murder.

One of the most dramatic losses the office suffered while I was district attorney came in the case of Eugene Baylis. Baylis said he had been disrespected by a fellow motorcyclist at an intersection in Colorado Springs. So he went to his home, which was a bunker in rural eastern El Paso County, and armed himself with grenades, pistols, and an AK-47 and went to search for the culprit. He wandered into a biker bar on North Nevada Avenue in the Springs. When he entered, he had no idea if the person he was looking for was inside. In fact, he was not. Because of his weaponry he was confronted by a bouncer who tried to take the weapons away. In the ensuing melee, Baylis killed two people and severely injured seven others. He alleged self-defense. The trial judge moved the case to Pueblo because of the pretrial publicity but did not go with the case. And in pretrial motions, he made two evidentiary rulings that had a profound impact on the outcome. The public defender's office was allowed to present evidence of the fact that the bar was a hangout for the Sons of Silence motorcycle gang and that the two decedents were associated with the gang, despite the fact that the defendant had no idea who the Sons of Silence were. Typically, such knowledge would be a prerequisite for any "bad character" testimony being presented in support of a self-defense theory. Secondly, a defense psychiatrist was allowed to testify what Baylis told him was going on in his head at the time of the incident, despite the fact that Baylis did not testify. Obviously, the shrink told a much better story than Baylis ever could and saved Baylis from a withering cross-examination by the prosecution. The psychiatrist opined that the bouncer should not have tried to stop him from entering the bar despite his arsenal of weapons. "If he just would have offered him a beer, everything would have been all right," he testified. The Pueblo jury bought the defense hook, line, and sinker and acquitted Baylis of all charges. The jury foreman, interviewed on TV moments after the verdict explained, "If the bouncer would have offered him a beer, everything would have been all right." I thought the verdict was a sad commentary on the collective analytical ability of the jury. If the exact same circumstances had occurred at a McDonald's, or at a respectable bar, Baylis may well have been on death row.

The highest profile murder case handled by the DA's office during my tenure was probably the case of *People v. Brian Hood and Jennifer Reali*. Hood and Reali were charged with murdering Hood's wife, Diane. The case had all the elements of a great soap opera. Brian Hood was a former all-American football player, tall and good looking. He was also a born again Christian. He and his wife, Diane, a former cheerleader, had two young children. He was a successful insurance salesman. Jennifer Reali was also a bright and attractive woman. She was married to an Army captain stationed at Fort Carson in Colorado Springs and they had two young children. But Brian Hood also had a dark side. He was a habitual womanizer. He had been cheating on Diane since they were married. After several years of marriage, he was looking for a way out without a divorce, which he believed would adversely impact his business because most of his clients were evangelical Christians.

Brian Hood met Jennifer Reali in a hot tub at a local fitness club. Eventually he convinced her to let him come by her house and try to sell her some insurance. They wound up having sex on top of a washing machine (the prosecutors in my office would nickname Hood "the Maytag Man") and a torrid affair began. Hood complained to Reali about his wife's deteriorating health. She had a mild case of lupus, but Brian greatly exaggerated its severity. He suggested to Jennifer that Diane should be put out of her misery. According to Reali's testimony, he would read Bible passages to her and argue that murder was no more serious a sin than adultery and that God would forgive them for both.

On a mid-September night in 1990, Diane Hood attended a lupus support meeting at a community center in a neighborhood park in Colorado Springs. As she came out and walked to the parking lot with friends, she was approached by a person dressed in

Army fatigues with a ski mask pulled over the head who grabbed Diane's handbag. "Take it," Diane screamed. But the attacker grabbed Diane's arm and dragged her some distance across the parking lot. Suddenly the attacker pulled out a long black handgun and fired it at Diane. "I've been shot," Diane yelled. With the handbag draped over an arm, the assailant walked closer to Diane, who was writhing on the ground, and stood above her pointing the gun with both hands. Diane screamed, "No don't." The attacker cocked the pistol and fired again from eighteen inches away. Then the attacker ran off down a nearby alley.

The morning after the murder of his wife, a tearful Brian Hood told the local paper that he could not conceive of how evil someone would have to be to murder his wife in such a fashion. He hoped law enforcement would catch the "scum." Family and friends from all over the country gathered to console Brian.

Jennifer Reali worked part-time at a floral shop in Colorado Springs, and as soon as the shop's owner read of the murder of Diane Hood he was disconcerted. A guy named Brian Hood had visited Jennifer at the flower shop on a few occasions and on one occasion the owner had seen them in Brian's car kissing. He called the police to tell them what he had seen. About the same time, ballistics tests on the bullet that killed Diane Hood were completed. She had been shot with an antique weapon. When the police began to look at Jennifer Reali, as a result of the call from the florist, they also asked questions about her husband, Army Captain Ben Reali. They learned he had an antique gun collection. It was time to interview Jennifer Reali.

Jennifer indignantly denied any involvement. But after many hours of questioning by Colorado Springs police detectives, Reali broke down and confessed to killing Diane Hood. She had left her kids at day care, dressed in her husband's fatigues and murdered Diane in a manner that she hoped would appear to be a robbery. She then went on to tell an intriguing story of how she had been put up to it by Brian Hood. She was immediately arrested.

Unfortunately, so was Brian Hood. I say unfortunately, because Brian Hood denied any involvement in the murder and, having retained high-priced defense counsel, began immediately to spin a tale that he had had an affair with Jennifer Reali and she had developed a "fatal attraction" that caused her to kill Diane when he tried to break off the relationship. The reality was that we could not prove a case against Brian Hood without Jennifer's testimony. Meanwhile, Jennifer had hired a very good lawyer of her own and wanted a sweet deal in exchange for her testimony against Hood. I discussed the matter at length with Bill Aspinwall and Bob Harward, the prosecutors assigned to the case. Faced with a dilemma, and unwilling to give Jennifer, who had plotted the crime and pulled the trigger, anything less than first-degree murder, we ordered the release of Brian Hood pending a grand jury investigation. The public, particularly local women's groups, were outraged. But we had to play hard ball with Reali. We told her attorney that if she testified before the grand jury and at the subsequent trial of Hood, we would do two things for her. First, we would give her use immunity, so that everything she told the grand jury and everything she testified to at Hood's trial could not be used against her in her own subsequent trial. Secondly, we would not ask for the death penalty as to her. If she chose not to cooperate, she would "take the fall alone."

Reali agreed to testify at the grand jury and provided great detail about the involvement of Hood, much of which we were able to corroborate with other evidence. Brian Hood was indicted for the murder of his wife and rearrested, much to the outrage of his family and friends, including Diane Hood's brother, a Houston lawyer who apparently could not psychologically cope with the possibility Brian was involved. The brother-in-law would testify for Hood throughout the case. Hood's attorneys publicly accused me of pursuing Hood because I needed "a great white defendant" to counteract criticism the office was receiving in other prosecutions.

Brian Hood was tried first. Because of massive pretrial publicity the case was moved to the small farming town of Fort Morgan in northeast Colorado. With a grant of use immunity, Jennifer Reali gave riveting testimony on direct examination and then was brutally attacked on cross-examination by Hood's attorneys, who were relentlessly pressing their "fatal attraction" theory. The details of the case were on the front page of every newspaper in Colorado for almost a month. Hood did not testify. Among the prosecution witnesses were two friends of Hood who testified Brian had asked them to kill Diane, although they were not certain he was serious at the time.

After lengthy deliberations, the Fort Morgan jury reached an apparent compromise verdict. They acquitted Hood of first-degree murder, thus freeing him of exposure to the death penalty. But he was convicted of conspiracy to commit first-degree murder and two counts of solicitation to commit first-degree murder. The judge sentenced Hood to thirty-nine years in prison. He would be eligible for parole in about sixteen years. But Hood was subsequently convicted of an attempted escape from prison and of using marijuana in prison, which significantly extended his parole eligibility date. He would be an inmate under my jurisdiction when I became director of corrections several years later.

Two trials of Jennifer Reali followed. She initially pled not guilty by reason of insanity, but a jury in Colorado Springs found her sane. The first-degree murder trial then followed in the western Colorado town of Glenwood Springs, near Aspen. In that trial, prosecutors Aspinwall and Harward faced a difficult task. While they could use evidence obtained against Reali before she testified at the grand jury, they could not directly or indirectly use evidence derived from her grand jury testimony or her testimony at the Hood trial. It was a tricky assignment. After several weeks of trial that were once again the subject of daily newspaper headlines throughout the state, Reali was convicted of first-degree murder, and pursuant to statute, was sentenced to life in prison. In her subsequent appeals she alleged the prosecution had used her immunized testimony against her. The appellate courts, including the Colorado Supreme Court, disagreed.

The Hood/Reali case was the subject of a Stephen Singular novel called *Sweet Evil* and was seriously considered for the subject of a movie. I would joke to various local gatherings that I became opposed to the movie idea when I learned that they wanted Arnold Schwarzenegger to play Brian Hood, Julia Roberts to play Jennifer Reali, and I would be played by Danny DeVito. But I never lost sight of the fact that the case was a terrible tragedy, resulting in five children from two families losing their mothers.

While the Hood/Reali case got the most publicity in Colorado, a much less serious but very bizarre case got the most international attention. A twenty-two-year-old male posing as an eighteen-year-old female enrolled at a local public high school and tried out for and made the cheerleading squad! The imposter even had a date to homecoming with the quarterback of the football team. When the fraud was finally exposed it was fair game for every tabloid newspaper in the world and every afternoon TV talk show in America. It was also the subject of a terrific skit at the next DA's Christmas party. A deputy DA who was a former college wrestler dressed up in a woman's cheerleading uniform amid several attractive young women in similar uniforms singing "There is Nothing Like a Dame," from the score of *South Pacific*.

Colorado in general and El Paso County in particular have a history of clean government and political corruption cases have been few and far between. One that arose during my term as DA involved the El Paso County Employee Retirement Fund. The veteran county treasurer, Sharon Shipley, who had been in office for over twenty-five years, was ex officio chair of the fund's board of directors. She had become close friends with the fund's administrator, Mike Witty, and used her influence to help him secure a very lucrative compensation package. Over time, Witty used his position to embezzle nearly $500,000 from the retirement fund. While there was no evidence that Shipley, or other members of the board, knew of the embezzlement, they had tolerated severe conflicts of interest that helped facilitate the theft, and Shipley and one other member of the board had borrowed money from Witty before voting on his compensation deal. Witty was convicted of theft charges and sentenced to sixteen years in prison. Sharon Shipley was convicted of official misconduct and resigned from office in disgrace. In the early 1990s, the voters of Colorado approved "limited stakes" gambling in the old mining towns of Blackhawk, Central City, and Cripple Creek. Because Cripple Creek was in my judicial district we had to prepare accordingly. Voters were led to believe during the campaign that merchants in Cripple Creek would simply convert some of their space for gaming. That, of course, was not the case. Local property owners were quickly bought out by gambling interests and only a fraction of the casinos had any local ownership at all. Law enforcement's job was to keep organized crime and sinister figures out of the business in Colorado. I helped set up a task force that monitored land purchases in Cripple Creek and gathered intelligence about those coming to town to cash in on gambling. We wanted to get a head start so we wouldn't be too far behind when the new state Gaming Commission came into operation. We were generally credited with avoiding many problems at the outset of legalized gambling and making for a relatively smooth transition from a law enforcement perspective.

The last murder case I personally handled as district attorney involved a very sad example of man's inhumanity toward his fellow man. An eighty-year-old woman named Cleo Lipkins suffered from mental health problems and lived a very transient life. She traveled across the country and eventually found herself in Colorado. An El Paso County woman named Theresa Roever took her in. Roever was essentially a squatter on some land in rural eastern El Paso County. She and her several children lived in a trailer on the land with no plumbing and stole electricity and water from a nearby source. Roever treated Lipkins like a slave, making her do numerous chores around the property. She also pocketed Cleo's monthly social security checks. One evening when Lipkins failed to wash the dishes as instructed, Roever and two elderly people who squatted on the adjacent property beat her and left her in a shed for the night. The next morning when Roever sent her teenage son to retrieve Lipkins, he found her comatose. Believing she would soon die, Roever and her two accomplices bound her and buried her on the property. Roever continued to receive and cash her social security checks. A guilty conscience on the part of one of the elderly accomplices led the sheriff's department to the discovery of the body. I was on homicide duty at the time and personally helped dig up the body. The coroner testified at trial that Lipkins had been buried alive. The key witness in the case was Roever's fourteen-year-old son Theo, who courageously refused to lie to protect her and testified in detail about the atrocities. Roever was convicted of first-degree murder and is serving life without parole. The case was known around the office as "the Grapes of Wrath."

During my eight years as DA, I took my turn as one of five lawyers who did two-week stints of on-call homicide duty, and probably responded to as many as thirty homicide scenes, some of which were quite grizzly and left a lasting impression on me, although I succeeded in remaining sufficiently detached to make sound decisions at such scenes. The worst in my opinion was at a residence in Woodland Park, west of Colorado Springs. A teenager, Jacob Ind, and his friend, Gabriel Adams, had walked into Ind's parents' bedroom in the middle of the night and shot them both in the head with a .22 caliber revolver. It did not kill them. So Ind and his friend sprayed them with bear mace and stabbed them repeatedly as they crawled around the dark bedroom on hands and knees. Finally, Ind got a .357 revolver and "finished them off" while they clung to each other in the corner of the room. The entire room was covered with blood. The scene looked like a picture I saw in the book, *Helter Skelter*, about murders committed by Charles

Manson and his family. Ind and Adams were both sentenced to life without parole. Their claim of self-defense, on the basis that the parents had been psychologically abusive, had little jury appeal given the circumstances of the murder.

My stints on homicide duty caused me to spend a lot of time at various crime scenes with a Colorado Springs Police Detective Lieutenant, Joe Kenda. After his retirement, Kenda would go on to become a high-profile cable television personality on his show called *Homicide Hunter*. All of us who worked with Detective Kenda marveled at how he turned his detective experience into a very lucrative television career.

Throughout my two terms as DA and for the rest of my career in public service, I did a great deal of public speaking. As DA, it was not unusual to do four or five speeches a week, sometimes more. I had become a popular public speaker under considerable demand. I spoke to service clubs, lawyer organizations, law enforcement groups, political groups, and student audiences about topics as diverse as legalization of drugs, the legal profession, and leadership and character. I developed a standard speech for Republican Lincoln Day Dinners that I gave in several counties. I was asked to speak at several commencement exercises. I was frequently called upon to speak at ceremonies to honor law enforcement officers, both living and dead. I could also give a very humorous speech when called upon to do so. I taught criminal law and procedure at the police and sheriff department's training academies. Finally, I made frequent appearances on radio and TV talk shows, even appearing on the *MacNeil/Lehrer NewsHour* on the Public Broadcast System in 1994.

In 1995, the DA's Office's public information officer, Liane Shupp, and I wrote a history of the Fourth Judicial District Attorney's Office entitled *On Behalf of the People*. Coincidently, Liane's husband, Gary, was my coauthor of the book on consumer fraud and white-collar crime written in 1980. This new book was the first time during the 120-year history of the office that anyone had comprehensively researched its past. It took hours of work to peruse microfilm at the local history section of the library. More than seventy-five past and present employees of the office contributed to the printing cost of the book.

Looking back on my tenure as district attorney, I am particularly proud of the legislative changes that occurred at least partially because of my efforts. From the point I took office in January of 1989, I was a very vocal and public critic of the existing juvenile justice system in Colorado. It had been created by statutory changes in the late 1960s after the US Supreme Court's decision in *In re Gault* (which extended many rights of adult criminal defendants to juveniles) and had not been changed over the ensuing decades to adequately deal with the increasingly violent crimes that were now being frequently committed by juveniles. I would tell audiences that a system designed to deal with youths stealing hubcaps and vandalizing mailboxes was now having to deal with murderers and rapists and it simply did not provide the tools to secure appropriate public protection. I gave a speech at the National District Attorneys Association Convention entitled "When the Best Interests of the Child are Not in the Best Interests of the Public" in which I detailed the nature of the problem. For three consecutive years in 1990-92, I helped draft a bill to expand the ability of prosecutors to charge violent juveniles as adults. It died all three years because of the fiscal note (the cost of imposing longer periods of incarceration). Then in 1993 Colorado experienced what became known as "the summer of violence" in which juvenile gang violence terrorized Denver. Colorado Governor Roy Romer was one year from a reelection campaign. Although he had never been much of an ally to the state's prosecutors, he suddenly got very interested in the subject of youth violence. In July of 1993 he came to the monthly meeting of the state's district attorneys and asked for our help in designing a bill that he would introduce at a special session he would call in September. While the DAs saw through the politics of the matter, we viewed the development as manna from heaven. We dusted off our earlier failed proposals and added a new creative one, a Youthful Offender System (YOS). Subsequent to the 1993 special session, every juvenile fourteen or over could be charged as an adult if he committed a violent crime, i.e., either he used a deadly weapon or the crime resulted in serious bodily injury or death. The judge would have the option of suspending the normal sentence to the Department of Corrections (DOC) and sentencing the youth to the YOS for a definite term of between two and seven years, much longer than the sentences available in the juvenile system. YOS, run by the Department of Corrections, had an intensive academic and vocational program that followed a boot camp initiation process. I would spend significant time trying to improve the operations of the YOS when I became DOC director six years later.

I served three years as the legislative committee chair for the state DA's council and became very involved with other legislative reforms dealing with the death penalty and other topics. I spearheaded a successful effort to do away with bifurcated sanity cases. Thereafter, only one trial would be necessary instead of two. During my time as DA, as head of the DOC and subsequently as attorney general, I became a "regular" at the state capitol during the annual 120-day legislative sessions, testifying before state legislative committees more than 100 times.

During my two terms as DA, I was also elected or appointed to several leadership positions in the legal profession. In 1991 I was elected president of the El Paso County Bar Association, an honor no previous DA had received. I defeated John Cook, a well-qualified local lawyer, in the contested election. It was the culmination of several years of involvement in the local bar in a variety of capacities. As my platform, I pledged to pursue additional judicial resources for El Paso County and was successful in helping secure three new judgeships from the legislature. In 1995 I was selected as the Senior Vice President of the Colorado Bar Association and in that capacity served my second stint on the

Association's board of governors. From 1992 until 1997 I served as a Colorado Commissioner to the Uniform State Laws Commission, having been appointed by the Colorado legislature. The commission promulgates and sends to the states proposed uniform legislation in order to deter the federal government from seeking new avenues of regulating the states. The prestigious commission is well over 130 years old, and my appointment came about as a result of my lifelong friendship with Chuck Berry, who had become Speaker of the Colorado House of Representatives. Finally, in 1994, I was given the honor of serving as the president of the Colorado District Attorney's Council (CDAC) by the other twenty-one DAs in the state. The CDAC president not only chairs the council's executive board but also frequently acts as public spokesman for the state's prosecutors.

It was generally acknowledged by the media in Colorado Springs that I had done a good job as district attorney. Even the *Gazette*, a Libertarian owned newspaper which was historically very restrained in its praise of public officials, editorialized to that effect on a couple of occasions. After a hard-fought battle to win the job in 1988, I was unopposed for reelection in 1992. In many respects, that was the ultimate compliment from the Colorado Springs legal community. The per capita rate of serious crime declined seven of eight years I was DA, a total of over 20 percent. At the same time, our budget requests grew at less than half the rate of inflation. Ours was clearly one of the best, if not the best, DA's office in Colorado. By mid-1995, it was pretty clear to me that I could easily win a third term in 1996, but I chose not to run for a variety of reasons. First, I had helped champion a term limit initiative that passed in 1990 limiting state office holders to two four year terms. While it would not kick in for DAs until 2004, I felt self-imposed term limitation was appropriate. Secondly, as I analyzed the careers of district attorneys that served many years, including my predecessor, Bob Russel, I observed two things. Long-term district attorneys rarely advanced to other political or public service positions. They also tended to become increasingly detached from the day-to-day operations of their office. I was open to further public service opportunities, although no specific opportunities presented themselves at the time. Therefore, despite the fact I thought it was a great job, I concluded it was appropriate to leave while I was on top and to return to private practice to await other challenges.

But the reasons I cited for not running again at the last DA's Christmas party were more humorous. They included: 1) No one should be called "honorable" more than eight consecutive years. 2) Several death threats a month get boring after a while. 3) No teenage boys will ask my daughters out. 4) I need to stop thinking of my in-laws as potential suspects. 5) Everyone tells me I look a lot like John Suthers.

Over the eight years I served as DA, I had become a great admirer of my Assistant District Attorney, Jeanne Smith. She was a fine lawyer and a good administrator, a rare combination. She was tough but had a great sense of humor. I strongly encouraged her to run for DA in 1996. Unfortunately, she was challenged in the Republican primary by another prosecutor in the office, Chief Deputy DA Bill Aspinwall. Bill and his wife belonged to our church and had been friends of Janet and mine. Bill was an excellent trial lawyer. He had done yeoman service as a prosecutor in the office, trying many of the toughest cases. I viewed him as a great warrior in the battle against crime. But it was my assessment, and that of virtually everyone in law enforcement that had worked closely with Bill, that he would not be a good manager of the DA's office. He had a volatile temper. Virtually no one in the office supported him. But Bill had many friends outside law enforcement, and he put together a good grassroots campaign. I worked very hard for Smith, personally walking dozens of precincts and doing radio ads. At the Republican Fourth Judicial District Nominating Assembly in June of 1996, I gave my farewell address as DA to the Republican faithful, and then nominated Smith to be my successor. The primary campaign was a tough one. Aspinwall ran negative TV and radio ads about the *Baylis* case, which Smith had prosecuted and lost. Some Christian conservatives quietly passed the word that Smith was the mother of two young children and shouldn't be working at all, let alone running for DA. On the night of the Republican Primary election in August of 1996, I was in San Diego as a delegate to the Republican National Convention. But I called back to Colorado Springs to get the much welcomed news that Smith had won the primary by 3,000 votes. She was unopposed in the general election and became the first woman to head a major DA's Office in Colorado.

District Attorney was the first elected public office I held. After eight years, I left the job with a sense of satisfaction that I had positively impacted the office during my tenure and with an understanding that I had a personal skill set that could lead to success in other public service endeavors.

Chapter XV
"I Just Want to Be a Good Ancestor"

On the second Tuesday in January of 1997, I walked out of the DA's office and strolled the two blocks to once again take up residence in the historic Alamo Building, the location of the Sparks, Dix law firm. The firm, and Ken Sparks in particular, knew that I entertained notions of possible future public service, and we negotiated a situation designed to meet both our needs. My title would be Senior Counsel. I would not be a shareholder. I would be paid a salary. I would be head of the firm's litigation section and attempt to assist the firm in new business acquisition.

I did bring in new work for the firm, and most importantly, was able to help it in securing Teller County government as a client. Adjacent to El Paso County to the west, Teller County was part of the Fourth Judicial District and as DA I had worked closely with the Teller County Commissioners. After rejoining the firm, I responded to a solicitation from the county for new legal counsel and made a presentation to the commissioners that led to them awarding Sparks, Dix the contract to represent the county. Over the next many years, Teller County became a very important client of the firm and contributed a healthy share of its revenues.

One of the fun things I did upon my return to private practice was to become an expert legal commentator for Channel 5/30, the NBC affiliate in Southern Colorado. They paid me a whopping $100 per appearance. I made frequent appearances to discuss proceedings in the trials of Timothy McVeigh and Terry Nichols for bombing the federal building in Oklahoma City. The trials were held in Denver.

In the course of the next two years back in private practice I would learn a lot about myself and what I would henceforth find occupationally satisfying. I had greatly enjoyed my first eight years in private practice. I found it fun and challenging to take on new clients, try to solve their problems, earn their trust, and to be paid well for the effort. But after spending eight years as district attorney, my perspective had changed. Much of what I had previously liked about private practice had lost some of its appeal. I found myself impatient at the pettiness of some of my clients. My duty to advocate for them sometimes conflicted with my personal sense of fairness. Lengthy depositions, which are the bread and butter of civil litigation and which many litigators find stimulating, I now found tedious and boring in contrast to my daily work at the DA's office. Most civil lawsuits, in which the ultimate goal was typically to transfer wealth from one party to another, now seemed relatively trivial to me in contrast to the risks and rewards present in a major criminal case. Discovery in civil cases was a money making machine for lawyers and a scourge for most clients. And too much civil litigation was just plain frivolous.

I also observed that in the twenty-two years I had been practicing law, Congress had passed, with the best of intentions, a myriad of new laws that had the practical effect of contributing to what some observers referred to as "the death of common sense." Particularly in the employment area, anti-discrimination laws were being routinely abused by plaintiffs and their attorneys to produce results that contributed to great inefficiency in the work place. Incompetent employees were tolerated because of the enormous legal and financial cost to deal with them.

But something else happened between my two stints in private practice that was clearly influencing my evolving mindset about what gave the most meaning to my career and to my life. When Jonas Salk, who developed the vaccine for polio, was asked why he spent his whole life in medical research with little compensation, he replied, "I just want to become a good ancestor." I was gaining a growing appreciation for his sentiment. In many respects it would become the essential goal of my professional and personal life. I began to analyze all the opportunities I was given by asking which presented the most opportunity to be a good ancestor. In fact, I would eventually publish a book in 2011 entitled *Becoming A Good Ancestor*. It contained my reflections on how to deal with unhealthy cultural trends and become a positive influence on those around you and those who follow you. Three decades after my father's death I was becoming more articulate in describing my search for meaning and purpose in life and my intent to lead an intentional and consequential life.

In the early nineties I had joined millions of Americans in watching Ken Burns's public television series about the Civil War. To this day I regard it as the best program I ever saw on television. It had a profound impact on me. I have watched it several times since. The series chronicled the incredible sacrifices of Americans on both sides of the war who were willing to fight and die for a cause. Because, as Burns pointed out, it was the first war fought by literate Americans, the most inspiring words came from the soldiers' own writings. The most memorable for me was an 1861 letter Burns had unearthed which was written by a young Union officer named Sullivan Ballou. Ballou was a lawyer and a member of the Rhode Island Legislature who had eagerly accepted his country's call to arms. The letter was written to his wife Sarah on the eve of the first Battle of Bull Run. Because of his responsibility to lead the charge, Major Ballou recognized that his chances of survival were slim. He eloquently expressed his conflicting emotions:

> Lest I should not be able to write again, I feel impelled to write a few lines that may fall under your eye when I shall be no more...

> I have no misgivings about or lack confidence in the cause in which I am engaged, and my courage

does not falter. I know how strongly American Civilization now leans upon triumph of the government, and how great a debt we owe to those who went before us through the blood and suffering of the Revolution. And I am willing—perfectly willing—to lay down all the joys in this life, to help maintain the government, and to pay that debt...

Sarah, my love for you is deathless. . . The memories of the blissful moments I have spent with you come creeping over me. . . and hard it is for me to give them up and burn to ashes the hopes of future years, when God willing, we might have lived and loved together, and seen our sons grow into honorable manhood...

But, Sarah, if the dead can come back to this earth and flit unseen around those they loved, I shall always be near you, in the gladdest days and in the darkest nights... and if there be a soft breeze upon your cheek, it shall be my spirit passing by. Sarah, do not mourn me dead. . . for we shall meet again.

Excerpted from letter by Major Sullivan Ballou,

Headquarters, Camp Clark,

Washington, D.C., July 14, 1861

Ballou died at Bull Run. A copy of his letter hangs in our bedroom.

Because of the Ballou letter and similar content, the Civil War series haunted me. I was also incredibly impacted by personal visits to the American Cemetery at Normandy, to Civil War battlefields at Gettysburg and Antietam, and to the *USS Arizona* Memorial at Pearl Harbor. In the words of Civil War hero Joshua Lawrence Chamberlain when he dedicated a monument at Gettysburg in

1889, "something abides" at places where heroic deeds have been done and great sacrifices have been made. How many modern-day Americans, in the age of relative hedonism, have Ballou's commitment to preserving our cherished freedoms? How many have the willingness to sacrifice exhibited by the World War II generation? How many would be willing to give up material prosperity, let alone their lives, to further the public interest? It was my perception that too many successful and materially prosperous Americans were content to leave politics and public service to the less successful among us, rather than allow their own prosperity to be diminished in any respect. I often harkened back to the words of Sister Georgetta. *Sic transit gloria mundi*. Life is short. You only go around once. You should make it as meaningful and purposeful as possible. At best, one typically has a career of forty to fifty years to make a contribution to the world. I also found myself asking, as a Baptist minister I once heard express it, "What do you want people to say about you when they are sitting around eating potato salad after your funeral?" That I made lots of money effectively advocating for the private interests of my clients? Or that I used my education and my abilities to pursue the public good? It's the difference between what author David Brooks called "resume virtues" (i.e., He was educated at Harvard) and "eulogy virtues" (i.e., He was loyal, compassionate and of high integrity). After two years back in private practice, the answer was clearer to me than before. Great material success was not my purpose in life. I was anxious to find further avenues of public service.

I believe that each person is born into a time and into circumstances which, in combination with that person's intellect, talent, and ambitions, will largely determine the parameters of their ability to contribute to society—determine their path to become a good ancestor. Over time it had become increasingly clear to me that the time and circumstances of my life, and the intellect, talent, and ambition that I exhibited dictated that my best opportunity to contribute to the public good would be in law and politics.

I knew I was very fortunate to have a profession that I could return to at any point when the public no longer desired (or tolerated) my public service. Having a means of livelihood like the law helps a public servant to maintain a certain level of independence. In a letter to one of his sons, founding father John Adams put it very well:

> Public business must always be done by somebody. If wise men decline it, others will not; if honest men refuse it, others will not; a young man should carefully weigh his plans. Integrity should be preserved in all events. His first maxim should be to place his honor out of reach of all men. To do this he must never become dependent on public employment for subsistence. Let him have a trade, a profession, a farm, a shop, something where he can honestly live, and then he may engage in public affairs, if invited, upon independent principles.

> Excerpted from John Adams's letter to Thomas Boylston Adams,

> 2 September 1789

The great thing about the law as a profession, from my perspective, is that the law itself presents many opportunities for public service, and one can readily combine the practice of law with service to the public.

During the Memorial Day weekend of 1997, I made a decision to run for attorney general of Colorado. It was frankly not something I had thought seriously about until a few months before. As district attorney, I had worked closely with the state attorney general, but I had not before that viewed the job as one I was interested in. The current AG, Gale Norton, who would subsequently became Secretary of the Interior under President George W. Bush, was term limited and could not run again in 1998.

The Democrats had a very strong candidate in Ken Salazar, who it appeared would face no primary opposition. Salazar was very close to Governor Roy Romer, having served as his legal counsel and in his cabinet as Director of the Colorado Department of Natural Resources. He was very well-known throughout Colorado. Two longtime state senators, Jeff Wells and Dick Mutzebaugh, had committed to running as Republicans. Norton had mentioned to me on a couple of occasions that I should consider running because she did not view either of the Republicans in the field as capable of winning. Based on my knowledge of them, I agreed that neither Wells nor Mutzebaugh were effective campaigners and I felt, given the current Republican lineup, I could win the Republican nomination. If I could then raise sufficient funds, I could give Salazar a tough race. I decided to take on the challenge.

The eighteen-month campaign for attorney general would prove to be exhausting and frustrating, but ultimately a very rewarding experience for me. In the summer of 1997, an unexpected development changed the whole tenor of the race for the Republican nomination. The primary field grew to four with the addition of Joe Smith, a very young section head in the Attorney General's Office. Unlike Wells and Mutzebaugh, he and his girlfriend were incredibly hard campaigners, and they would build a good grassroots organization. He clearly designed his campaign to win the nomination at the Republican State Convention where delegates are typically more conservative than the party as a whole. Smith was also ruthless, frequently making uncalled for attacks, and in the course of a very heated primary campaign, I grew to dislike him, his girlfriend, and several of his campaign staff.

I quickly learned just how large Colorado was geographically and that I was not well-known outside of the Fourth Judicial District. I traveled all over the state and slowly built a statewide campaign organization. It took an enormous amount of work. For the first nine months I would attend events in Colorado Springs and Denver during the work week, and travel to various Republican events throughout Colorado on the weekends. My law partners were very supportive, even as my billable hours declined steadily as the election got nearer. In the last six months I was campaigning almost full time. Often, I would get up at 4:30 a.m. and drive to Denver for an early morning breakfast event and a few fundraising calls, drive the seventy miles back to Colorado Springs and practice law for a few hours, and then return to Denver for an evening event, sometimes not getting home until after midnight. Weekends found Janet, me, and our hard-core campaign volunteers spreading out all over the state. Drivers became the most-needed volunteers and one in particular, Bill Dinnebeil, drove with me many of the 72,000 miles I put on my car during the twelve months before the election. One weekend alone we drove almost 2,000 miles, crisscrossing the Continental Divide four times. It took the help of more than two dozen dedicated volunteers to cover the multiple Lincoln Day Dinners or multiple county conventions occurring on the same day.

I met lots of great people when campaigning across Colorado and some of them became friends and political allies for years to come. One young man, Jason Dunn, had recently graduated from college and was hired to run the campaign in the Denver Metro area. He would leave the campaign in the fall to start law school at the University of Colorado. But that would not be the last I saw of Jason.

I also learned that a candidate from Colorado Springs started at a disadvantage in a statewide campaign. Over the years, Colorado Springs had produced some high-profile political agitators that were viewed as conservative extremists in other parts of the state, even among Republicans. It was clear I had the burden of proving to them that I wasn't one of them.

The 1998 Republican State Convention was held in Colorado Springs on May 30th, our daughter Kate's sixteenth birthday. Two weeks before the convention it was fairly apparent the Republican race was between Joe Smith and me. Wells and Mutzebaugh, despite their claims to the contrary, had nowhere near the 30 percent of the delegates needed to make the primary ballot. Our goal at that point was to get the 30 percent needed to make the ballot and get access to the more moderate Republican electorate in the August primary election. Smith was publicly voicing confidence that he was going to shut everyone else off the ballot.

But in those two weeks we gathered considerable momentum. Two well-designed mailings went to delegates emphasizing my experience in contrast to Smith's inexperience. One brochure listed many residents of Colorado who would not be supporting John Suthers. It was a list of all the heinous felons who had been sent to prison by my DA's office. Two prominent supporters of mine, former US Senator Bill Armstrong and former Secretary of State Natalie Meyer came to events the night before the convention to work the crowd for me. In my opinion they changed many delegates' minds. On the morning of the convention, in addition to our regular campaign volunteers, Janet got dozens of our social friends to surround the arena carrying signs and passing out brochures. Janet and I separately worked every aisle of the arena. Armstrong and Meyer nominated me. My speech at the convention was well designed, well delivered, and well received. When the votes of the 3,500 delegates were tabulated, I had not only made the ballot, but won the top line with 43 percent of the vote. A stunned Smith got 37 percent. Wells and Mutzebaugh failed to make the ballot with 13 percent and 7 percent respectively.

With the top-line designation we knew we would beat Smith in the August primary. I would have an easier time than he getting contributions, and he would be less attractive to primary voters than he was to the more conservative convention delegates. But it would prove to be painful. Unfortunately, the Smith campaign chose to make a desperate attempt to regain momentum by going very negative in the month after the convention. They tried to get the media to publicize a frivolous lawsuit that had been filed against me by the litigious husband of a woman who had embezzled several hundred thousand dollars from a small business in Colorado

Springs that I represented. The tactic backfired badly for Smith, but I wound up spending $175,000 to win the primary. We operated campaign offices in Denver and Colorado Springs and did mailings, newspaper ads, and radio ads. Meanwhile, Ken Salazar had not spent a dime of his considerable war chest to gain the Democratic nomination.

The week after my primary victory, I traveled the state by bus with all the other Republican statewide candidates. We stopped for political rallies in virtually every town of any size, giving essentially the same speech each time. But it was a great way to get the attention of the many small-town newspapers that are read faithfully by the rural residents of the state. I also got to know Bill Owens, the Republican candidate for governor, and Colorado's US Senators Ben "Nighthorse" Campbell and Wayne Allard, much better as a result of the tour. Those relationships would subsequently prove very valuable.

The campaign was a family affair. Janet worked incredibly hard. She spent evenings and weekends and vacation time making phone calls, managing databases and mailing lists, and traveling with me all over the state on the campaign trail. Toward the end of the campaign, she worked half day at HP and half day at the campaign. Our daughter Kate used her new driver's license to drive me to campaign events around the state. Alison attended parades and picnics while she was home from college.

In contrast to the primary, the general election was a much more enjoyable experience. Ken Salazar was a true gentleman, and I came to like him personally. We had many joint appearances. Unfortunately, from my perspective, they got very little press coverage. Only the governor's race garnered much coverage. Most objective observers, and even many Salazar supporters, gave me very high marks for my performance in the head-to-head encounters. I was certainly better informed on criminal justice issues. I also did very well at editorial board interviews, but it did not matter. Salazar had the endorsement of both major Denver newspapers wired as a result of his longtime Denver-area associations. The editor of the *Rocky Mountain News* confidentially told me that they could not pass up the chance to endorse a Hispanic candidate of Salazar's caliber. Both papers took time in their endorsement of Salazar to point out how well qualified I was for the job. I received the endorsement of a few much smaller newspapers.

Being from Colorado Springs, I was unable to garner much support from Denver's 17th Street. The big law firms and corporate interests that line 17th Street are a significant source of financial support for statewide candidates. Salazar was much more familiar to them than I was.

Unfortunately for my campaign, the state Republican Party in Colorado was at a low ebb in 1998. The party had typically been headed by well-connected businessmen who were able to raise considerable funds and use them to assist candidates in tough races. The chair for the 1998 election cycle, Steve Curtis, had no such ability, having been elected more for his conservative social agenda than for his connections or record of success.

Polls that appeared a month before the election gave Salazar a sizable lead. With his campaign war chest not depleted by a primary, he was able to start his TV ads two to three weeks earlier than mine. In hindsight, I would love to have had the $175,000 we spent in the primary to add to our TV buy during the last month of the campaign. We campaigned very hard on street corners in Denver and Colorado Springs and our TV and radio ads were well done. In the last few days of the election, the polls tightened considerably. I was certain we had momentum and that it would be a very close race. But I was totally uncertain of the outcome.

In fact, it was very close. Late into the election night the media had the race neck and neck. Even at midnight reporters were saying it was too close to call. But our campaign had been carefully analyzing the returns throughout the night and we sensed a few serious problems almost immediately. The turnout in heavily

Democratic areas of Denver and surrounding suburbs was much heavier than in Republican El Paso County and rural Colorado. Several controversial ballot issues, including a new stadium for the Denver Broncos, were on the ballot in the Denver Metro area but not in the rest of the state. In a non-presidential election year, that had a considerable impact. The issues turned out blue-collar Democrats in unusually large numbers. That in turn led to smaller than hoped for margins of victory in Arapahoe and Jefferson Counties for both me and Bill Owens, the Republican gubernatorial candidate. Also, a Libertarian candidate for attorney general got 33,000 votes, much more than we had anticipated. In the absence of a party candidate, Libertarians typically vote Republican. In the wee hours of the morning the results were final. Owens had won the governorship by 0.5 percent of the vote. I had lost the attorney general race by 2 percent (49 percent to 47 percent). A swing of 16,000 votes out of the 1.3 million cast would have changed the result. I called Ken Salazar at 6 a.m. to concede. The result clearly had a big impact on Colorado politics. Salazar would eventually become a US Senator, Secretary of the Interior under President Obama, and ambassador to Mexico under President Biden.

I was disappointed at having come so close and not succeeding, but I was generally pleased with the campaign we had run. Several newspapers commented on the quality of the attorney general race in contrast to other statewide races. Both Ken Salazar and I were praised for the high minded campaign we had waged. In the course of the campaign, Salazar and I had come to admire each other. While I was not certain of it then, politics would take some strange twists and turns in the ensuing years and my unsuccessful effort in 1998 would lead to future career opportunities.

Chapter XVI
The Director of Corrections

I told my law firm and my family the day after the 1998 election that I was ready to practice law for at least the next few years and significantly elevate my income in the process. Janet was pleased at that prospect though she expressed some concerns that my enthusiasm for private practice had waned. But I was upbeat and determined to make the best of it.

However, three days after the election I got a phone call from Bill Owens, the Governor-Elect of Colorado. After some small talk about the razor-thin margins in our respective races, he got to the point. He wanted me to join his cabinet. It was something that totally caught me by surprise. I had been so engrossed in my own election campaign that I had not thought about the ramifications of the Republicans winning the governor's office for the first time in twenty-four years. I asked him what he had in mind, and he mentioned the possibility of running the Department of Personnel and Administration or the Department of Regulatory Agencies. I knew enough about those jobs to immediately tell the new governor that I did not view either of them with sufficient interest to cause me to move to Denver or commute there every day. He asked me to think it over and let him know if I might be interested in another cabinet department. "I really want you in the cabinet," he said. I told him I would think about it.

Over the next few days, I spoke to several friends and professional colleagues who had extensive knowledge of the cabinet departments in Colorado state government. I concluded I only had genuine interest in two of the departments, Public Safety (which consisted of the Colorado State Patrol, the Colorado Bureau of Investigation and the Division of Criminal Justice) and Corrections, which included the state's prison, parole and community corrections systems. Corrections had the significant added benefit of being headquartered in Colorado Springs. It was the only cabinet department not based in Denver.

When I called Bill Owens and told him I would only be interested in heading public safety or corrections, there was a long silence on the phone. He then explained that those were the only two positions for which he made commitments before the election. Both would go to Democrats. Ari Zavaras, a former Denver police chief and current head of corrections, would move to public safety. A former state senator from Pueblo, Larry Trujillo, who was the deputy director of corrections, would get the director's job. I reiterated to Owens that he certainly did not owe me anything and that I was simply not interested in the other cabinet positions. I thought that was the end of the matter.

About three weeks later, Owens called again. He said he had changed his mind and offered me the corrections job. I accepted the following day and three days later, at a press conference in Denver, I was introduced as the governor's nominee to be the Executive Director of the Department of Corrections. I was among the first three cabinet members to be appointed. In hindsight, I believe Owens was getting strong encouragement from his political advisors to make sure I was part of the cabinet. I was the only contender for a cabinet position from El Paso County, with the largest Republican population in the state. The governor had won his race by 8,000 votes. His margin of victory in El Paso County was 38,000 votes. It also did not hurt that I had garnered over 600,000 votes in the attorney general's race.

My nomination was unanimously confirmed by the State Senate, and I was sworn in as Colorado's eleventh director of corrections on January 12, 1999. I had taken the job with some reservations and apprehension. As a prosecutor I had observed the department from the periphery and viewed it as a large bureaucracy that would be hard to manage in a meaningful way. Further, several predecessors in the position had fared poorly with the legislature and/or governor and had been unceremoniously vanquished from the job.

As it turned out, I made a great decision and wound up enjoying the job very much. I also learned a great deal about managing a very large organization. DOC was indeed a large bureaucracy. At the end of my thirty-two-month tenure, the department had 18,000 prison inmates, 5,000 parolees, and almost 6,000 employees. There were twenty-two state-operated prison facilities and contracts with four private prisons. The department had parole and community corrections offices throughout the state and had contracts with over thirty private community corrections programs. The Correctional Industries program consisted of thirty businesses and included factories, farms, ranches, and various other enterprises to provide inmate jobs. Prison education programs, food services, and health care were complicated undertakings. The department's operational budget was $525 million, and we had at least $100 million of capital construction underway at all times. From a management perspective, my tenure as head of the Department of Corrections was the best experience I had to prepare me to subsequently become mayor of a large city.

The enormity of my management challenge was brought home to me one night when I had only been at the job for two weeks. I had just given a speech in Cañon City, fifty miles southwest of Colorado Springs, where eight DOC facilities were located. I stopped to get gas about 9:30 p.m. at a combination gas station and convenience store. When I went inside to pay, I saw about a dozen uniformed correctional officers buying snacks for their lunch buckets in preparation for going on the swing shift at nearby prisons. It occurred to me right then that as hard as I would try, I would never personally meet a significant portion of the 6,000 employees of the department that worked three shifts seven days per week. To many of them I would only be Director Suthers on memos and department regulations. The DOC did not yet have email in its facilities. How do you manage such an organization?

I learned to do so by sending very clear messages down the chain of command. And my personal example was very important. I was surprised how soon low-level managers learned of the things I said and did at high-level management meetings. I met with the sixteen division directors at DOC twice a month. I met with my three deputy directors no less than weekly. By holding high-level managers accountable and demanding they do the same for their subordinates, you could in fact impact a large organization. We carefully monitored a wide variety of performance indicators throughout the department as a means of enforcing accountability. I believe I got good marks from the vast majority of DOC employees.

With some luck, I was able to put together what I considered to be an excellent executive management team. The former deputy director, Larry Trujillo, left to become Director of Personnel and Administration and took a regional director, Carl Zennon with him. Bob Cantwell, who had been chief of staff to my predecessor, Ari Zavaras, left after six months to join Zavaras at the Department of Public Safety as director of the Colorado Bureau of Investigation. That provided me with a great opportunity to reorganize the upper levels of the department.

Before deciding whether or how to reorganize, I met with all division directors and wardens in the department. When I met separately with each of the eighteen wardens, several of them complained of the micromanagement and in some cases inconsistency that occurred as a result of accountability to both a deputy director and a regional director. I concluded they were right and proceeded to eliminate the four regional director positions. Under the director, I had three deputy directors with specifically-defined responsibilities and all wardens and division heads reported directly to the deputy directors. The deputy directors were Jerry

Gasko, in charge of Prison Operations; Dr. Mary West, in charge of Special Operations and Community Services; and Brian Burnett, in charge of administration. Burnett in particular had a "can do" attitude that was extremely helpful to me in motivating the executive management team and effecting some meaningful changes in DOC. He was especially helpful in identifying appropriate performance indicators to monitor as a means of measuring the progress of the department. The streamlined management structure saved over $400,000 per year and worked quite well for the department. I considered it a significant accomplishment of my tenure. I was disappointed when one of my successors returned to the regional director format.

I was so impressed with Burnett that I recommended him to Governor Owens as a successor when I left DOC. He was not chosen and moved to higher education, eventually doing a great job as Vice Chancellor of the University of Colorado at Colorado Springs, as Chief Financial Officer for the University of Missouri and University of Minnesota systems, and at the University of Alabama at Birmingham.

The Department of Corrections faced two large logistical challenges during my first year as executive director, and Brian Burnett was instrumental in successfully meeting both of them. In August of 1999, we hosted the American Correctional Association annual convention in Denver. Hosting 5,000 people for a convention is a huge organizational task, but it went off flawlessly. At the end of 1999 came the new millennium and every large organization with complex computer systems spent a great deal of time preparing for Y2K. The public was besieged with doomsday scenarios. Some pundits suggested computer malfunctions would lead to prison security systems shutting down and dangerous criminals escaping to prey on the public. We took things so seriously that my executive management team assembled a "war room" at the DOC headquarters in Colorado Springs on New Year's Eve to monitor any system-wide problems. When the clock struck midnight without incident, we drank champagne and went home. Our feverish preparation for Y2K strikes me as humorous in hindsight.

Managing a para-military organization such as DOC was a unique and interesting experience for me. Chains of command are rigorously adhered to out of necessity. Preparing for an emergency response is a constant undertaking and discipline is extremely important. I was treated like a general. There was a reserved parking spot for me at most of the prison facilities, despite the fact that I would visit most of them no more than once per quarter. My periodic appearances at various facilities for inspections or ceremonies were treated as a big deal, as were my monthly visits to the training academy to talk to the new class of recruits.

The biggest downside to the job was the inflexible Colorado personnel system that made it difficult to effectively deal with the 1 percent of employees who were problematic, and the litigious nature of the inmate population. In the thirty-two months I was the corrections director, I was named as a defendant in approximately 475 lawsuits. One time a process server staked out my house and jumped out from behind a tree to serve me when I went out to get the newspaper at 6 a.m. The Attorney General's Office was kept busy fighting off all the frivolous litigation.

I received dozens of letters from the inmates each day. A few were threatening, some were sad, and some were humorous. I found particular humor in the letters from inmates that complained they were being treated like criminals. I would often write back to remind them that they were.

Managing prison inmates also involved me in some unique problems. One inmate was in the middle of a sex change from male to female when he came into the system for armed robbery. Under the law at the time Colorado taxpayers were required to maintain his female hormone treatments but were not required to pay for his very expensive sex change surgery. After extensive psychiatric evaluation we put the individual in a women's prison. The experts' conclusion was that the inmate was much more female than male. But the female inmates complained that the inmate would "wave" his penis at them in the shower. When we put the inmate in a male prison, he was assaulted by other inmates. When we put him in protective custody, he sued us, demanding to return to general population. Finally, we found a prison facility in California that specialized in transsexual inmates. Unfortunately, I had to agree to accept a few "Charlie Manson type" inmates from California in return. But it was deemed a very good trade from a management and financial standpoint.

My tenure at DOC definitely strengthened the conviction I developed as a prosecutor about the significance of the family in preserving social order. An inordinate percentage of inmates had been born out of wedlock. The lack of a father led to social problems that spiraled into serious crime. Very few inmates were from intact, viable families. The fact of the matter was that no amount of government or private programming, however well intentioned, was an adequate substitute for a stable family. I viewed the primary purpose of prison as isolation of criminals from the community they victimized. But I was intent on ensuring that the time offenders spent in prison was as constructive as possible and placed a great deal of emphasis on academic and vocational programs in the department, as well as the Correctional Industries.

In my monthly reports to Governor Owens, I cited several significant accomplishments of the department in addition to the streamlining of its upper management. Through the establishment of a Private Prison Monitoring Unit the department achieved a stable and productive contractual relationship with the four private prisons in Colorado, and the unit was looked at as a model throughout the country. I was also able to secure additional resources for the Offender Reintegration Program, which I saw as the one area where we could do a better job of impacting recidivism rates.

I also felt we created a five-year bed plan that proved visionary in its flexibility and efficiency. By limiting larger capital requests to high security and special needs beds and relying on private prisons for anticipated growth in medium security and below, the department insured that the state could appropriately respond to population growth that proved to be significantly faster or slower than anticipated. That also helped the department weather a budgetary crisis that hit the state as a result of an economic downturn in 2002 and 2003 and to significantly cut expenses when the inmate population declined beginning in 2010.

We increased inmate accountability by implementing a system-wide smoking ban, a system of child support and restitution collection, and further enhancing our inmate Drug Reduction Program. Stopping inmate smoking was a more daunting challenge than some might think. Almost 30 percent of the inmates smoked. We did about 16,000 random drug tests during my last year at DOC and our positive rate of less than 1 percent, including alcohol, was among the very lowest in the country, and much lower than the illicit drug use rate of non-incarcerated persons in Colorado. We also increased employee accountability by implementing physical agility and psychological suitability testing and spearheaded changes in the Colorado Criminal Code to deter staff sexual misconduct. I personally shepherded a bill through the legislature that made consensual sexual contact between inmates and staff a felony offense for the DOC employee.

After evaluating the Inspector General's Office in DOC, which was responsible for investigation of crimes committed in prison as well as internal affairs matters, I decided to bring in a new IG from outside the department. Mike Rulo, who I knew when I was DA and who served as Woodland Park police chief, was hired for the job. Under Rulo the department increased the effectiveness, accountability, and professionalism of its Inspector General's Office.

I also worked hard to reverse the traditional antagonism between corrections and the legislature. My first hire as DOC director was Alison Morgan as the department's lobbyist. She did a great job. Our high level of financial accountability and our professional presentations to various legislative committees contributed to a relationship between the department and the legislature that was envied by other Colorado agencies, as well as other departments of corrections around the country.

I met quarterly with all the inmate advocacy groups at a library in Denver. The crowds, which generally included forty-five to sixty people, often included difficult and antagonistic individuals. I understood that was unavoidable and tried hard to deal with the organizations in a straightforward and candid manner. While we rarely agreed philosophically, I believe they appreciated my willingness to meet and directly address their concerns.

I also felt I contributed to an increase in the morale of the DOC employees by instituting two special projects. Prior to my arrival the department had not had a single memorial in tribute to the thirteen employees who had died in the line of duty. On March 11, 2000, department employees, public officials, and the relatives of decedents gathered in Cañon City to dedicate a Fallen Officer Memorial. At the ceremony, I spoke with an eighty-year-old man whose father was the warden of the Colorado State Penitentiary during a riot and hostage taking in October 1929 in which eight DOC employees and six inmates were killed. His description of the event and its impact on his father was riveting. I also commissioned the writing of the first comprehensive history of the department, which was completed in September 2001. It was well received by the DOC employees.

The job of a correctional officer has always been a difficult one. While technology has made the job much safer than it used to be, it is still dangerous work. A correctional officer is essentially a cop that walks a beat inside a prison—a beat that includes nothing but thieves, robbers, rapists, and murderers. And because they work behind the walls of a prison and outside the scrutiny of the general public, their work is largely unheralded. But I found many officers took pride in their work and were quite good at it. The history of the department was replete with stories of courage and heroism. When I met with new correctional officers, I liked to tell them the story of Robert Wiggins, a guard at the Colorado State Penitentiary, who died during the 1929 riot. Wiggins was in his late sixties and on the verge of retirement when he was taken hostage by the inmates. They were executing an officer every half hour as long as the warden refused their demands for transportation out of the prison. Wiggins was asked by the inmates to write a letter to the warden begging him to save his life. Wiggins refused. When it was his turn to be executed, the ringleader of the inmates asked him if he had any last statement to make. He said simply, "Show me where you want me to stand." He was then shot point-blank in the head. I told the audience of correctional officers that Wiggins let everyone know where he stood—on the side of law and order. As a result of my tenure as a prison administrator, I will always have great respect for those who work in prisons.

When I accepted the job as head of corrections, I knew that my statutory responsibilities included acting as executioner if a death row inmate was ordered by the court to be put to death. While I didn't relish that aspect of the job, given my views on the death penalty I was willing to perform the function if required by law. As fate would have it, no one was executed during my thirty-two-month tenure. One inmate had been executed the year before my appointment and the next in line, a man named Frank Rodriguez, died of hepatitis before he could be executed.

I continued doing a lot of public speaking as director of corrections. In addition to speeches to service clubs and law enforcement groups, I routinely accepted invitations to speak to groups of inmates at ceremonies marking their graduation from educational programs in DOC. In addition to whatever certificate they would receive, I would personally give each inmate a copy of the "Desiderata." I told them I had always kept a copy of it on my wall as an inspiration and suggested they periodically read it as a possible inspiration on how to conduct their lives from this point forward. I emphasized to them that despite their past breaches of the social contract they were nevertheless, as the "Desiderata" described, "a child of the universe" who "no less than the trees and the stars, has a right to be here" and that "with all its sham, drudgery and broken dreams, it is still a beautiful world." I saw a few copies of the document on the walls of cells as I toured prisons.

In June of 1999, Governor Owens came to Sterling, Colorado to dedicate the new Sterling Correctional Facility which, with 2,500 beds, was by far the largest prison that Colorado had ever constructed. As part of the festivities Janet, our daughter Kate, and I spent the night in prison cells. My most vivid memories of the experience were the uncomfortable flame-retardant vinyl pillow, the one-inch-thick vinyl mattress on top of concrete, and the institutional sounds of steel clanging against steel and toilets flushing throughout the night.

I very much enjoyed being in the cabinet of Governor Bill Owens and later working with him as attorney general. As the first Republican governor in twenty-four years, his election bought an air of anticipation about constructive change to the state, and it was fun to be a part of that. In my opinion, Owens did a good job of focusing on just a few main themes to start with: tax reduction, education reform and transportation, and staying focused on those issues. He was clearly the most ideologically consistent of the three governors I worked with. I also appreciated his management style. He let us know early on that he felt he had put together a solid cabinet and that he would not be attempting to intervene in the day-to-day management of our departments. We met twice a month as a cabinet, once with the governor for breakfast at the governor's mansion and once with Roy Palmer, his chief of staff. I submitted a short written report to the governor monthly, advising him of major developments in the department. Like most political managers, the governor simply emphasized that he did not want any surprises that he had not been adequately briefed on in advance.

I had first come to know Bill Owens when he was a state senator, and I was the DA in Colorado Springs. I had publicly criticized then Governor Roy Romer in 1989 for suggesting there were too many minor offenders taking up space in prisons. In response to his comments, the district attorneys in Colorado commissioned a study showing that roughly 80 percent of inmates in Colorado had committed a violent offense at some point in their criminal careers. The 20 percent that had only committed nonviolent crimes averaged 2.9 prior felony convictions apiece. In other words, the prisons were filled with violent offenders and highly recidivist nonviolent offenders. Owens, who championed a lot of tough-on-crime legislation, frequently corresponded with me about various articles and studies that supported our mutually shared position that people in prison deserved to be there. With that background, it did not surprise me that as governor, Owens proved supportive of corrections. In light of that, I was pleased to see the department move forward during my tenure to the point that I could confidently claim to the governor that Colorado had one of the very best corrections departments in the United States. I was also glad that during my tenure the department had avoided any of the kind of controversies that can plague governors and sometimes bring them down.

Although Governor Owens's initial cabinet was quite strong, I personally was less impressed by some of his subsequent cabinet selections, particularly during his second term. I also believe it's more difficult to attract high quality people to the cabinet as a governor gets close to the end of his term in office. To his credit, Bill Owens continued to make good selections for judgeships. In eight years, he managed to turn the bench in Colorado from one of the most liberal and "activist" in the country to one that included many good, solid conservative jurists, although he made only two appointments to the state's Supreme Court. I had some influence in the selection process and was proud to play a small role in the appointment of several very good judges to both the trial courts and the appellate courts.

While Bill Owens was a consummate politician, he was also a really decent guy. He was not wealthy and had very simple tastes. He regularly passed up a fancy dinner for a McDonald's hamburger. He appeared to be a great family man, frequently leaving state business behind for a short while to attend a child's soccer match. The governor did not live in the governor's mansion so as not to disrupt the education routine of his children, who attended suburban public schools. Many of us who knew him were surprised when he and his wife, Francis, separated in September of 2003.

Owens did a very good job during his first term, and it was clear to me he would cruise to reelection (in fact he won with 63 percent of the vote) and that his future political prospects were bright. Immediately upon his reelection in November of 2002 he began being mentioned by national columnists, including George Will, as a potential presidential candidate in 2008. That discussion ended with the separation from his wife and a few political setbacks that occurred during his second term.

In November of 1999 we put the Suthers family's fine-tuned knowledge of grassroots politics to work to get Janet elected to the Board of Education of Cheyenne Mountain School District 12. It was an exceptionally well-organized local campaign, and she was the top vote getter. Having lost the AG's race in 1998, I got a laugh at subsequent public appearances when I introduced Janet as the "successful politician in the family." Two years later she would be elected by her fellow board members to serve as President of the School Board, and she would again be the top vote getter when she was reelected in 2003. It was just the beginning of Janet's incredible work as a volunteer public servant.

In the spring of 2000 Colin Powell visited the Department of Corrections YOS in Pueblo. Powell was a retired four star general who had served stints as National Security Administrator to President Reagan and Chairman of the Joint Chiefs of Staff under George H. W. Bush. He was now Chairman of America's Promise, a national organization of groups dedicated to serving the country's at-risk youth. I met with Powell and was incredibly impressed. He had accepted an invitation from a counselor at YOS to speak with a group of young inmates and had arrived without fanfare and insisting that his visit receive no publicity. He spent an hour with the young men and showed genuine interest in them. Within a year, Powell would be appointed secretary of state by George W. Bush.

In June of 2000, I was awarded a fellowship by the Gates Foundation to attend a Government Executives Program at Harvard's John F. Kennedy School of Government. The six-week program tended to attract many more liberals than conservatives to the class of about 125 and the professors who led the discussions were "politically correct" to the extreme. The smaller cadre of law enforcement executives, including myself and my roommate, the chief of police in Winnipeg, Ontario, Canada, constituted the heart of the conservative minority. The pervasive indoctrination into the notion that government was an effective solver of virtually every conceivable social or economic problem did not convince me of that fact, but it did increase my appreciation of the necessity that public service not be allowed to become the exclusive province of the left. It strengthened my commitment to stay involved. It also gave me a much better understanding of where liberals are coming from and hopefully a more effective ability to communicate with them. Two of the lecturers were immensely entertaining. Dan Fenn, now in his eighties, had been a close friend and advisor of John F. Kennedy's and the first director of the Kennedy library. He had a delightful commonsense view of the world. Professor Gary Orren was one of the best speakers I've heard on the politically necessary art of persuasion. The Harvard campus itself was a great place to spend a summer contemplating the problems of the world.

In the course of the year 2000, Janet and I also made a difficult decision regarding our continuing membership in the Cheyenne Mountain Country Club. For several years we had been troubled that the exclusive club still had no Hispanic or African American members. And it was pointed out to us that the club still did not have any Jewish members. There were several identifiable Jews in the community that were clearly appropriate for membership because of their business or professional status. We had discussed the subject on several occasions with other prominent members, including Bill Hybl, the President of the El Pomar Foundation and president of the US Olympic Committee. Hybl suggested that a prominent Jewish businessman, Marvin Strait, should be nominated for membership. Strait was a CPA who had been president of the American Association of CPAs, the Chamber of Commerce Citizen of the Year, and was a member of other prestigious clubs in town. In Hybl's words, the membership could not dismiss Strait as a "politically correct" nominee. A fellow member, Jon Medved, and I approached Strait and he agreed to let us nominate him. I also discussed the matter with Dusty Loo, the president of the club. Loo was a friend of Strait's and told me, "Marvin would be a great member, and I'll personally expose anyone on the membership committee who votes against him." With that assurance, Strait was nominated for membership.

Months later it was apparent that there was considerable resistance to the nomination. Two or three members of the membership committee apparently resented the attempt to "force the issue." I called Dusty Loo. He confirmed the fact there was opposition. When I reminded him what he had said earlier, he said he did not want to "tear the club apart over this." When I said I was uncomfortable belonging to a club that would not admit a person of Marvin Strait's stature and that I could not help but think there was some anti-Semitic motive, he told me I should probably think about quitting. I am not sure if he was serious. But I was. Janet and I resigned in the summer of 2000. Two other members who told me they would quit if Strait did not get admitted changed their minds. They said they wanted to continue to "work the issue from within." I was not surprised.

I believe very strongly that a private social organization, which is privately funded, has a right to admit or deny membership to anyone it wants for any reason it wants. But it is up to individuals to decide whether they want to join or continue to belong to an organization which excludes members for reasons they do not agree with.

From Top Left clockwise: 1) My parents, Pat and Bill Suthers, in Colorado Springs in June of 1942, before he shipped off for North Africa. They agreed that if he survived the war they would move to Colorado Springs.; 2) My adoptive home was a warm and loving one. Even as a small boy there were signs I'd grow up to be a nerd.; 3) As an alter boy with our parish pastor, Monsignor Michael Harrington. He was a fixture in my youth.; 4) An all-city second baseman at St. Mary's High school. Even "the Goose" couldn't strike me out.; 5) Janet and I on our wedding day, May 21,1976. It was the best decision I've ever made.; 6) Campaign for District Attorney in 1988 was a family affair. Our daughters liked the parades.

From Top Left clockwise: 1) As U.S. Attorney for Colorado, getting a pep talk from the Commander in Chief after the terrorist attacks of 9/11.; 2) Colin Powell visited the Department of Corrections when I was the Executive Director. He would shortly be appointed Secretary of State.; 3) With U.S. Attorney General John Ashcroft and Deputy A.G. Larry Thompson announcing indictments against executives of Qwest.; 4) Arguing before the Supreme Court is a daunting and memorable experience. I did so in Kansas v. Colorado (2008). They don't allow cameras.; 5) Fly fishing on the South Platte River with Supreme Court Justice Antonin Scalia. He was perhaps the best conversationalist I ever met.

From Top Left clockwise: 1) Visiting a COVID ward at a local hospital in the fall of 2020. The COVID epidemic called for a different kind of leadership.; 2) At a press conference with U.S. Attorney General Eric Holden, HUD Secretary Shaun Donovan, and other state AGs to announce the $25 billion National Mortgage Settlement.; 3) Meeting President Trump to lobby him to keep U.S. Space Command Headquarters in Colorado Springs.; 4) Announcing for Mayor of Colorado Springs in January of 2015. It was a difficult job, but a great opportunity for political leadership.; 5) At an impromptu press conference when the Planned Parenthood shooter was arrested after a long and deadly stand-off with the police.; 6) With Israeli President Shimon Perez at his residence in Jerusalem. As Colorado Attorney General I had numerous international travel opportunities.

From Top Left clockwise: 1) With Colorado Governors Bill Owens, John Hickenlooper, and Bill Ritter. As Attorney General I had a very good working relationship with all three of them.; 2) Swearing in as Colorado Attorney General. For a good lawyer interested in public service, it's a fantastic job.; 3) This needlepoint has hung in every office I've occupied. "Thus passes the glory of the world" is a reminder that life is fleeting, and character is all that endures.; 4) Janet and I with our daughters and their husbands. The tragic death of Mark Karla (second from left) left a huge void in our lives.

Chapter XVII
The United States Attorney

In January of 2000, I became involved in the presidential campaign of George W. Bush, then the governor of Texas. Colorado Governor Bill Owens was a friend of Bush. He had grown up in Ft. Worth, Texas and had been a fellow young Republican of "George W." Owens put together a group of about forty Coloradans to go to Iowa for the five days before the Iowa caucuses. We attended rallies, manned phone banks, and stood on street corners with signs in -10 degree weather. We were in charge of three northwest Iowa counties which included Sioux City. Bush comfortably defeated Steve Forbes and other contenders at the caucuses.

Owens asked me to co-chair the Bush presidential campaign in El Paso County. As the largest Republican populated area in the state, Bush would need to win it big. We put together a grassroots effort that was better than I had ever seen for a presidential campaign on a local level. We wound up delivering a 70,000 vote victory for Bush over Al Gore, the third largest margin in any county in the country.

In the summer of 2000, I was elected a delegate to the Republican National Convention in Philadelphia. It turned out to be a real family affair. Our daughter Alison took off the fall quarter from her senior year at Stanford to be the only paid employee of the

Bush campaign in Colorado. She also worked for the campaign at the convention. Our daughter Kate was a page at the convention. Only Janet was without any obligation other than to party. We had a great time.

It was also in the summer of 2000 that Governor Owens suggested the possibility that I might be an appropriate candidate for US attorney for the district of Colorado if Bush won the presidency. "You're clearly the most qualified," he remarked. The notion gained some momentum before the November elections through conversations with Colorado's Senators Wayne Allard and Ben Nighthorse Campbell, both of whom I had gotten to know fairly well during the 1998 election campaign. The US attorney's job was one I was very interested in. Based on my observations as a district attorney, it was at the pinnacle of public prosecution. So for the first time in my life, I had something personal at stake in the presidential election on November 7, 2000. As a consequence, it was one of the longest nights of my life.

Because our daughter Alison had worked so hard on the Bush campaign in its Denver Office, we started out there on election night. By 8 p.m. Mountain Standard Time the news was very grim. The national networks declared Al Gore the winner in Pennsylvania, Michigan, and Florida. I had followed the election analysis closely and knew that Bush could not win unless he carried one of those three states. We headed back to Colorado Springs to see the local returns in a state of depression. About half way my cell phone rang. My Bush campaign co-chairs were informing me that the networks were taking Florida out of the Gore column and declaring it too close to call. We arrived at the Republican campaign headquarters in Colorado Springs around 9:30 p.m. and spent the next three hours obsessing over the incredibly close vote count in Florida. About 12:30 a.m. the networks declared Bush the winner of Florida and the presidency and the crowd of about 250 erupted in wild celebration. I gave a victory speech thanking our local campaign team. I then drove home to watch the Gore concession speech and the Bush victory speech. But neither occurred. Janet and I stayed up into the wee hours of the morning in disbelief as the networks once again retracted their earlier declaration and pronounced the Florida vote too close to call.

And there it stayed for over a month. Every day I would watch the incredible intrigue of the Florida recount on television and in newspapers wishing it had no impact on me. I tried to be detached and take a what-will-be-will-be attitude, but I was not entirely successful.

When a 5-4 decision of the US Supreme Court finally decided the matter, and Bush was the victor, Janet and I quickly secured our inauguration tickets. Despite the huge crowds and the lousy weather, we had a great time at the myriad of events surrounding the inauguration. It was made more fun by the fact that a large group from Colorado, and El Paso County in particular, were able to attend.

During January and February of 2001, Governor Owens, Senators Allard and Campbell, and all of Colorado's Republican Congressmen wrote letters to the presidential transition team recommending me to the president for the US attorney position. In late March, I was contacted by the White House and the Justice Department. After spending approximately forty hours filling out forms and questionnaires about every aspect of my life, past and present, I flew back to Washington for interviews with officials from DOJ and the White House Counsel's Office. The questions were generally unremarkable, except those by David Margolis, a legendary senior DOJ prosecutor, who asked whether I had ever used illicit drugs, had an affair, or had done anything else that could embarrass the president. Fortunately, my answers were short and emphatic. In May, I was informed the White House had requested a "priority one" FBI background investigation. The investigation took thirty days and included almost 100 interviews by fifteen agents. They talked to college roommates, fellow employees at every job I had ever had, supervisors and subordinates, friends and neighbors. I referred to the process as the "revenge of the nerds." My downright boring personal life was finally starting to pay off.

In June I returned to Washington for an interview with Attorney General John Ashcroft and Deputy Attorney General Larry Thompson. During the meeting, Ashcroft outlined the Bush administration's law enforcement priorities as 1) prosecution of federal gun laws, 2) prosecution of major drug distribution organizations, 3) the growing threat of Russian and Eastern European organized crime, and 4) cybercrime. I felt the meeting went well. On July 30, 2001, President Bush formally nominated me to be the thirty-ninth US attorney for the district of Colorado since it became a territory in 1861.

The previous US attorney, Tom Strickland, had unsuccessfully run for the US Senate in 1996 before being appointed US attorney by President Bill Clinton in 1999. It was clear he had designs on running again for statewide office. (In fact, he ran again in 2002 and lost, again, to Senator Allard.) So, the White House was quick to request and receive his resignation effective April 1, 2001. The office was then run by an interim US attorney, Dick Spriggs, who had been chief of the criminal division under Strickland. In mid-August, the Department of Justice indicated they were unsure how quickly the Senate would act on my nomination. Because they could foresee no serious opposition, they asked if I would consider being appointed interim US attorney pending confirmation of my nomination by the Senate. I agreed, and after approval of the appointment by the federal judges in Colorado, I was sworn in as the interim US attorney on August 31. I was the first lawyer from Colorado Springs ever to become US attorney. My first day on the job was the day after Labor Day, Tuesday, September 4, 2001. I met that morning with all the employees in the office to share my vision and expectations with them. But I did not know then that the timing of my interim appointment would prove to be providential.

One week later, on Tuesday morning, September 11, I was to fly to Las Vegas to attend an Indian Country Conference. The US attorneys in Arizona, Colorado, New Mexico, and Utah met annually to discuss problems on Indian reservations in the "four corners" states. While walking to the gate at Denver International Airport I heard a report on a television monitor that a plane had crashed into one of the World Trade Center Towers. I remember thinking to myself that it must be a small private plane with a highly incompetent pilot. I remarked to a colleague that the pilot must have a serious inner ear infection. But as I was about to board my plane, my pager and cell phone went off simultaneously. I was informed by my office that a second airplane had crashed into the World Trade Center and a terrorist attack on the United States was underway. Within minutes we learned that a third plane had crashed into The Pentagon. The US attorney general was directing all US attorneys to return to their offices pending further instructions. As Dick Spriggs, once again the chief of the criminal division, and I drove back to the office, we listened on the radio as reporters described the horror of the collapse of both World Trade Center towers and yet another crash of a plane in Pennsylvania, this one apparently intended to target the White House or US Capitol building. I recall turning to Spriggs and saying, "I think this is going to change the nature of this job."

Within twenty-four hours of the events of September 11, all ninety-three US attorneys participated in a highly secure phone conference with Attorney General John Ashcroft and shortly thereafter received a written directive from him. It said, "Until further notice, anti-terrorism will be the first and overriding priority of the Justice Department." Each of the US attorneys was instructed to set up an anti-terrorism task force to coordinate intelligence gathering and dissemination in their district and to respond to any terrorism threat that occurred in their district. I was fortunate that mine was one of thirty-one districts nationwide that had a pre-existing Joint Terrorism Task Force with fourteen agencies involved under the direction of the Denver FBI office. We did not have to start from scratch in the all-important task of gathering intelligence. The attorney general told us that ultimately our success would be measured by whether or not we were able to prevent another major terrorist attack on American soil.

Largely due to the events of September 11, the process of nominating and confirming many US attorneys was accelerated. I was among the first of the Bush nominated US attorneys to be unanimously confirmed by the Senate on October 11, 2001. I was sworn in as the presidentially appointed US attorney on October 16.

On November 29, 2001, many of the newly appointed US attorneys met in Washington, DC with President Bush and Attorney General Ashcroft to discuss how the domestic war on terrorism would be conducted. Bush talked to us for half an hour about how the challenges facing law enforcement had changed since September 11. It was no longer acceptable that we be good at "sifting through the rubble" and apprehending terrorists after the fact. We must prevent them from perpetrating the attacks. He told us that he viewed the US attorneys as his "battlefield commanders" in the domestic war against terrorism. When he shook my hand he told me, "I need your help, you are on the front lines of this war." Ashcroft took us to The Pentagon bombing site and implored us to do everything "legally and constitutionally permissible" to make sure a terrorist incident of such magnitude did not occur again. For the first time in my life, I was serving my country in a time of war, and I relished the challenge. It also occurred to me as I left Washington that not everyone gets a personal pep talk from the most powerful man in the world.

Over the next six years, I would meet with George W. Bush on three more occasions. I found him a very likable man. Without TV cameras in his face, he came off as very engaging and very sincere. He did not fare as well with the cameras on. Bush genuinely believed he had a mission after 9/11 to prevent another attack on American soil. His success in that regard was not as likely as it is often perceived in hindsight. It may be the greatest accomplishment of his presidency.

A year later, in the fall of 2002, the US Attorneys Conference was held in New York, and we visited Ground Zero, the site where the World Trade Center had stood. All ninety-three US attorneys and their spouses joined Attorney General Ashcroft in a ceremony at the bottom of the forty-eight-acre excavated site, seven floors below street level. It was an incredibly moving event. It also served as great motivation to all of us to aggressively pursue the domestic war on terrorism.

On November 10, 2001, a crowd of 300 people gathered in Colorado Springs for a "Friends of John Suthers" tribute organized by a small group of friends and political supporters. Family, friends, and political allies roasted me unmercifully. The consistent theme of their affectionate barbs was the "astonishingly boring life" the "straight arrow" had led. At the end, I roasted my roasters and then made some serious remarks which chronicled my life from a ward of Catholic Charities to the US Attorney's Office, thanking all the people, both living and dead, who had helped me along the way. I had turned fifty just three weeks prior to the event. As I contemplated the events of my life up to that point, I had to concede that I had not led a flamboyant life. But on the other hand, it had been interesting beyond all expectations. And I was very much looking forward to the challenges of the future.

Anyone who follows the news in the paper or on radio or television hears frequently about US attorneys, but I quickly found out that very few people have much knowledge about what the job of a US attorney actually entails.

The US Constitution is largely silent about the structure of the federal court system, saying only in Article III that there will be one Supreme Court and such other inferior courts as Congress shall designate. It said nothing about who would exercise the prosecutorial powers of the United States. When Congress convened for the first time in 1789, it quickly enacted legislation to give shape to a federal legal system. The Judiciary Act of 1789 created the position of the US attorney general to serve as the chief law enforcement officer in the country. But in the spirit of decentralization that was very much a part of the founders' philosophy, it also provided that the president would appoint, with the consent of the Senate, "a person learned in law" in each federal district to serve as US attorney and represent the United States in all criminal and civil matters occurring within the district. The US attorney would be the chief federal law enforcement officer in the district.

George Washington appointed the first thirteen US attorneys in 1789. They included future Chief Justice of the Supreme Court, John Marshall, who was appointed US attorney for Virginia. Since 1789, Congress has divided the United States and its territories into ninety-three federal districts. Populous states like New York, California, and Texas have multiple districts. Others like Louisiana and Oklahoma have multiple districts because they exercised inordinate political clout in bygone days. But Congress has not created any new federal districts in several decades and all the western states, other than California and Washington, constitute single federal districts.

When I became US attorney, the Colorado office, headquartered in downtown Denver, had 135 employees including sixty-five lawyers called assistant US attorneys. It also had two field offices, one in Grand Junction to deal with the myriad of federal agencies and extensive federal land holdings on the west slope of Colorado, and one in Durango primarily to deal with all the criminal and civil issues arising from two large Indian reservations in southwest Colorado. The Criminal Division of the US Attorney's Office represents the US in prosecuting violations of the federal criminal code ranging from bank robbery, firearms offenses, drug trafficking, and counterfeiting to cybercrime, health care fraud, and public corruption. The Civil Division represents the United States as plaintiff against contractors, environmental polluters, fraudulent federal program providers, and delinquent debtors. It represents the US and its agents as defendants against actions brought by contractors, employees, patients in federal health care facilities, and federal prison inmates.

All the employees in the US Attorney's Office are civil servants, but the US attorney is permitted to bring in his or her own first assistant, the second highest job in the office. I chose Bill Leone, whom I had practiced law with for about a year at Sparks, Dix in the mid-1980s. Bill had gone on to be a highly successful partner in a national law firm, Cooley Godward. He was very bright, very professional, and I was pleased to get someone of his caliber to be my first assistant US attorney. He made a significant financial sacrifice to take the job. For the third time in three successive public service jobs, I was extremely fortunate to have outstanding support on the executive level. Bill's expertise in corporate and securities law matters would prove extremely beneficial to the office. I've always maintained that the key to being a good manager is a willingness to surround yourself with people that are smarter than you are. That was easy to do at the US Attorney's Office. I relied on several veterans of the office like Jim Allison, Dave Gaouette, Tom O'Rourke, Gina Rodriguez, and Michael Hegarty to guide me through the intricacies of federal law and the federal bureaucracy.

Because a daily commute from Colorado Springs to Denver would have been impractical and exhausting, I rented a two-bedroom condominium in the LoDo (lower downtown) area of Denver, just two blocks from the office. It was in a forty-one-story complex called Brooks Towers. Friends of ours in Colorado Springs owned the condo and gave me a reasonable rate. They used it occasionally on weekends when I was in Colorado Springs. The condo was close to everything in downtown Denver and had a good workout room and other amenities. Four years later Janet and I would purchase a one-bedroom condo in Brooks Towers so that the monthly payments would create equity. I found urban living four or five days a week to be quite enjoyable. During my first year as US attorney, our oldest daughter Alison lived at the condo with me.

After graduating from Stanford, she had planned to join the Peace Corps. But her assignment to Mauritania, an Islamic country in West Africa, was canceled after the terrorist attacks of September 11. She went to work as a research director for Governor Owens's reelection campaign and deferred her admission to Georgetown Law School until the fall of 2003. She would also live with me while she was doing an internship in Denver in the summer of 2005.

In many respects the job of US attorney was similar to that of district attorney. But there were significant differences. As US attorney I spent much less time dealing with the victims of crime and their families. Because of the nature of many federal crimes, most of my constituents were the many federal, state, and local agencies that brought cases to the US attorney. The bureaucratic overlay of the Department of Justice was also much different. I had little to do with budgeting and had to get permission from Washington for certain major decisions such as a request for the death penalty. Many of the cases we handled, particularly drug cases and white-collar crime cases, were much larger and more complex than on the local level. Others were not. The caseloads in the US Attorney's Office were smaller than big city DA's offices and there was less plea bargaining. In general, federal sentences were harsher than state sentences, primarily because there was no parole eligibility until you had served 85 percent of a sentence.

Many federal crimes are more regulatory in nature, whereas most state crimes seem rooted in the Ten Commandments. A former US attorney in Colorado, Bob Miller, once described the situation as follows: "A district attorney knows a crime has been committed and is trying to prove the defendant did it. A US attorney knows the defendant did something wrong and is trying to prove it's a federal crime."

As DA I had the privilege of meeting and working with the governor, state attorney general, state legislators, and others. As the US attorney, I was privileged to make acquaintance with not only the president and US attorney general, but also with a wide variety of high-ranking federal officials. The fact I had been promoted really dawned on me in April of 2002 at the funeral of former Supreme Court Justice Byron White. I sat next to Senator Ted Kennedy. At a reception after the funeral, I spent a considerable time in a room alone with Ted Olson, the US solicitor general and five sitting justices of the US Supreme Court. I also had the opportunity to accompany Supreme Court Justice Antonin Scalia on a fly fishing trip on Colorado's South Platte River. I had dinner with Scalia on two of his subsequent trips to Colorado. He had an amazing breadth of knowledge about a wide variety of subjects and was perhaps the most interesting conversationalist I've ever encountered. The renowned American historian, David McCullough, who I was privileged to have dinner with when I was attorney general of Colorado, also ranks very high in that category.

My fellow US attorneys were a talented and interesting group. More of them had extensive prosecution backgrounds than had been the case under Bill Clinton. One of my most memorable compatriots was the brash US attorney for New Jersey. Chris Christie went on to become the brash governor of New Jersey and make quite a splash on the national scene. Matt Mead, my neighboring US attorney in Wyoming, became governor of his state. Other US attorney colleagues were elected to Congress or took other government appointments, including several to the federal bench. One, J. B. Van Hollen, was elected Attorney General of Wisconsin, and we would work together for several years. My work as US attorney also caused me to meet two Justice Department officials I came to admire very much. One was FBI Director Bob Mueller, a former US attorney who took his stellar reputation as a prosecutor to the Bureau and the other was James Comey, US attorney for Manhattan and subsequently deputy attorney general under Ashcroft. Both would go on to considerable notoriety when Donald Trump became president.

I found the job of US attorney very much like that of district attorney in one important respect. It was a great public service opportunity. As DA and as US attorney I went to work every day knowing that I would confront many interesting and important challenges. For a lawyer interested in public service, I don't think it gets any better.

The quality of lawyer applicants to the US Attorney's Office was astonishing. Assistant US attorney jobs paid well and were viewed by the best law school graduates in the country as very prestigious. We also got applications from many very good private practitioners looking for more trial experience or more meaningful work. Many successful assistant DAs wanted to move up to the US Attorney's Office. We interviewed only one out of every three hundred applicants. We hired even fewer. I was very pleased with the quality of the hiring that we did. In many respects good hires are the best legacy a US attorney can leave his office. They will impact the work of the office for years to come.

The greatest downside to the job, as I saw it, was responding to the bureaucracy at Main Justice in Washington. Although the Judiciary Act of 1789 made US attorneys ultimately accountable to the president, over the years the federal prosecutorial power has become more centralized in Washington. In 1933 Franklin Roosevelt issued an executive order giving the US attorney general supervisory oversight over US attorneys. Since that time the Department of Justice has acquired immense control over the budgets, the personnel policies, and the prosecutorial policies of US attorneys, although they have retained considerable discretion in filing decisions. Main Justice expected US attorneys to get approval for a remarkable number of things. That aspect of the job was particularly irksome for those of us who had formerly been elected state prosecutors with a great degree of autonomy. I found the federal budget process irrational. In order to get any additional resources for US attorneys' offices, DOJ would go to Congress with a particular program. For example, they might ask for more prosecutors to prosecute federal firearms violations. Congress would grant the request, but all such new positions would be "dedicated" and could do *only* firearms cases. If, several years later, other priorities emerged, it was virtually impossible to switch dedicated employees to other responsibilities. This was true of both lawyer and support staff. It made for great inefficiency and great frustration. As to the budgeting function, I yearned for my days at the DA's office where I had virtually complete discretion as to how the allotted funds were expended, as long as they were not overspent. Not surprisingly, it was also virtually impossible to fire federal employees absent serious misconduct on their part. Poor job performance typically wasn't enough. Luckily, I was blessed to inherit an office with great employees, and I made it even better with outstanding hires.

In my opinion, the quality of the federal district court judges in the district of Colorado was a mixed bag. Lewis Babcock, the chief judge, was a good jurist and a decent guy. He had some reservations about me because I was pushing the judges to put judicial resources in Colorado Springs, and they were opposed. In a letter to the United States Judicial Conference, I accused the federal judges of being "Denvercentric" and Babcock did not appreciate that. Judge Richard Matsch and Judge Edward Nottingham were plenty smart but had difficult personalities and a barely disguised anti-government bias. Nottingham in particular could become irrationally angry at the slightest provocation. He would later resign from the bench amid a scandal involving his patronage of prostitutes. A few other federal judges were nice people but unimpressive when it came to the intricacies of the criminal law and the rules of evidence. Fortunately, subsequent appointees to the bench, Robert Blackburn, Marcia Krieger, and Phil Figa, were pretty solid and contributed to the improvement of the overall performance of the federal trial bench in Colorado. Blackburn in particular was an outstanding jurist. Our office had a generally favorable view of the Tenth Circuit Court of Appeals, which included eventual Supreme Court Justice Neil Gorsuch.

As US attorney I continued to do a great deal of public speaking. At least a dozen times per month I would talk to service clubs, law enforcement groups, and various other organizations. Favorite topics would include the role of the US attorney and the domestic war on terrorism. I was also invited to address the employees of federal agencies regarding particular challenges confronting them and the nature of the attorney-client relationship between the US attorney and the federal agencies.

The US Attorney's Office, just like the District Attorney's Office I had managed, was involved in thousands of interesting cases. But unlike the DA's Office, over half of the cases were civil. I cannot possibly chronicle all the interesting cases and issues we were involved in, so I will limit myself to a few I found most memorable.

In April of 1999, Colorado had endured the worst episode of school violence in the nation's history. Thirteen students and one teacher were killed at Columbine High School; many others were seriously injured. The school had been attacked by two well-armed students, Eric Harris and Dylan Klebold. When I took office as US attorney in the fall of 2001, two-and-a-half years had passed since the incident. But the controversy surrounding the tragedy still lingered. The parents of some of the victims had filed suit, alleging the police had caused their children injuries or death by failing to enter the building and confront the perpetrators immediately upon their arrival. One parent maintained that his son had been killed by police fire rather than that of Harris or Klebold. In January of 2002, in an event heavily covered by the media, an attorney for the families delivered a letter to me as US attorney alleging federal civil rights violations had occurred and requesting a federal grand jury investigation. Every newspaper in the state listed the "29 lies" the parents alleged the police had perpetrated on the public. I personally reviewed voluminous documents and received a lengthy briefing from the FBI, which had been in on the investigation from the beginning. Despite the attention the parents' claims had gotten

All This I Saw, and Part of It I Was

from the media, I found their contention that any crime had been committed by anyone other than Harris and Klebold to be totally without merit. I concluded the police had made tactical mistakes and that the main investigative agency, the Jefferson County Sheriff's Department, had been very inept in its communications with the media and the public, but only the perpetrators were criminally culpable. There was no purpose to be served by a federal grand jury investigation. I was vilified in the media by some of the parents, but I was very confident of the appropriateness of my decision. All subsequent inquiries by other governmental agencies and by the media vindicated my decision.

One of the things that makes the work of a large public prosecution office so interesting is that important, high-profile cases can occur at any time and under surprising circumstances. As a longtime prosecutor, I've come to understand the reality of the phrase, "Truth is stranger than fiction." One such case involved the largest wildfire in the history of Colorado.

In the summer of 2002, the state was suffering the worst drought on record. Mountain snowpack from the winter before had been only 5-10 percent of normal. The whole state was under severe water restrictions and a complete ban on open fires. On June 8, 2002, a fire broke out near Lake George, Colorado about fifty miles west of Colorado Springs. Efforts to suppress the blaze by early responders failed and the fire spread incredibly fast. Over the next month, 140,000 acres were engulfed, by far the most in the state's history at that time. Nearly 200 structures were destroyed. Fire suppression and forest restoration costs were enormous. A total of over $100 million in damage was done.

The fire was initially reported by a veteran forest service employee, Terry Barton. She said she was on duty in the forest enforcing the fire ban when she smelled smoke and responded to a campsite where it was coming from. She described the size of the fire when she arrived and said that despite her best efforts, she was unable to suppress it. When expert fire investigators were called in to examine the point of origin, they quickly became suspicious of Barton's version of events. Eventually they confronted her with their forensic findings, and, in a videotaped interview, she finally admitted that she started the fire. She claimed she had burned a letter from her estranged husband in an old campfire pit and thought the fire was out, but that it ignited the surrounding grass and timbers, and she was unable to put it out. She then called for help and constructed her original story. Investigators still didn't buy her story completely. They found no trace of paper ash in the fire pit and believed rocks around the pit had been intentionally arranged in a fashion to facilitate the fire escaping the pit. A possible motive? Probably to be the hero who first encountered the danger and put it out before it engulfed the forest. She had been pushing her supervisor to promote her to fire investigator and probably felt such a heroic act might assist in that quest.

Barton was arrested on June 16, 2002, and indicted by a federal grand jury a few days later. For a week I found myself in front of cameras from every national network and cable channel and on the front page of the *New York Times*, *Washington Post*, and every major newspaper in America. Connie Chung, then working for CNN, called me early one morning on my office cell phone. Only a few of my fellow employees were supposed to have the number. She wanted to talk "off the record." I declined. Publicity wise, it was a very big case.

In addition to federal charges for willfully setting fire to National Forest lands and lying to investigators, Barton also pled guilty to state arson charges for the private property damage she had done. My successor as District Attorney of the Fourth Judicial District, Jeanne Smith, handled the state prosecution and our offices worked very closely together. Barton was sentenced to six years in federal prison and to a term in state prison, to be served concurrently. She served a total of about six years in prison before parole. Federal District Court Judge Richard Matsch refused to order Barton to pay millions of dollars in restitution to the government, despite the seemingly clear directive of federal statute. In March of 2004 I personally argued an appeal of Matsch's order to the Tenth Circuit Court of Appeals. The appellate court reversed and directed Judge Matsch to order restitution to the government in the amount of $14.7 million for reclamation efforts. Unless Barton someday wins the lottery, the chances of recovering much of the restitution is negligible.

In 1999 a building in Colorado Springs housing an IRS office was burned to the ground. Shortly thereafter another IRS office was destroyed by fire. Both cases clearly involved arson and various anti-government groups were the prime suspects. It took over two years, but eventually four members of a group called the Sons of Liberty were arrested. Their leader, as it turned out, was the former son-in-law of a state senator from Colorado Springs. He himself had tried to run for district attorney against Jeanne Smith in 1996 before being disqualified because he wasn't licensed to practice law. Three of the four were convicted of the crime and given lengthy prison sentences.

In late June of 2002, our office got directly involved in the nation's war on terrorism. A young man named James Ujaama was arrested by the FBI in Denver on a material witness warrant from the Eastern District of Virginia. Ujaama, who had previously been known as James Thompson, was an American citizen, born in Denver and raised in Seattle. In the last six years he had become very involved in Islamic fundamentalism and had gone to London for training at the Finsbury Park Mosque. The mosque was headed by Sheikh Abu Hamza Al-Masri, an Egyptian-born Islamic extremist and cleric. Abu Hamza had lost an eye and an arm fighting the Russians in Afghanistan and had subsequently become a principal player in *mujahideen* (Islamic warriors engaged in jihad). He was a longtime associate of Osama bin Laden and an early member of Al-Qaeda. According to a confidential source who was taken prisoner by US forces in the liberation of Afghanistan after the terrorist attacks of 9/11, Ujaama, known in the Islamic extremist movement as Balil Ahmed, had become a high-ranking assistant to the sheikh. He was responsible for maintaining websites and assisting in the transport of volunteers into Afghanistan and Pakistan. The informant indicated Ujaama had personally delivered laptop computers to the Taliban in Kabul in August 2001. Further, the FBI had procured documentary evidence that Ujaama had scoped out a possible terrorist training camp for the sheikh in a remote area of Oregon.

Ujaama had recently returned to the state of Washington from London, through a very circuitous route that included Zurich and Montreal. He had escaped FBI surveillance in Seattle before being located in Denver. He had purchased a plane ticket back to London, through Zurich. Nervous that he might escape the country, the anti-terrorism unit of the Justice Department had sought his arrest on a material witness warrant pertaining to the ongoing grand jury investigation in eastern Virginia. We had several closed hearings in Denver regarding Ujaama's objection to being transported to Virginia. The press was angry about being excluded from the hearings and sued to gain access. Commentators blamed the secrecy on John Ashcroft, George Bush, and the USA PATRIOT Act of 2001 (Uniting and Strengthening America by Providing Appropriate Tools Required to Intercept and Obstruct Terrorism). In fact, the hearings were secret under Rule 6 (e) of the Federal Rules of Criminal Procedure which required all matters pertaining to a grand jury be closed to the public. Ujaama was eventually indicted for providing material support to a terrorist organization and the prosecution was pursued in the Western District of Washington. He eventually pled guilty to providing material support to the Taliban. He was sentenced to three years in prison and agreed to testify against Abu Hamza Al-Masri.

As the war in Iraq raged in 2003, we charged several Iraqi and Pakistani nationals with immigration violations and money laundering offenses. The FBI considered some of them to be national security threats because they had attended training camps in Pakistan.

Our office was involved in several other classified matters pertaining to the domestic war on terrorism and consulted with the FBI and Justice Department frequently regarding surveillances under the Foreign Intelligence Surveillance Act (FISA) and other law enforcement operations, primarily in the Denver Metro area. When I first occupied my rather plush office in September of 2001, I questioned whether I would ever have occasion to use the secret and top-secret phones installed in the office. In fact, they were used several times. I am quite certain we disrupted some potential terrorist activity.

In September 2002 our attention to national security concerns caused us to conduct an operation at Denver International Airport which resulted in the indictment of 110 workers at the airport. All the workers, the vast majority of whom were illegal aliens, had used fraudulent documentation to get security badges which gave them access to the most secure areas of the airport including airplanes, luggage handling, and the tarmac. While we were criticized for this "disruption project" because it did not turn up any terrorists, we were vehement that such operations had to be undertaken to determine the true identities of everyone who had access to our critical infrastructures. We subsequently did similar operations at military bases and the US Air Force Academy.

When President Bush tapped John Ashcroft to be attorney general, his confirmation process had been quite contentious. Despite being a former US Senator, governor and Attorney General of Missouri, he was portrayed as being an extreme conservative and liberal interest groups tried desperately to block his nomination. While they failed, they helped create an image of Ashcroft as being so conservative that he was out of the mainstream. In the aftermath of the September 11th terrorist attacks, Ashcroft led the domestic efforts against terrorism and quickly became the whipping boy for the ACLU and both liberal and conservative media who felt the

Justice Department's efforts to fight terrorism were infringing on civil rights. As a US attorney, I had considerable exposure to Ashcroft, in both formal and informal settings. I talked with him dozens of times. In January of 2003 we spent an afternoon hiking together in the foothills west of Denver. He came to Denver to meet with our Anti-Terrorism Advisory Council. I shared the platform with him at a few press conferences, including one to announce the first indictments in the Qwest case. I heard him give speeches to large and small audiences. As a consequence, I had ample opportunity to form some impressions of my own about Ashcroft. I admired him. The man was incredibly sincere. Depending upon his audience, he could be a motivating and inspiring speaker. He had extensive knowledge of history. His evangelical beliefs were entirely genuine. Several evangelical politicians I've encountered were phonies. Not Ashcroft. He was a true public servant who always pursued the course he felt was best for the country, even if not the most politically expedient. He was consumed with protecting America from terrorism, believing that was the mission God, through George W. Bush, had chosen for him after his defeat for reelection to the Senate in 2000. It is well documented that on September 12, 2001, the day after the terrorist attacks, George Bush told John Ashcroft it was his responsibility to make sure that such attacks on America did not happen again. Ashcroft took the directive literally and seriously.

I believe the course Ashcroft set for the DOJ, in light of the nature and extent of the threat the country faced from terrorism, was fairly balanced and largely effective. I believe most of the initiatives would have been pursued regardless of who was attorney general. It would have been irresponsible not to pursue them. In my opinion, critics greatly exaggerated the threat posed to civil liberties from those initiatives, including the PATRIOT Act.

But, in my opinion, Ashcroft also gave his critics too much material to work with. His problem was often in the delivery. His message rarely had any warm edges to it. Instead of calling critics of the anti-terrorism efforts "unpatriotic," or accusing them of aiding the terrorists, he should have politely dismissed them as critics at a time when the country needed doers. He also needed to publicly emphasize more frequently the primacy of protecting constitutional rights while still waging the war on terrorism. I have found that conservatives are most effective, and most able to gain widespread public support, when they display sufficient warmth and humor to soften any suggestion of self-righteousness. George W. Bush had that ability at times. John Ashcroft did not.

Despite his success in leading the department's anti-terrorism efforts, Ashcroft remained a much maligned figure by the time of the 2004 election, and I was not surprised that he resigned soon thereafter. It was apparent that he was physically exhausted from the work of the past four years.

In the three years after the terrorist attacks of September 11, 2001, I spoke to almost 100 groups defending the Justice Department's anti-terrorism initiatives, including the PATRIOT Act. There were only a few provisions of the act I thought should be modified. I debated the ACLU and other critics at least two dozen times. In July 2004 I prepared Governor Owens for a debate on the PATRIOT Act with Vermont Governor Howard Dean, who had recently dropped his presidential campaign. The debate took place at the ACLU National Convention in San Francisco. I felt I was very effective in debates by always beginning with an acknowledgment of the primacy of constitutional rights, and then arguing that DOJ's anti-terrorism efforts were necessary to preserve an environment in America where the free exercise of those rights could continue to flourish.

The easiest aspect of the PATRIOT Act to defend was its removal of the "wall" that the 1974 FISA had created between the intelligence community and criminal investigators. US Attorney Patrick Fitzgerald, who had prosecuted the first World Trade Center bombing case in 1993 and several other international terrorism cases, described the problem to the Senate Judiciary Committee in 2003:

> I was on the prosecution team that began a criminal investigation of Osama bin Laden in early 1996. We had access to a number of sources... We could talk to local police. We could talk to other US Government agencies. We could talk to foreign police officers. Even foreign intelligence personnel. And foreign citizens... We could even talk to Al-Qaeda members. But there was one group we were not permitted to talk to. Who? The FBI agents across the street from us who were assigned to a parallel intelligence investigation of Osama bin Laden and Al-Qaeda. We could not learn what information they had gathered. That was the "wall."

> From US Department of Justice,

> Report from the Field: The USA PATRIOT Act at Work

Many who analyzed the failure to learn of the 9/11 attack before it occurred blamed the "wall" for preventing an exchange of information within the FBI which would have uncovered the plot. I was not surprised that most of the PATRIOT Act had remained intact in the ensuing years.

In the spring and summer of 2002, a series of corporate scandals swept the United States and wreaked havoc on investor confidence and consequently on American stock markets. It began with the collapse of Enron Corporation which was followed closely by the failure of WorldCom and Global Crossing. They all involved accounting abuses that included hiding debt or booking income and revenue in a fraudulent fashion in order to meet very aggressive growth projections. The other thing they had in common was their

All This I Saw, and Part of It I Was

accountant, Arthur Andersen, a company which wound up imploding as a result of the scandal.

In the case of Enron and Global Crossing, one of the problem areas involved the exchange of fiber optic capacity. There was no real market for the capacity and the exchanges or "swaps" were done to create illusory revenue. Further, in some cases the sale portion of the exchanges was booked as immediate revenue while the cost portion was expensed over time, giving shareholders a misleading view of actual valuation. Both companies had done such exchanges with the largest company based in Colorado—Qwest Communications—and the Securities Exchange Commission opened an investigation into the accounting at Qwest. Qwest's accounting of such deals had been even more aggressive. On the recommendation of the SEC, my office authorized the FBI to open a criminal investigation of Qwest in late June of 2002.

The *Wall Street Journal* reported the existence of the criminal investigation in its Friday, July 5th edition, based on sources close to the investigation. We suspected SEC investigators leaked the information. Qwest lawyers called our office to confirm the report. After speaking with Deputy Attorney General Larry Thompson, our office was authorized to acknowledge the existence of the investigation to Qwest. We knew that as a publicly traded company they would then be obligated to inform the public. When they did so Wednesday July 10th, Qwest stock fell by 40 percent in one day and the entire market plummeted several hundred points. It occurred to me that the ability to impact the market in that fashion was not something I had as a local district attorney.

In early June *The Denver Post* newspaper called and indicated that it had learned from searching records at the Secretary of State's Office that during my 1998 campaign for attorney general I had received a $1,000 contribution from Qwest's major shareholder, Philip Anschutz. They asked if I would be recusing myself from the investigation as a result. I indicated I would have the matter reviewed by the Justice Department, but that on the basis of my knowledge of the law and ethical guidance, I did not have an actual conflict of interest. I did not own Qwest stock. I had no business or personal relationship with any of its officers, including Mr. Anschutz. In fact, I had never met Anschutz at the time. He had responded to a solicitation that was mailed to 5,000 Republicans. It wasn't until several years later that I would become well acquainted with Mr. Anschutz.

The Denver Post ran two articles and one editorial pushing the notion that I should recuse myself. One article quoted the chair of the Democratic Party saying I should recuse myself because of ties to Senator Wayne Allard, who had received sizable Qwest contributions. My predecessor as US Attorney, Tom Strickland, was running against Allard for the US Senate seat and the Dems apparently thought they could score some points in what had turned into a very nasty campaign. The Republicans lashed back at Strickland in the article by once again labeling him as a "millionaire lawyer lobbyist" who had once lobbied on behalf of the now bankrupt and scandalized Global Crossing.

The Denver Post editorial was entitled "Suthers on a Tightrope." They insisted they just wanted to make sure the matter was reviewed in Washington. While The Denver Post is traditionally no friend of Republicans, the editorial did point out that as a prosecutor I had earned a reputation as the kind of guy that "would prosecute his own mother if the circumstances warranted it." I laughed when I read it because that characterization stemmed from an actual confrontation I once had with a defense attorney many years earlier when, as a deputy district attorney, I had rejected his plea bargain offer. Angered by my apparent lack of compassion for his client's circumstances, the defense lawyer heatedly blurted out, "Suthers, you'd prosecute your own mother." I thought for a moment and replied, "No I wouldn't. . . unless there was probable cause to believe she committed a crime." The encounter became part of the folklore at the DA's office.

Shortly after the editorial appeared, the Justice Department ruled I had no conflict of interest and need not recuse myself from what would become a very extensive investigation and prosecution of Qwest and its mismanagement. Philip Anschutz would eventually be subpoenaed before the grand jury and be found not to have any role in Qwest's misconduct. My first assistant, Bill Leone, headed up the investigation and prosecution, directing the numerous FBI and SEC investigators and the legal team in our office. The complex case was divided into several manageable components for purposes of investigation. The prosecution team did a masterful job of managing the more than six million documents we received. I was also touched by Bill Leone's willingness to pass up a chance to be nominated for a federal judgeship in January of 2003 in order to stay on the case. It was a genuine sense of duty and loyalty to the office that caused him to do so.

The first phase of the investigation was concluded with the indictment of four vice president level Qwest executives on February 25, 2003. They were accused of accounting fraud by booking revenue in the second quarter of 2001 in order to meet the company's very aggressive revenue projections, when they met none of the accounting criteria necessary to do so. Leone and I took a red eye to Washington to stand with John Ashcroft, Larry Thompson, the Deputy AG, and SEC Chairman William Donaldson when the first indictments and SEC charges were announced. My picture with Ashcroft at the press conference appeared on national television and in major newspapers throughout the country. *USA Today* followed up with a feature story about Bill Leone and me. The Qwest case was a big national story. Both Denver papers carried a story about it almost daily. There was much speculation as to where the investigation would lead.

It was clear to us that the root of the problem was the corporate culture created by Qwest's CEO, Joe Nacchio, who had pocketed $230 million in stock options alone during his brief tenure. Nacchio would make public pronouncements of extremely aggressive quarterly revenue targets and had a make-the-numbers-work-or-I'll-find-someone-who-will management style. He also offered incredible levels of compensation to those willing to get it done. But he didn't appear to get personally involved in the details as to *how* they got it done. Not surprisingly, his name did not show up on the myriad of incriminating accounting documents, including emails, that we uncovered.

While the prosecutions of mid-level executives at Qwest had mixed results, including a hung jury as to some of the defendants, we eventually procured pleas from several of them and secured their cooperation in a prosecution of Joe Nacchio. We chose to simplify the case against Nacchio by avoiding the accounting complexities that had been problematic in the earlier trials. We charged Nacchio with insider trading, alleging he sold his shares at great profit knowing the house of cards was about to collapse, while at the same time painting a very rosy picture of Qwest's performance for stock analysts and the public at large. The choice to use that strategy proved to be a good one. After I left the US Attorney's Office to become Colorado attorney general, Nacchio was convicted at trial of insider trading and eventually served a six-year federal prison sentence. He was also ordered to pay restitution of over a $100 million.

Largely because of the Qwest case, Bill Leone and I made numerous appearances to speak about corporate fraud and related topics.

The office performed well in a number of other high-profile white-collar crime cases. In the Best Bank case, several bank executives were charged with a fraud that led to one of the largest bank failures in a decade, involving losses to the FDIC in the range of $225 million. The cases went to trial after I left the office and resulted in convictions of all those involved. They all received significant prison sentences. One of the principals died by suicide before he was to report to prison. We also prosecuted a fraudulent

Ponzi scheme involving so-called prime notes. The fraudsters got over a thousand investors to put up over $56 million in hopes of getting ridiculously high yields on their money. In a very similar prime note case we successfully prosecuted, the Coors Family Foundation was victimized to the tune of $40 million. We were able to recover all but four million dollars. I was very pleased that the performance of the US Attorney's Office during my tenure included successful prosecutions of many very large white-collar cases.

In 2004 our office became involved in a fairly far-reaching investigation of Russian organized crime. We pursued several cases in Colorado that appeared to the public to be fairly small in scale, but which were part of a significant nationwide effort against Russians engaged in drug trafficking, health care fraud, and insurance fraud. Also in 2004, federal investigators uncovered a commercial driver's license scam in the Colorado Department of Revenue. Crooked employees in the department were taking payments of several hundred dollars per license and giving truck driving licenses to totally unqualified people, oftentimes illegal immigrants. A truck driving school was also implicated in the scam.

As district attorney, I had prosecuted several members of pacifist groups that insisted on violating the law by trespassing on sensitive government installations and sometimes engaging in minor vandalism. The cases had not generated much more than local publicity. So, when the US Attorney's Office charged three Dominican nuns for cutting through a fence at a nuclear installation and pouring their blood on a missile silo, I had no notion how high profile the case would become.

The nuns, members of the national "Plowshares" movement, got a very flamboyant Denver attorney, Walter Gerash, to represent them and were intent on milking the case for all it was worth. That meant turning down a reasonable plea offer in order to use the trial as a stage. But the judge and the jury were not impressed and convicted them of two felonies for damaging government property and interfering with government operations. Because they each had an extensive criminal record for doing the same type of thing numerous times over the last twenty years, the federal sentencing guidelines called for sentences ranging from five to eight years. The pacifist community and the liberal media reacted with outrage and our office was the perceived oppressor. Editorials appeared in newspapers across the country. Between the trial and the sentencing in July of 2003, the nuns made public appearances all over the country and our office and the court were inundated with letters. A *Denver Post* columnist called me brain dead for pursuing the prosecution. The liberal media blamed George Bush and John Ashcroft for stifling dissent, despite the fact that we had never discussed the case with anyone in Washington. The trial judge, Robert Blackburn, did a great job maintaining some semblance of dignity at the trial and sentencing, despite the fact 350 protestors gathered in and around the courthouse. He gave the nuns a "downward departure" for their life of "good works," but severely chastised them for their reckless behavior and failure to appreciate the many means of lawful protest available to them. He sentenced them to prison for terms ranging from two-and-a-half to three-and-a-half years.

Our office called the sentences fair and reasonable. The sentencing was covered nationwide, and I did interviews with several national news outlets. The day after the sentencing, the *Rocky Mountain News* ran a fairly favorable piece about how a good Catholic boy found himself sending nuns to prison in order to uphold the rule of law. It even included the Sister Georgetta story from my high school days.

In the summer of 2003, I got a call from the executive director of the US Anti-Doping Agency (USADA) based in Colorado Springs. The agency, charged with policing drug abuse in sports in America, had once been part of the US Olympic Committee but had been spun off to avoid conflicts of interest. Jim Allison, the head of the Criminal Division, and I met with the executive director, Terry

Madden, and the agency's attorney, Rich Young. USADA had received an anonymous communication that several high-profile American athletes were using a steroid, THG, that was undetectable under current testing methods. The informant even sent a syringe containing the substance. He alleged a lab in Northern California named BALCO (Bay Area Laboratory Co-operative) and its owner, Victor Conte, were the source of the drug. Madden asked us how to proceed. Given the jurisdictional issues, I arranged a meeting with Main Justice in Washington and a decision was made to conduct the investigation through the federal grand jury in the northern District of California. What followed was one of the biggest drug scandals in the history of sport in America. Many high-profile Olympic and professional athletes were implicated, including Olympic gold medalist Marion Jones and Barry Bonds, baseball's home run king. Victor Conte served a prison term but refused to testify against his famous clients. Marion Jones was convicted of a felony, served time in prison, and was stripped of her numerous Olympic medals. Barry Bonds was indicted and convicted of lying to a grand jury, although the conviction was subsequently overturned on appeal. Several athletes were excluded from the 2004 summer Olympics in Athens and Major League Baseball overhauled its drug policies in response to the public outrage that followed the scandal.

I am also proud of the great work the Civil Division of the office did during my tenure as US attorney. The division had an excellent record of effectively defending the United States in all sorts of cases and occasionally suing on behalf of the US to recover debts, damages to government property, or losses due to fraud against the government. It had many talented and experienced lawyers. The heads of the division during my tenure were Regina Rodriguez and Michael Hegarty. I would subsequently assist Hegarty to become a federal magistrate and Rodriguez to become a federal district court judge.

As district attorney and Director of the Department of Corrections I had spearheaded projects to compile and publish the history of the respective agencies. The Colorado US Attorney's Office had been around for 140 years when I got there and had no written history whatsoever. So, I once again took on the task of compiling one. Aided by a committee of employees, we published a book that chronicled the history of the office including profiles of all prior US attorneys. It was a fun and interesting task. A paralegal in the office, Melba Duprey, did yeoman work researching the files of Colorado newspapers and the state archives. Jeff Dorschner, the public information officer, prepared the manuscript for publishing.

Jeff Dorschner also did a great job of public relations for the office. Prior to Jeff being hired by my predecessor, Tom Strickland, the office had not had a full time PR person. It made all the difference in the world. Jeff built and maintained great relationships with the media, particularly the print media which regularly covered the federal courthouse. Despite his past involvement in Democrat politics, he was very loyal to me as US attorney and did a great job of promoting the office. I learned a great deal from Jeff about public relations in general and media relations for public law offices in particular.

In October of 2004, a family tragedy occurred that could have been even more devastating than it was. My father-in-law, Bud Gill, had turned eighty-five in July of 2004. His physical health was failing but he had remained mentally pretty sharp. His children's efforts to get him to move from the family home, which had gotten more aggressive after the death of my mother-in-law in 1999, had been unsuccessful. "They'll have to carry me out of here feet first," he would always say. His words proved prophetic.

On the night of October 14, Bud called Janet about 8 p.m. In the course of the conversation, he said he was not feeling well and blamed it on his erratic blood sugar count. He was diabetic and on oxygen. The complaint was not unusual. He declined Janet's offer to come over that evening, but requested she stop by before going to work the next morning. I happened to be in Colorado Springs at the time because of a speaking obligation. Janet arrived at her father's house about 7:30 a.m. When she walked in, she found him slumped in a chair, fully clothed, at the kitchen table. He was dead. He still had his oxygen tubes in his nose. Janet assumed he had suffered a heart attack and called 911. She then called me, and I said I would come over immediately.

When I arrived at the Gill home a half hour later, an ambulance with lights and sirens was arriving at the scene at the same time. I thought it was strange for an ambulance to pick up a dead body. I also noticed that two fire trucks were there.

I was met in the front yard by a woman who was my father-in-law's nurse. She stopped by a twice a week to take his blood pressure and address his other health issues. She told me Janet was in the backyard and that "she was overcome." I thought she meant Janet was very upset. But when I got to the backyard, I found Janet on a stretcher with an oxygen mask on. She was being attended to by emergency medical personnel and was being placed in the ambulance to go to the emergency room.

When emergency personnel responded to Janet's call to 911, they had confirmed Bud was dead and began to get information about him from Janet. In the course of that she had suddenly passed out. Suspicious that something was wrong, they then cleared out the house and secured a carbon monoxide monitor. It gave an incredibly high reading. Another half hour of investigation by masked utility workers determined that Bud's Ford Explorer was running with the engine on in the downstairs garage. As it turned out, the car had been running since 2 p.m. the previous day, over eighteen hours! It appeared Bud had returned home at 2 p.m. from a dentist appointment. He had a phone in the garage with a long extension cord from the adjacent family room. He kept the phone in the garage because he would frequently wait there for a friend to pick him up. The friend would call him when he pulled into the driveway. Apparently, the phone was ringing when Bud had pulled into the garage on this particular day. Phone records revealed it was his dentist's office. He apparently got out of the car, picked up the phone and walked into the family room, and closed the garage door behind him. When he got off the phone, he forgot the car was running in the garage and proceeded to go upstairs.

He had died after 9 p.m., because he talked to his sister on the phone at that time. The reason it took so long for the carbon monoxide to overcome him was that it was competing against the direct flow of oxygen from his oxygen tank. Had Janet visited her father the night before, or delayed in calling 911 the next morning, she likely would have been overcome by the odorless gas and died.

As it was, she spent the rest of the day at the hospital in a hyperbaric chamber and had to go back for two more hyperbaric chamber sessions before her system was purged of carbon monoxide. She suffered no permanent effect. Unfortunately, three fire department personnel and two police officers also had to be treated.

The tragic incident turned into a big media event. Three TV stations camped out at the Gill house all day and filmed Bud's body being wheeled out feet first, just how he wanted it. Frankly, knowing Bud, he would have delighted at the prospect that TV cameras were rolling at the time. All the largest newspapers in the state carried a front-page article the next day indicating the US attorney's father-in-law had died of carbon monoxide poisoning. The news cameras even showed up at his funeral, which was attended by about 800 people.

It's only natural that US attorneys get nervous about elections where the president that appointed them is seeking a second term. Such was the case in the November 2004 presidential election. I loved being US attorney and hoped President Bush would be reelected. Given how close the race had been in 2000, the political pundits were certain it would be close again. And indeed, it was. On Election Day, results of media exit polls began to leak out on political blogs. They showed the key states of Florida and Ohio trending toward John Kerry. But when actual results started coming out after the polls had closed, Florida went to Bush by a comfortable margin and all eyes focused on Ohio. But the intrigue did not last as long as it had four years before. The networks correctly called Ohio for Bush about 1 a.m. EST and Kerry conceded shortly thereafter. It seemed my job was safe.

But something else interesting happened in Colorado that same election night. Ken Salazar, who had beaten me in the attorney general's race in 1998, won a US Senate seat over Republican Pete Coors. It was the culmination of a very strange political year in Colorado. Just a few months before it seemed the incumbent Republican US Senator, Ben Nighthorse Campbell, was cruising to reelection. In fact, Democrat opposition had not yet been identified. But Campbell suddenly dropped out, citing his age of seventy-two and the fact he was tired of the political grind. But it was also clear he was concerned about a federal investigation of financial misconduct by a member of his staff.

When Campbell announced he wouldn't run, all eyes turned to Governor Bill Owens. If he ran, he would be the clear choice of the Republican Party and it was unlikely a formidable Democrat would take him on. But after a few weeks of contemplation, the governor decided not to run, citing family considerations. A mad scramble ensued. Attorney General Salazar and fellow Democrat Congressman Mark Udall played a game of political chicken, both saying they'd run and hoping the other would blink. Several tense private meetings took place before Udall said he was out, and Salazar climbed up on the state capitol steps to make it official. Former Republican Congressman Bob Schaffer announced he'd run. While that was fine with the right wing of the party, many others felt he couldn't beat Salazar and looked for someone else to run. There were several stops and starts before Pete Coors, the CEO of Coors Brewing Company, jumped into the race shortly before the party nominating convention. Coors eventually won the Republican primary over Schaffer, and Salazar won the Democratic nomination over a political newcomer, Mike Miles. Because the US Senate majority hung in the balance, outside money poured into Colorado. Salazar eventually won the race by a comfortable margin. He was headed to Washington and there were two years left in his term as attorney general. Under the Colorado Constitution, the governor would nominate the new AG and the nominee would have to be confirmed by the state Senate. That created further intrigue. For the first time in forty years, the Democrats had won control over both houses of the Colorado legislature. So, Owens's attorney general nominee would face confirmation before a Democrat-controlled Senate.

From the outset of the Salazar-Coors race, it was apparent Salazar had a good chance to win. So, a lot of backroom maneuvering began by Republican lawyers interested in succeeding Salazar. Several let the governor and others know they were interested long before the election. I stayed quiet for several reasons. First, I liked my job as US attorney and was not eager to leave it. Secondly, as US attorney I could not, under Department of Justice guidelines, be involved in a public pursuit of a political office. Finally, I thought it was bad form for Republicans to be outwardly suggesting it was clear to them a Democrat would win the Senate race. (The governor later told me he also thought it was bad form.) I had only one relevant discussion before the election. At a social function, the governor's chief legal counsel, Cynthia Honssinger, asked if I would be interested if the attorney general job became vacant. I told her the question was premature but if that did happen and the governor asked me to consider it, I would consider it.

The day after the election several Republican lawyers publicly acknowledged to newspaper reporters their interest in being appointed attorney general. In response, a few Democrat state senators indicated a few of the interested Republicans would be unacceptable. I gave no comment to anyone. But about a week later I got a phone call from the governor's chief of staff, Bob Lee. He told me the governor wanted to appoint a Republican with a legal background that would be difficult for Senate Democrats to publicly oppose and asked me to consider being nominated with the understanding I would run for election as AG in 2006. He cautioned that the governor couldn't guarantee the confirmation process wouldn't get ugly for any Republican nominee.

I then did two things. As was my custom whenever new career opportunities presented themselves, I consulted my loving wife, who had borne the financial and family burden of my many public service endeavors. We discussed the job's downsides. It meant a huge cut in pay, from $142,000 to $80,000. It meant assuming a much higher political profile. State AG was typically a higher-profile job than being district attorney or US attorney. It meant another exhausting statewide political campaign in 2006. On the upside, it meant impacting public policy by shaping the state's legal policy, and it meant being involved in many of the most significant challenges that would face Colorado in the years ahead. It also meant being involved in some of the most interesting legal cases and issues on a national level. As usual, Janet said she would support me if I wanted to go for it.

I then made a call to Ken Salazar who, with his Senate race victory, was the preeminent force in Democratic politics in Colorado. Through our very close but very professional race in 1998, and working together over the ensuing years, we had become friends. I asked Salazar if he would publicly support me if Owens nominated me for AG. Without much hesitation he said he would, but he would also want to have some advance notice so he could cover his bases with his Democrat constituents.

I called Bob Lee, the governor's chief of staff, and told him I was interested in being nominated for AG and informed him of my conversation with Salazar. A few days later, around Thanksgiving, Governor Owens called to offer me the appointment, again cautioning me that it could get ugly if the Democrats were inclined to make it so. I told him I thought Salazar's support could be of great help. He agreed and said he was meeting with Salazar the next day. Because of that and the fact I had to negotiate a departure date with the Department of Justice, we agreed the matter needed to remain confidential until all bases were touched.

I confirmed with DOJ that I would have to resign after being nominated and could not wait to see how the confirmation process evolved. That made my decision very high stakes. I told the governor it was my desire to be appointed acting attorney general on January 4, 2005, the day Salazar's resignation was effective, and to go through the confirmation process while occupying the office. If I was not confirmed I would be out of a job.

When Ken Salazar met with Governor Owens, he confirmed he would support me and suggested a process that would assist him politically. Salazar would write a letter to Owens and provide a copy to the media and all state senators. The letter would list all the people Salazar thought would make a good attorney general to replace him. There were twenty-five lawyers on the list, only three of whom were Republicans. I was near the bottom of the list. The newspapers published the list the next day and interviewed the various candidates who said they were flattered or honored to be on the list. That covered Salazar's bases with his party. No one other than the governor, the Senator-elect, and I knew that a deal had been struck.

On December 9, 2004, at 2 p.m. Governor Owens held a press conference in his office. In front of a large crowd of media, Owens, Salazar, and Janet and I walked in and ended the month of political intrigue. The governor said that my background and experience made me the most qualified lawyer in Colorado to be attorney general. Salazar strongly endorsed me, saying I would make a great attorney general. I thanked both of them and promised that if I was confirmed as attorney general, "no person in Colorado will be beyond the reach of the law, and no person in Colorado will be without the protection of the law."

Immediately after the press conference, I met with all the employees of the US Attorney's Office to inform them of my departure. I told them how fortunate I felt to have been US attorney at such a critical time in the nation's history. I was very proud of the efforts we'd made to prevent further acts of terrorism, to deter corporate fraud, and in helping bring violent crime rates to a thirty-year low. And I told them it was a great privilege to work with so many great lawyers.

As agreed with the Department of Justice and the White House, I then sent letters of resignation to President Bush and US Attorney General John Ashcroft resigning as US attorney effective January 4, 2005, when I would become acting attorney general of Colorado. John Ashcroft was kind enough to call me a few days later to congratulate me and wish me luck. In the course of the conversation, he said something I found very intriguing. Having served as Missouri attorney general, governor, US Senator, and attorney general of the United States, he told me being state attorney general "was the best job I ever had." I would soon learn why he said so.

Chapter XVIII
General Suthers

A t 10 a.m. on January 4, 2005, simultaneously with Ken Salazar's swearing in as US Senator, I took the reins of the Colorado Attorney General's Office. The state legislature convened a week later and set a confirmation hearing before the Senate Judiciary Committee. The hearing was set for January 31st.

Between the governor's announcement of my appointment on December 9th and my confirmation hearing, I personally met with all but one of the eighteen Senate Democrats. I met with or talked on the phone with all seventeen Republicans. I made sure I met with the Democrat leadership first, including Senate President Joan Fitz-Gerald. The meetings went well, and their public statements were encouraging.

Members of the AG's management team that were holdovers from the Salazar administration proved very helpful to me during this period. Several section heads who were Democrats told senators the transition was going smoothly and lobbied on my behalf. I'm particularly indebted to Renny Fagan, a longtime acquaintance and former Democrat state representative from Colorado Springs, who served as the interim Chief Deputy AG during the transition period.

Frankly, the biggest problem during the confirmation process came from a Republican state senator who was deeply disappointed he had not been nominated. In a conspiracy with a former assistant US attorney who had resigned after I disciplined him, the state senator attempted to clandestinely undermine my confirmation by "leaking" inaccurate information to the press, but his scheme was transparent and quickly fizzled.

The confirmation hearing itself had some amusing aspects. After Governor Owens and I gave opening statements, the heads of the state district attorneys, police chiefs, and sheriffs all appeared to express the support of their organizations for my nomination. But when it came time for people to speak in opposition, a strange cadre of citizens appeared. Two nuns and a career peace protestor argued that I was unsuited for the job because I had prosecuted and sent to prison three Dominican nuns for trespassing and destroying property at a nuclear missile facility. A priest testified against me because I had asked for the death penalty as a prosecutor. The irony of it all struck me and was quite amusing to Janet who was seated in the audience. I was a dedicated former altar boy who went to Catholic schools for sixteen years and nuns and priests were my main antagonists! Where were Monsignor Harrington and Sister Georgetta when I needed them? Other dissidents included a lawyer, Rob Corry, who demanded an apology for statements I made critical of medical marijuana. I respectfully declined. Another activist criticized me for not opening a federal grand jury investigation of the Columbine High School shootings.

After the parade of witnesses, the judiciary committee members asked questions about water law, affirmative action, abortion, and gay marriage. I answered the questions candidly, expressing a generally conservative but well thought out viewpoint, but emphasized that my personal views on controversial issues of the day would not interfere with my obligations to enforce the law.

After the hearing, the committee voted 6-0 to recommend my nomination to the full Senate. The chair, Democrat State Senator Dan Grossman from Denver, abstained, indicating he was seriously considering running for AG in 2006. A few days later the full Senate voted 30-1 to confirm my nomination. The lone dissenting vote came from Senator Peter Groff, an African American from

All This I Saw, and Part of It I Was

Denver, who said he did not like the fact I spoke against racial quotas as an appropriate way to pursue affirmative action.

At 3 p.m. on Friday, February 7, 2005, I was sworn in as Colorado's thirty-seventh attorney general by Supreme Court Chief Justice Mary Mullarkey. Janet held the same family Bible that had been present at my swearing in as district attorney and US attorney. The Bible had been a gift from my mother to my father in 1952. In my remarks to the crowd of about 400, I indicated I felt as though I had won the legal trifecta. To be a DA, a US attorney, and an attorney general in one legal lifetime was beyond my dreams, let alone my expectations.

I inherited an AG's office with about 380 employees, including about 240 lawyers. The office had a budget of about $45 million. We handled 10,000 distinct legal issues each year on behalf of Colorado state government and Colorado citizens, including 1,500 cases in the state and federal courts and about 1,000 water rights cases.

I made no official appointments until after the confirmation process was complete, but then I worked quickly to put a team together. I hired Jason Dunn as my Deputy AG for Legal Policy. Jason had worked on my 1998 AG campaign, was now a water lawyer in private practice, and had remained involved in politics and public policy. He would be the office liaison to the legislature and to a wide variety of lobbyists and interest groups. He would be responsible for the legislative agenda of the office and advise me on various public policy issues. Jason hired Kristen Hubbell to be the communications director. She would be the day-to-day contact with the media and plan the public outreach efforts of the office.

I hired Cynthia Honssinger, the governor's chief legal counsel and former assistant AG in Georgia to be the Chief Deputy AG, the second ranking position in the office. She would be primarily responsible for the day-to-day administration of the office. Soon thereafter Cynthia married Mike Coffman, who served as Colorado treasurer, secretary of state, and US congressman.

I was able to convince Allison Eid, a University of Colorado law professor, to take a two-year leave of absence to serve as Solicitor General (SG). Allison had clerked for US Supreme Court Justice Clarence Thomas. The SG is in charge of shaping the legal policy of the state as reflected in litigation, including recommending what cases to appeal and what position the state takes in appellate litigation across the country as an *amicus curiae*. Allison would serve as S.G. for less than a year before being appointed to the Colorado Supreme Court by Governor Bill Owens. She would later be appointed to the Tenth Circuit Court of Appeals.

When I took over the office it had seven sections, each headed by a deputy attorney general. Four of the section heads were departing—two to join Ken Salazar in Washington, one to become a judge, and another to become a district attorney. I consolidated two of the sections, Civil Litigation and Employment Law, into one. That meant I needed to hire three new section heads for Natural Resources and Environment, Business and Licensing, and Criminal Justice. After interviewing numerous interested parties inside and outside the office, I decided to promote from within for Natural Resources and Business and Licensing. I believe that had a positive effect on office morale, as did my decision to retain three section heads, Renny Fagan, Jan Zavislan, and Beth McCann, who were Democrats and had been Salazar appointees. As for the Criminal Justice Section, I had no doubt what I wanted to do. Jeanne Smith, my former assistant DA and successor as DA in Colorado Springs, was term limited and leaving office. I had tremendous respect for her abilities and was very pleased to appoint her as Deputy AG for Criminal Justice.

On a day-to-day basis, the AG's office is engaged in a diverse and fascinating variety of legal matters. The State Services Section represents the governor, the treasurer, the secretary of state, and the judicial branch of government. It represents several cabinet departments of state government, the state board of education, and all the state's colleges and universities. The section is also involved in some of the most interesting litigation in the office, including constitutional issues, ballot issues, and disputes between the branches of government. In one such case, the legislature had sued the governor alleging he could not veto headnotes in the annual appropriation bill. Governor Owens, like several governors before him, felt legislative headnotes in the bill inappropriately micromanaged the governor's control over the executive branch and infringed on his executive powers. The AG's office represented the governor and prevailed in the case. While the office is required to defend legislation passed by the legislature, it is the one branch of government the office does not represent as a party to litigation.

In another case waged soon after I took the job, the City and County of Denver sued the state alleging a concealed-carry law passed by the state legislature, which made issuance of concealed weapons permits uniform throughout the state, was an unconstitutional restriction of Denver's powers as a home rule city. The court ruled otherwise.

As counsel for the secretary of state, the State Services Section would defend various constitutional amendments passed by the voters and would defend repeated challenges to the state's Taxpayer Bill of Rights (TABOR). The section also helped draft many of the formal opinions of the office issued as required by Colorado law. While the office issued dozens of informal opinions each year to guide state agencies and offices, we also issued an average of a half dozen formal opinions each year. Such opinions were binding on state government but not on courts who subsequently addressed the issue. In one such formal opinion we determined illegal aliens were not entitled to in-state tuition (subsequent legislation in 2013 granted such tuition to illegal aliens who attended and graduated from state high schools), but in another we determined the children of illegal aliens who were born in the US and domiciled in Colorado were entitled to in-state tuition. I also issued an opinion to the Commissioner of Education that under a Colorado statute a school could not prohibit a student from wearing clothes displaying an American flag. A junior high school principal had issued such a ban so as not to offend the sensibilities of Mexican nationals attending the school. Needless to say, such political correctness ignited a firestorm of protest from parents.

A highly respected three decade veteran of the AG's office, Maurie Knaizer, was the institutional memory of the State Services Section and helped navigate through so many of the tough issues we faced. When he retired at the end of 2012, we would rename the annual Attorney General Distinguished Service Award after him.

The Business and Licensing Section was the largest in the office. The state legislature decides as a matter of public policy what businesses, professions, and commercial activities will be regulated. They typically do so through formation of a board, commission, or office that conducts the regulation, including issuing licenses and revoking them if necessary. The AG's office represents all such boards, commissions, and regulatory offices, ranging from the highly complex Public Utilities Commission and Oil and Gas Conservation Commission to the vital to public health agencies like the state medical, dental, and nursing boards. Colorado has approximately fifty such regulatory entities and the Business and Licensing Section represented most of them. After eight years as AG, growth of the Business and Licensing Section would cause me to carve out a new section to represent the Department of Revenue and the Public Utilities Commission.

While the representation of regulatory bodies can be fairly routine, license revocation can be highly contentious, particularly in high paying professions and lucrative businesses. Take for example a medical license revocation proceeding against a neurosurgeon who makes over $2 million per year, or a new car dealer facing a $500,000 loss for a thirty-day license suspension. It was not unusual for such matters to involve lengthy hearings and very expensive expert testimony.

Under Colorado law, the attorney general directly regulates certain financial industries. The AG appoints an Administrator of the Uniform Commercial Credit Code who regulates state licensed consumer lenders, debt collectors, debt settlement companies, and pay day lenders. Laura Udis did a very good job at this task before and during most of my tenure.

The Civil Litigation and Employment Law Section of the office handles all tort and civil rights litigation against the state and defends against all claims of state employees alleging improper discipline or termination. As a general proposition, a state is immune from suits brought by its citizens under a legal doctrine known as sovereign immunity. But the legislature of virtually every state, including Colorado, chooses to waive such immunity and allow citizens to sue the state for negligent or reckless conduct of its employees. For example, someone injured in a car accident because of the carelessness of an on-duty state employee can bring a claim against the state, and people injured because of negligent maintenance of state infrastructure, including highways or bridges, can also bring suit. Every year in Colorado, motorists are killed or injured by falling rocks on mountain highways. In one such incident several years ago, a rockslide hit a tourist bus and several people were killed and many others injured. Wards of the state, including prison inmates and mental health patients, can also bring claims for injuries caused by state employees. Because taxpayer dollars are used to pay such claims under state law, the legislature can set caps on possible recoveries. During my tenure as AG the cap was $150,000 per person and $600,000 per incident until 2013, when it was raised to $440,000 per person and $900,000 per incident. Unfortunately, at least from the taxpayers' perspective, there is no sovereign immunity and no such liability cap on claims against the state under federal civil rights statutes, including 42 USC § 1983. Such claims brought against police officers and corrections officers can result in large verdicts. One false arrest claim brought against a state patrolman in federal court during my tenure resulted in a $1 million jury verdict. Fortunately, it was overturned on appeal. But another case where a state patrolman shot and killed a drunk driving suspect led to a $1 million settlement. As attorney general, I sat on a claims board with the state treasurer and the executive director of the state Department of Personnel and Administration, and we had to approve any settlement by the state in excess of $100,000. On average we paid out $2-4 million per year in settlements.

In every state Attorney General's Office, the Natural Resources and Environment section is important, but that's particularly true in the West because of water and mining issues. In Colorado, the work of the section is vital to the future of the state. I joined virtually every previous Colorado AG in listing as a top priority the preservation of every possible drop of water for the state. That's because all the water flows out of Colorado; no water runs into the state. How much Colorado is allowed to keep and how much it must provide to eighteen other downstream states is determined by nine interstate river compacts to which the state is a party. Coloradans like to say, "Whiskey is for drinkin' and water is for fightin'." And oftentimes the fights are long and expensive.

In 1983, Kansas sued Colorado for over $300 million alleging Colorado had violated the Arkansas River Compact of 1949 by not delivering the amount of water Kansas was entitled to. It was the latest of many disputes between the two states over the river dating back to 1902. All interstate water suits are heard by the US Supreme Court, pursuant to its original jurisdiction under Article III, Section 2 of the US Constitution. This particular case went on for twenty-two years before Kansas was awarded $29 million plus $5 million in interest in 2005. A dispute over costs and fees in the case would result in my personal appearance before the US Supreme Court in 2008.

The most contentious river basin for the twenty-first century will certainly be the Colorado River Basin. Extraordinary population growth in Southern California, Phoenix, and Las Vegas has brought about growing demands on the river and Colorado is spending considerable time and effort protecting its interests under the Colorado River Compact. In 2006, the AG's office received funds from the legislature and the Colorado Water Conservation Board to create a Defense of the Colorado River Compact Unit in the office. The unit's mission is to compile all the relevant documentary evidence to support Colorado's interests and to participate in any litigation necessary to do so. We were quite effective in that regard.

On the basis of my transition discussions with Ken Salazar, I made it a high priority to resolve long pending claims brought by Colorado against entities that had operated hazardous waste sites in the state. Under federal law, a state can sue to force cleanup of such sites and to recover money for any permanent damages to the natural resources of the state. Colorado had filed several such cases in the early 1980s and a few of the biggest were still pending when I became AG in 2005. Over the first several years of my tenure, we made a concerted effort to bring the cases to final resolution. In the case of Rocky Mountain Arsenal, an eighteen square mile parcel northeast of Denver that had housed a chemical weapons plant for the Army in World War II and subsequently been leased to Shell Oil for a pesticide plant after the war, I was personally very involved in the negotiations. To their credit, the Army and Shell had spent $2.5 billion to clean up the site, but the continuing controversy involved Colorado's claim for permanent damages to ground water. Prior to my tenure, the defendants had not offered more than $1 million to settle the claim. I met personally on several occasions with a vice president of Shell and the top Department of Justice lawyer for the Army. After such meetings and some carefully orchestrated pressure from editorial pages in major Colorado newspapers, we were able to settle the claims for $35 million, which was reinvested in trails, open space acquisition, and water resources in the South Platte River Valley around the Arsenal. With the cooperation of local governments who matched our investment, we were able to make the Northeast Corridor Greenway a model of conservation excellence. I considered the effort a major accomplishment of my administration. I was pleased to attend a ceremony turning over the Arsenal to the Department of the Interior for a national wildlife refuge.

We were similarly successful in finally resolving long-standing natural resource damage claims at Rocky Flats, which had been operated by the Department of Energy as a plutonium manufacturing site, and at California Gulch, which involved molybdenum pollution in the upper reaches of the Arkansas River near Leadville, Colorado. In the case of California Gulch, we recovered $21 million in natural resource damages. Rocky Flats also became a national wildlife refuge.

Along with the executive directors of the Department of Natural Resources and the Department of Public Health and Environment, I served as a Natural Resource Damages Trustee for Colorado. We determined whether to bring claims for damages to the environment and how to invest any funds recovered to help mitigate such damage.

The consumer protection sections of state attorneys general offices were relatively low profile before 1998. They enforced state consumer protection laws and antitrust laws but attracted little attention from Wall Street and the national media. That all changed with the nationwide tobacco litigation that culminated in 1998 when forty-six states settled with the major tobacco companies for an estimated $250 billion. Since then, state AGs are routinely involved in multi-state actions against alleged corporate wrongdoers. Such AG activism, personified by Eliot Spitzer of New York, has become the subject of much criticism by the US Chamber of Commerce, the *Wall Street Journal*, and other advocates of free enterprise who believe that the AGs are pursuing public policy changes through litigation and destabilizing the marketplace in the process.

My view of the proper role of consumer protection litigation stems from my experience as a prosecutor and law enforcer. I did not hesitate to pursue cases against businesses, both large and small, when I believed Colorado law had been violated and the evidence was sufficient to prove the case. My office joined in numerous multi-state litigations where we believed laws had been violated. On the other hand, I sympathized with the critics of AG activism. It was clear to me that some of my colleagues did see it as their role to bring cases to advance their public policy views and ingratiate themselves to the public, rather than to simply redress violations of the law. One example of such activism was *Connecticut v. American Election Power*, a case brought by several East Coast attorneys general seeking to force several coal-fired utility plants to reduce carbon emissions, despite the fact the plants were not located in their states, and they were in full compliance with all state and federal regulations. By a 9-0 vote the US Supreme Court held such regulatory efforts were beyond the AG's powers.

Colorado's Consumer Protection Section, led by Deputy AG Jan Zavislan, had limited personnel but accomplished a great deal by carefully choosing and prioritizing the cases it pursued. We filed more Consumer Protection Act cases than any prior administration of the AG's office. We joined multi-state cases against large pharmaceutical companies for antitrust violations and against various national mortgage lenders, including Ameriquest and Countrywide, for a variety of fraudulent practices. The cases resulted in settlements that brought hundreds of millions of dollars to Colorado and its citizens. Settlement funds that were not directed for restitution to victims were made available in grants to Boys & Girls Clubs, drug prevention organizations, Children's Hospital, and other worthy organizations to support public education programs. We even brought antitrust actions to prevent further consolidation in the beef packing industry, which would have had adverse consequences for cattle producers and beef consumers in Colorado, and successfully sued Apple, Inc., and several large book publishers for price fixing e-books. And we pursued hundreds of scams throughout Colorado that involved every sort of fraud and deceit imaginable.

In Colorado, twenty-two elected district attorneys have primary jurisdiction to enforce the state's criminal laws. But over the years, the legislature has given the attorney general "concurrent" or shared jurisdiction in several areas including environmental crimes, securities fraud, insurance fraud, workman's compensation fraud, and Medicare and Medicaid fraud. Such cases are handled by the Criminal Justice Section of the office. The section also has a special prosecution unit to assist DAs in complex multi-district cases involving drugs, gangs, organized crime, and other matters of statewide concern. While the DAs were once reluctant to refer cases to the unit, that wasn't the case in my tenure. In part, I believe it stemmed from the fact I was a former DA and was trusted by the state's prosecutors. But I also think growing caseloads were a factor. We were regularly involved in the largest drug cases in the state. We also prosecuted mortgage fraud schemes, sex trafficking, intellectual property theft, and tax fraud cases. The Criminal Justice Section also had a violent crime assistance unit that assisted DA's offices throughout Colorado in pursuing the death penalty and prosecuting high-profile crimes of violence. That unit was of particular assistance to rural prosecutors.

One of my highest priorities during my first two years as AG was to increase the resources and expertise that the office brought to the prosecution of white-collar cases, particularly securities fraud and insurance fraud. I went to the legislature in the 2005 and 2006 sessions and was able to get two additional securities fraud investigators, one additional lawyer, and three investigators to do insurance fraud cases. We would expand the unit again in 2012. The resources resulted in much greater activity in those areas over the ensuing years. We were successful in prosecuting large Ponzi schemes throughout Colorado and receiving long prison sentences for the perpetrators. One such case involved a man from Colorado Springs, Alan Hamilton Bird, a well-connected evangelical who preyed on hundreds of fellow churchgoers and defrauded them of over $20 million. We call it *affinity fraud* when the perpetrator exploits his religious, ethnic, or other type of connection to his victims.

The Criminal Justice Section also had an appellate division that very competently handled all criminal appeals taken by defendants convicted in the trial courts of the state. The thirty-six lawyers in the appellate division were a brainy group that handled approximately 1,200 cases per year, consistently prevailing in well over 90 percent of their cases.

As attorney general I had the statutory responsibility to chair the state's Police Officer Standards and Training Board (POST) and to manage the board's staff. The POST Board determined the requirements for becoming a peace officer in Colorado. It did so by setting the curriculum for the various police academies and approving standard examinations. The board, appointed by the governor, also awarded grant funding for training and continuing education opportunities for law enforcement. By the end of my tenure as AG, the board was awarding over $2 million per year in grants. Assistance to rural law enforcement agencies was a priority. Finally, the board determined which peace officers would have their certification revoked for various transgressions. The board did a good job of quickly dispatching cops who committed felonies or misdemeanor offenses involving moral turpitude.

Soon after I became attorney general, the office became embroiled in an ongoing controversy involving the University of Colorado football team and the university administration. Several women on the Boulder campus had accused football players of sexually assaulting them. Governor Owens had appointed my predecessor, Ken Salazar, to investigate possible criminal conduct surrounding the football program when it became apparent the Boulder DA's office would be unable to because of a perceived lack of objectivity. The Boulder DA, Mary Lacy, had made many public statements concerning the lack of oversight of the football program, while at the same time indicating there was insufficient evidence to prosecute anyone. The AG's office convened a grand jury that explored both issues of sexual assault and possible mishandling of summer football camps. The grand jury returned only one indictment, a misdemeanor theft charge against an assistant football coach. He was accused of and pled guilty to charging numerous personal calls, including calls to prostitutes, to the state. But the grand jury also prepared a report that was extremely critical of the financial management of the football camps and also of the lack of cooperation of university officials and University of Colorado Foundation officials in the grand jury investigation. A judge refused to allow the report to become public, but it was somehow leaked to the media. An investigation by the grand jury judge was unable to determine who had leaked the document. I conducted an internal investigation and was convinced no current employee of the AG's office had leaked the report. Nevertheless, officials of the CU Foundation, stung by the criticism in the leaked report, threatened to sue the AG's office.

The football scandal and the way it was handled greatly eroded public confidence in the University of Colorado. Before it was all over, the university president, the athletic director, the football coach, and the executive director of the CU Foundation all resigned. The University Regents appointed former US Senator Hank Brown as CU's president and he quickly and effectively moved to restore public confidence in the university and the credibility of its administration.

As indicated earlier, my highest priorities during my first two years as attorney general were to protect Colorado's water interests, resolve long pending hazardous waste site litigations, and increase the office's capabilities in prosecution of complex white-collar crimes. But we also pursued several public safety initiatives that I was proud of. In the first few months in office, the governor appointed me chair of a task force to deal with several apparent loopholes in the Sexually Violent Predator's (SVP) law in Colorado. Largely through the work of Jeanne Smith, we were able to move quickly and effectively to draft and get enacted legislation that closed the loopholes.

Based on input from many officials in Colorado concerned about the level of mortgage and foreclosure fraud in the state, I convened a task force to examine the problem. Our timing was very good. Within months, Colorado was leading the nation in the per capita rate of foreclosures largely because of the high percentage of creative sub-prime loans being originated. But it was also clear that mortgage fraud, including misleading advertising, fraudulent documentation, bogus appraisals, and various creative scams were contributing to the problem. Colorado was identified by the FBI as one of eight hot spots in the country for mortgage fraud. My task force was divided into public education and legislative subcommittees. The education subcommittee prepared a statewide brochure to be given to everyone in foreclosure about the legal process and warning them about foreclosure scams. The legislative committee did several things. It supported legislation to require registration of mortgage brokers, the posting of bonds by them, and the exclusion of felons from the industry. Prior to that, Colorado was one of only two states that did not regulate mortgage brokers and we were becoming a haven for other states' miscreants. Within another year Colorado would fully license and regulate brokers.

The task force, largely through the work of Deputy Attorney General Jan Zavislan, drafted and got passed a Foreclosure Fraud Protection Act which dealt with the growing cottage industry of foreclosure "consultants." These predators would identify homes in foreclosure that had equity and contact the owner and tell them they "were here to help." They'd offer to pay off the current indebtedness if the person in foreclosure would quitclaim the property to them during a "workout period" in which they could stay in the property and pay rent until they got back on their feet and could buy the property back. But the rent and fees were more than the mortgage payments. The victim was soon evicted, and the "consultant" had successfully stolen the equity in the property. The legislation said all foreclosure consultant agreements had to be in writing and include a "cooling off" period to withdraw from the agreement. Most importantly, it prohibited foreclosure consultants from winding up with title to the property. The legislation put a real damper on the fraudulent activity.

Throughout the financial crisis that lasted several years, we remained very aggressive in criminal and civil prosecutions of a wide variety of mortgage and foreclosure fraud schemes. In January of 2010, I appeared before the Financial Crisis Inquiry Commission, appointed by Congress to ascertain what had caused the financial collapse of 2007-2008 and to recommend legislation that would prevent a repeat of the economic debacle that led to the Great Recession. The testimony centered around the deregulation of the financial industry, the resulting securitization of sub-prime mortgages, and the bursting of the housing market bubble that caused banks to become insolvent.

In the 2006 legislative session the General Assembly established a statewide methamphetamine task force to deal with the scourge of meth in Colorado. The problem was costing the state hundreds of millions of dollars each year in crime, health care costs, and social services expenditures. Approximately two-thirds of the identity theft in Colorado was attributable to meth addicts. The meth epidemic, in contrast to previous illicit drug epidemics, had disproportionate impact on women and residents of rural areas. The task force consisted of twenty-four experts in prevention, treatment, and law enforcement. The attorney general was statutorily designated as its chair. We were able to attract considerable government and private foundation grants to assist our work and partnered with the Colorado Drug Endangered Children program to help carry out our mission. The task force was successful enough that it was extended by the legislature through my tenure as attorney general and was given the task of addressing other emerging substance abuse problems, including prescription drug abuse. It became known as the Colorado Substance Abuse Trend and Response Task Force.

Montana businessman Tom Seibel started the Montana Meth Project, which used very edgy media advertising to discourage meth use by teenagers. It also had a very effective online presence. I helped bring the Meth Project to Colorado in 2007 and over several years, with the help of foundations and individual donors, we were able to accomplish a reduction in meth use in the state. In 2013 the Meth Project also reorganized as Rise Above Colorado to take on the emerging problems of prescription drug abuse and recreational marijuana, which had been legalized by Colorado voters in the 2012 election. The Attorney General's Office gave a substantial grant from civil recoveries against drug companies to get the revamped organization off the ground.

Another public safety initiative I was very proud of was our internet safety effort, the Attorney General's Safe Surfing Initiative. It had two components, public education and legislation. We traveled around the state educating kids and their parents about the dangers posed by sexual predators on the internet. We worked closely with law enforcement, particularly the Internet Crimes Against Children (ICAC) task force, to shape new legislation that would better protect children. In the 2006 legislative session we successfully advocated for "internet luring" and "internet sexual exploitation" laws. Prior to the passage of the internet luring law, an undercover police officer posing as a young teenager could not make an arrest unless and until the predator showed up for a meeting with the "teenager." The new law allowed law enforcement to intervene earlier, after the predator engaged in a sexually-explicit communication and issued an invitation to meet. The exploitation law allowed police to arrest a predator for exhibiting himself on a web cam or soliciting a child to do so. We also passed legislation making it a felony to possess child pornography. It had previously been a misdemeanor. We were very heartened by the fact that these new laws were used to arrest seventy-five sexual predators in the first six months after their passage. Over 500 predators would be arrested over the next five years. It was a great example of being able to use your office to genuinely make a difference in terms of public safety.

In the 2007 legislative session, I sought to require the 9,000 registered sex offenders in Colorado to register their email addresses and computer identifications as well as their physical addresses. This would be of benefit to law enforcement policing the internet for predators and social networking sites seeking to preclude participation by sex offenders. Amazingly enough, the bill was initially defeated by a straight line party vote in the House Judiciary Committee. The six Democrats sided with the ACLU and sex offenders that testified in committee hearings and against law enforcement. But after I went on *The O'Reilly Factor* to publicly criticize them on national television, one of the Democrats on the committee reintroduced the bill as his own and it was successfully enacted.

The governor called a special session of the legislature in July of 2006 to deal with issues of illegal immigration in Colorado. The state had an estimated 225,000 illegal aliens and the costs of incarceration, medical care, and education for them were substantial. The legislature passed a series of bills to attempt to reduce the burden on Colorado. Some were constructive, like requiring an applicant for state benefits to prove citizenship or imposing sanctions for employers who knowingly hired illegal workers. Others were largely symbolic, like a voter referendum directing the attorney general to sue the federal government for non-enforcement of the immigration laws. Six states had previously pursued such a suit unsuccessfully. While the voters overwhelmingly passed the referendum, Colorado fared no better. My office spent a great deal of time and effort working with state agencies to implement the legislation passed in the special session. Some of the legislation was rescinded when the Democrats took control of both houses of the legislature in 2012.

From the beginning of my tenure as attorney general, I worked hard to promote professionalism and high morale among AG employees. I instituted an Employee Appreciation Day at the end of each fiscal year. Each such event had a theme and employees won awards for the best costumes. More importantly, we also instituted Attorney General Awards for Excellence which, over the ensuing years, became highly valued by the employees.

As attorney general I was privileged to be involved in some interesting travel opportunities. Each year the Israeli government and the American-Israel Friendship League hosted about a half dozen AGs on a week-long tour of Israel. I went in January of 2006 and in June of 2011. We could take our spouse if we personally paid the costs, and Janet made it very clear she wanted to go. It was an incredible experience for both of us. We met with high-ranking government ministers including the acting prime minister, the Israeli Supreme Court, the attorney general, military leaders, leaders of the Palestinian cause, and former Russian dissident Natan Sharansky. On our second trip, I had a very memorable meeting with Shimon Peres, who had served as prime minister three times and was then, well into his eighties, serving as President of Israel. We spent several days in Jerusalem and visited all the major sites in the country. We got security briefings at all the various borders. I was particularly inspired by our visits to Masada, near the Dead Sea. Masada is the "Israeli Alamo." In AD 72, nine hundred Jews held off 15,000 Roman soldiers and mercenaries for nine months. When it appeared the Romans were finally going to overtake them, the Jews committed mass suicide rather than be taken prisoner. When one walks through the ruins of Masada and looks down from the cliff on the ruins of the Roman encampments that surround it, the ghosts of ancient history can almost be seen and felt. To this day Israelis explain their commitment to preserve a Jewish state by exclaiming, "Masada will never fall again." As a consequence of our visit to Israel, Janet and I acquired a much better appreciation and understanding of both Middle Eastern politics and biblical history.

Janet and I also joined government delegations to Taiwan in 2008, Turkey in 2011, and Thailand and Cambodia in 2014. A meeting with President Ma was the highlight of the Taiwan trip. An audience with Patriarch Bartholomew, the Pope of the Greek Orthodox Church, was a highlight of the Turkey visit. A visit to the Killing Fields in Cambodia was a sobering highlight of the Southeast Asia trip. Such travel opportunities greatly expanded and clarified my international perspectives.

As I had done as district attorney and US attorney, I formed a committee of employees to research the history of the Attorney General's Office, which dated back to 1861, something that had never been done before. In 2007, *The People's Lawyer: A History of the Colorado Attorney General's Office* was published and has been well received by employees, interested lawyers, and state history buffs.

My first two years as Colorado attorney general went very well. The transition had gone smoothly. I was largely seen as bipartisan in the way I managed the office, and we received a lot of positive press. Despite the poor pay, I loved the job. That being the case, I decided to stand for election as attorney general in 2006.

I had actually started to put a campaign together in March of 2005 by filing appropriate paperwork, and Governor Bill Owens hosted my first fundraiser in April of that year. I found fundraising much easier as an incumbent. I hired a campaign manager, Rich Coolidge, who went full time in January of 2006 and hired Katie Behnke of Phaseline Strategies to help with fundraising. Behnke would later form her own political consulting firm, The Starboard Group, and would manage subsequent campaigns. The combination of good press and a well-organized campaign left the Democrats somewhat discouraged about the prospects of beating me. Several high-profile Democrat lawyers passed on the opportunity to run, including State Senator Dan Grossman, who had previously indicated he was a likely candidate.

Finally, in the spring of 2006, two Democrats entered the race. One was Bobby Johnson, a lawyer in his seventies who'd been involved in politics for decades, including unsuccessful campaigns for district attorney and the Denver city council. A more serious candidate was a business lawyer from Boulder, Fern O'Brien, who I believe was recruited by the House Majority Leader, Alice Madden, also from Boulder. O'Brien easily won the Democrat nomination at the state convention.

Fern O'Brien was my age but had only practiced law for a dozen years. Although her private practice credentials were good, she had no significant public service on her résumé and had very little name recognition in Colorado. She also had a bigger problem. By the time she entered the race, I had secured the support of most of the legal community, including several large traditionally Democrat law firms in Denver who would typically supply the bulk of campaign funds to a Democrat running for AG. She got little momentum in her fundraising efforts. Further, unfortunately for her, she had been convinced to hire expensive political consultants and her campaign expenses were unusually high given the modest money she was raising. I raised $525,000 for the race and had about $300,000 to spend on mailings and television in the last month. The Republican Attorneys General Association also bought radio ads on my behalf. O'Brien raised about $200,000 and could only afford a small radio buy in the last few months.   We did everything a good campaign should do. With the help of volunteers, we covered virtually every Republican event and all the important bipartisan campaign events leading up to the election. We were in most of the summer and fall parades. We put out 10,000 yard signs and 100 billboards across the state. I traveled about 30,000 miles around the state campaigning, and we had two dozen fundraising events. We ran a well-produced, very positive, television ad on network channels in Denver. Denver TV channels are seen by 76 percent of the state's population. We went out of our way not to mention our opponent because her name recognition was so low.

My dozen or so joint appearances with Fern O'Brien went very well. While she was cordial and professional, she was not well versed in the intricacies of the AG's office and the disparity in our respective knowledge about the job was painfully obvious to anyone who observed our debates.

I secured virtually every newspaper endorsement in the state of any consequence, including traditionally liberal papers like *The Denver Post*, *Boulder Daily Camera*, and *The Durango Herald*. They all conceded I'd done a good job as AG and that I was extremely well qualified to continue in the job. I was also the first statewide Republican candidate to be endorsed by the state teacher's union in a very long time. Although I didn't align with the teachers on labor issues, they also conceded I was fair, impartial, and very well qualified. As it turned out, I needed all the endorsements, liberal and conservative, that I could get because the national and state political environment became very adverse to Republicans.

By early 2006, Colorado Republicans had rallied around Congressman Bob Beauprez as their gubernatorial candidate to replace term limited Bill Owens. I liked Beauprez a lot and felt he'd be a great governor. He'd been successful as a dairy farmer, land developer, and banker and had done good work as chair of the state Republican Party. He was a practicing Catholic and a very ethical guy. Beauprez had been elected to Congress in 2002 in a very competitive district by a 120-vote margin and reelected very comfortably in 2004. His only Republican opponent, Mark Holtzman, had lots of money and a huge rolodex. He had recently come to Colorado and served briefly in the cabinet of Governor Bill Owens. He had phenomenal contacts as a result of having worked as a Republican activist, an aide to Ronald Reagan, and as a successful international investment banker. Unfortunately, Holtzman "ran to the right" of Beauprez and forced him into some positions that ultimately hurt his electability. In the 2004 election, Colorado voters approved Referendum C, which was a five-year reprieve from the impacts of the state's TABOR. The TABOR Amendment, in combination with other peculiarities of Colorado law, had put the state in a real budget squeeze and even an anti-tax fiscal conservative like Bill Owens had seen the need to support Referendum C. Holtzman led the charge against C and, in my opinion, caused Beauprez to also come out strongly against it in order to court the very conservative Republican base that would be delegates to the state Republican convention in May 2006. The problem was that the state's business community, primarily Republican, overwhelmingly supported C and financed the campaign supporting it.

Holtzman did not get enough votes at the state convention (30 percent) to make the ballot, but he indicated he would attempt to petition his way onto the ballot. The secretary of state ultimately ruled he did not have sufficient valid signatures on his petitions, and he appealed that ruling. Unfortunately, although it was fairly clear throughout the process that he wouldn't be the nominee, Holtzman spent a ton of money, much of it his own, running very negative TV ads which labeled Beauprez, "both ways Bob." While Holtzman's campaign ended in the summer of 2006, the moniker "both ways Bob" stuck all the way through the general election in November.

The Democrat side of things was also intriguing. A friend of mine, Bill Ritter, had announced early on that he was running for governor. Frankly, until I was appointed AG to replace Ken Salazar after the 2004 election, insiders thought Ritter would probably run for AG in 2006. When I got the job, Ritter told me he wouldn't run against me and set his sights even higher. Ritter was the former Denver district attorney until term limited in 2004, and we had worked closely together during my last four years as DA in Colorado Springs and during my tenures at the DOC and as US attorney. Very few people thought Ritter would be the Democrat nominee. He was a pro-life moderate and everyone was sure he could not defeat a prominent Democrat on the left. Going from DA to governor was a huge leap. But as it turned out, no prominent candidate from the left side of the Democrat Party emerged. In the spring of 2006, most of the Democrat establishment, believing Ritter could not beat Beauprez, turned to the popular Denver Mayor John Hickenlooper as their possible savior. For almost two months the media speculated every day as to whether Hickenlooper would enter the race. Ritter told me he felt like a "side-show." It was high drama. Finally, Hickenlooper said he would not run. To their credit the Democrats reluctantly closed ranks behind Ritter and only a few vehemently pro-abortion Dems refused to support him. And from that point forward Bill Ritter led a charmed life.

On the national level, things deteriorated badly for Republicans in the summer and fall of 2006. The war in Iraq was going badly. President Bush's approval rating was abysmally low, and scandals plagued the Republican majority in Congress. The national mood, and the mood in Colorado turned strongly against Republicans.

To add to the Republican woes, Bob Beauprez ran a poor campaign. His TV ads were uninspiring. One featured the back end of a horse. The issues he went after Bill Ritter on, including plea bargaining, fell flat. *The Denver Post*, angered by his opposition to Referendum C, seemed determined to torpedo him, and ran a negative article almost every day. By mid-October, polls consistently showed Ritter would beat Beauprez by a wide margin.

Some polls also showed I was only leading Fern O'Brien by 2 or 3 percent with almost a third of voters undecided. The Republican Attorneys General Association was panicking and calling my campaign and asking me to put personal funds in the campaign. I absolutely refused. We had a poll that showed me with a more comfortable lead and our TV ads would hit the last two weeks of the campaign.

I spent every morning of the last three weeks of the campaign on street corners. Our daughter Alison, who had just passed the

Colorado Bar exam, joined the campaign for the last month, and we enjoyed some father-daughter bonding on the street corners.

On election night, the Republicans met at the Denver Marriott Tech Center. My campaign had a suite. Janet and I started out the evening at a political function in Colorado Springs and by the time we arrived at the hotel about 9:15 p.m., it was a sad scene. The election was a debacle for Republicans. Bill Ritter completed his improbable journey besting Bob Beauprez by 16 percent. Mark Hillman, a terrific young Republican state legislator, lost the treasurer's race. The secretary of state's race was too close to call. The Democrats won large majorities in the Colorado House and Senate. Colorado now had a 4-3 Democrat majority in Congress. Despite the adversity, I garnered almost 800,000 votes and won by 9.5 percent. A lot of unaffiliated voters had voted for me but not for my Republican colleagues. Given what else had occurred it was a satisfying win. When I went downstairs at the hotel to give my victory speech, I also did a series of media interviews. The first TV reporter who interviewed me during a live segment began by saying, "And here's John Suthers, the only Republican left standing." Sadly, it was all too true.

After the election, I was looking for some rest; but it was not to be. A statewide campaign is particularly exhausting. A few days before the election I was contacted by the American ambassador to Saudi Arabia, James Oberwetter, who was referred to me by Governor Bill Owens. The ambassador asked me to go on a diplomatic mission to Saudi Arabia leaving four days after the election.

In August of 2006 a Saudi national living in Colorado, Homaidan Al-Turki, was convicted in Arapahoe County District Court of enslaving his Indonesian maid and sexually assaulting her. She had come with Al-Turki's family to Colorado in 2000. She had worked twelve hours per day, seven days per week, without pay. Another Saudi tipped off immigration authorities. When they removed her from the house, she alleged she had been sexually assaulted by Al-Turki. The Arapahoe County DA had filed charges and the trial had been very contentious. Al-Turki's top-notch defense attorneys, hired by the Saudi government, claimed the prosecution was a pretense because the FBI had been unable to make a terrorism case against him in the aftermath of 9/11. The maid testified for several days through an interpreter. Al-Turki did not testify. After about eight hours of deliberation the jury convicted him, and the judge sentenced him to twenty years to life in prison.

The case became an international incident because Al-Turki's family was very influential in Saudi Arabia. His father had been an imam of the holy mosque at Medina and a respected Islamic cleric from the Wahhabi sect (the most conservative in Saudi Arabia). The Al-Turki family went to the Arab media and claimed he had been the victim of American bias against Muslims in the wake of the 9/11 attacks. The Arab media was generating numerous articles critical of the American justice system and suggesting America was not a safe place for Saudi students to study. Alarmed by the nature and extent of the anti-American sentiment, Ambassador Oberwetter sought out an expert on state and federal law and the American criminal justice system to confront the allegations. He contacted Governor Owens who recommended me for the mission.

I carefully studied the case during the week before I went. I also met with the FBI for a briefing. The FBI was very concerned about my trip, believing the Saudis' ploy would be to try to negotiate a release of the defendant. While I'm unable to relate all I learned from the FBI, I did learn that Al-Turki was personally acquainted with five of the nineteen 9/11 hijackers and it was clear why he had been of interest to the FBI. The agents I met with told me the good news was that the royal family would ensure Al-Qaeda would not kill me while I was in the kingdom. The bad news was I would be under constant electronic surveillance and the Saudis might attempt to compromise me by sending an attractive woman to my room. I assured them there was nothing to worry about in that regard.

I traveled with the governor's chief legal counsel, Jon Anderson. Four days before we left, the US ambassador learned I had an Israeli stamp on my passport from my trip to Israel ten months earlier. "Not even the president of the United States can get into Saudi Arabia with an Israeli stamp on his passport," the ambassador said. In a rare but impressive display of US government efficiency, I got a new passport in twenty-four hours. Before we left, we were told we would be guests of the American embassy and would meet with the Saudi press and Saudi leaders. But when we arrived in Riyadh, we learned that we had been upgraded to guests of Saudi King Abdullah. We stayed in the king's palace hotel. I had a six-room suite to myself. It was luxurious, although I'm confident the FBI was right about constant surveillance. The "smoke alarms" on the ceiling of each room were unusually large with small opaque windows. The US ambassador gave me a "diplomatic" cell phone to call Janet each day. He still suggested I say nothing to her about the business I was conducting.

Over the course of four days, I had a very busy schedule of meetings. I met with King Abdullah for an hour. We met in a palatially decorated throne room where he regularly received foreign dignitaries. He seemed very engaged and interested in what I had to say. Despite the extravagant surroundings, King Abdullah, then eighty-three years old, seemed to me to be a humble man. He had been raised in Saudi Arabia before the discovery of oil made his family fabulously wealthy. His interpreter, Adel al-Jubeir, was very savvy and the King appeared to grasp the legal issues. It was apparent he wanted to meet with me to give him cover with the Wahhabis who were frequent critics of the royal family. A short time after my visit, Adel al-Jubeir was appointed Saudi ambassador to the United States and in 2011 he would be the subject of an assassination plot orchestrated by the government of Iran. The Crown Prince, whom I met with for half an hour, was much less engaged. He told me how much he liked Las Vegas. I also met with the Minister of Interior (domestic security), the Minister of Justice, and the highest-ranking religious judge. The religious leader was very critical of our justice system that gave credence to an "illiterate maid" and asked me where our laws come from. After I explained in some detail how elected representatives enact our laws that must comply with our constitution and which the courts enforce, he condescendingly responded by declaring that Sharia (Islamic) law comes from Allah. I had contentious meetings with members of the Al-Turki family and with Saudi human rights lawyers. The irony of being cross-examined by Saudis about human rights was not lost on me. The ambassador had a dinner in my honor to which sixteen prominent lawyers in Riyadh, many of whom represented American corporate clients, were invited. Everywhere I went was by a lights-and-siren escort with heavily armed vehicles in front and back. It was clear, as the FBI had indicated, that the Saudis were intent on ensuring my safety. At that point in time, Al-Qaeda was in open war with the royal family. My visit was heavily covered in the Arab print media and on *Aljazeera*, the Arab TV network.

My job was to defend the American judicial system, assure the Saudis that Al-Turki had not been the victim of a witch hunt against Muslims, and to relate some details about the case that the Arab press was not reporting and that supported my arguments. I also explained the appeal process. Two facts were particularly relevant in my conversation with the King and with Saudi lawyers. In addition to the Indonesian maid, two other women had testified as "similar transaction" witnesses that Al-Turki had attempted to sexually assault them. Also, while Al-Turki's refusal to testify was not significant in the US because of the right against self-incrimination, it was a devastating fact under Islamic law, which draws strong inferences of guilt from silence in the face of such serious accusations.

I certainly didn't change anyone's mind. The cultural divide was too enormous. The Saudis simply couldn't understand how American courts could view the Indonesian maid as a competent witness. Under Islamic law, you must have four eyewitnesses to prove sexual assault. Female witnesses are less credible than male witnesses. Sexual assault convictions are a rarity. And even upon conviction, the victim can and often does accept a monetary settlement in lieu of execution of a sentence. The interior minister betrayed the essence of the problem when he said to me, "The accuser is a foreign maid. She's not an American. Why do you care?"

Nonetheless, the ambassador was very pleased with my visit. The additional facts I explained about the case caused Saudi officials to be less strident about the alleged injustice. Everyone involved, including the Al-Turki family, acknowledged the respect shown by the visit. Despite the fact I had been unapologetic about the American justice system, some newspaper columnists in Colorado and authors of letters to the editor were critical of my trip to kowtow to the Saudis. But I had no regrets, and I had some amazing experiences I wouldn't soon forget. Seven years later, in 2013, the Al-Turki case would take a bizarre twist that would cause me considerable anxiety.

On January 9, 2007, I took my oath of office on the west steps of the state capitol building with Janet and our daughter Alison once again holding the family Bible. Kate had just received a new assignment from the Navy to Pearl Harbor and was unable to attend. In light of what had transpired in November, there were very few Republicans in the inauguration crowd of 1,500 and very few Republicans among the 4,000 who attended the inaugural dinner a few days later. It had been fifty years since the Democrats had held the governorship and both houses of the legislature at the same time, and they were ready to party.

After the 2006 election, I enjoyed the additional legitimacy that comes with having been elected (as opposed to appointed) attorney general. The next four years would prove to be very eventful.

There were some major changes in the management of the office. I appointed Dan Domenico to serve as S.G. upon Allison Eid's elevation to the Colorado Supreme Court. Dan would serve as S.G. for the next nine years of my tenure and then be appointed a federal district court judge. Jason Dunn left to make big bucks as an attorney at the Denver-based Brownstein law firm. He would subsequently be appointed US attorney for Colorado by President Trump. Jeanne Smith was appointed by the new governor, Bill Ritter, to head the Colorado Division of Criminal Justice. I promoted Tom Raynes, a former DA from the west slope, to replace her as head of the Criminal Justice Section. During the term, we also hired a great communications director, Mike Saccone. Mike was a Northwestern University journalism school graduate who had covered the US Supreme Court and most recently had been a reporter for the *Grand Junction Daily Sentinel*. Mike took our office public relations to a new, higher level.

The office continued to have great results in criminal prosecutions. Successful prosecution of large investment schemes became routine. Various drug task forces brought their largest cases to our office, and we effectively used court approved wiretaps to take down criminal organizations, including Mexican cartels. One high-profile insurance fraud case involved a well-known and controversial Black minister in Denver, Acen Phillips. He was buying group life insurance policies for members of his church with funds donated by them. He was keeping a larger-than-agreed-upon portion of the proceeds upon the death of a church member and not accurately reporting to the insurance company who was covered by the policies. Some families had no idea he collected policy proceeds when their loved one died.

We continued to effectively investigate and prosecute mortgage fraud cases, environmental cases and a variety of other matters, including sex trafficking of minors. I would become passionate about that issue and spearheaded efforts to educate Colorado law enforcement to more effectively deal with the problem. Senior Assistant Attorney General Janet Drake prosecuted a number of sex trafficking rings and became a national lecturer on the issue. We made changes in Colorado law to facilitate successful investigations and prosecutions of traffickers. Through the special prosecution unit in the office, we continued to effectively deal with Mexican nationals who had committed murder in Colorado and fled to Mexico before capture. Under Article IV of the Mexican Criminal Code, AG investigator LuzMaria Shearer translated all the police reports into Spanish and presented them to Mexican courts. If the court found the case meritorious, it issued an arrest warrant, and the defendant was subject to prosecution and sentencing in Mexico. Shearer started the unit in 2004 and it successfully secured prosecution in Mexico of over two dozen cases in the next eight years. LuzMaria frequently traveled to Mexico and was well-known by Mexican law enforcement.

On two occasions, I was appointed by the governor to manage rural district attorneys' offices for a period of time. In one case the DA was killed in a motorcycle accident and my office needed to run the office until a successor could be named by the governor. In another, the Montrose DA, Myrl Serra, was charged with sexually assaulting female employees, and we ran the office until a resignation could be secured and a successor appointed. My office also prosecuted Serra. He was convicted and sentenced to prison.

In 2007 a judge in Fort Collins granted a new trial to a defendant who had been convicted in 1995 of a murder that occurred in 1987. Tim Masters had been convicted by a jury of murdering Peggy Hettrick. Hettrick had been found dead in a vacant field near where Masters lived. She had been stabbed to death and her nipples and vagina had been mutilated. The evidence against Masters consisted of a footprint near the body, an admission that he had passed by the body the morning after the murder, and bizarre drawings in his possession that depicted a woman stabbed in the back being dragged by the arms. A Fort Collins police detective had relentlessly pressured prosecutors to bring the case and they did so eight years after the murder. A psychiatrist testified at the trial for the prosecution and made some bold observations about the significance of the drawings. Masters and his defense counsel vehemently maintained his innocence, even after conviction. DNA testing done by a Dutch laboratory in 2005 found no DNA of Masters but did find the DNA of an ex-boyfriend on the victim's clothing. A hearing on a new trial motion also revealed the Fort Collins detective had withheld evidence. A judge granted Masters a new trial. The DA in Fort Collins dismissed the case, citing insufficient evidence to go forward. Masters was released from prison and filed a suit against the City of Fort Collins that was eventually settled for $10 million. Governor Bill Ritter did not feel it appropriate for the Fort Collins police and DA to continue investigating the now-unsolved murder and, by executive order, appointed the attorney general to do so. We put our best prosecutors and investigators on the case, and they began to methodically reconstruct the case. By the fall of 2010 we began presenting evidence to a statewide grand jury. Despite identifying another prime suspect, the evidence was insufficient, and no new indictment emerged. But the grand jury requested, on the basis of their review of the evidence, that I publicly exonerate Masters, and I did so.

The Consumer Protection Section also continued to do great work. The Colorado Humane Society, a venerable institution that had existed for over a century, had been taken over by a small group of people who were using charitable contributions for their personal benefit. Under the AG's power to oversee charitable institutions, we wound up putting the Humane Society in the hands of a receiver. Though we weren't successful in saving the institution, the name was sold to another animal protection organization which continued its philanthropic work.

The section also did dozens of civil cases against mortgage brokers for advertising fraud and operating without a license. We continued to be involved in multi-state litigations against banks, mortgage brokers, and lenders who had contributed to the financial collapse and its aftermath. Throughout the severe recession that began in 2007, we aggressively pursued debt settlement and mortgage modification companies that were operating illicitly. When General Motors and Chrysler went bankrupt, we monitored the proceedings to protect Colorado consumers and Colorado car dealers. We intervened with several other states in the GM bankruptcy to ensure future manufacturer-dealer disputes would be subject to the jurisdiction of Colorado authorities rather than the bankruptcy court in New York. Our intervention also saved several Colorado dealerships that faced closure by the manufacturers.

Our consumer outreach effort concentrated on senior citizens through our ElderWatch program, a partnership with the AARP Foundation. During my tenure as AG, I traveled to every corner of Colorado speaking to seniors about fraud scams. ElderWatch included a hotline for seniors to call. We published an ID Theft Repair Kit and distributed approximately 100,000 copies across the state. We also created a widely circulated pamphlet telling small businesses how to protect against data security breaches. In cooperation with the Drug Enforcement Administration, we sponsored prescription drug take-back events at which seniors, and everyone else for that matter, could dispose of unused drugs that could be abused by others. The events were very successful, collecting over fifty tons of drugs in the first five years.

The Natural Resources and Environment section of the office continued to be very effective. After successfully resolving several large hazardous waste cases during my first few years in office, we were able to settle another long-standing case against the City of Denver and several other responsible parties involving the Lowry Landfill. We also resolved cases involving contamination at a research facility on the campus of the Colorado School of Mines and involving pollution of the South Platte River by Suncor, a petroleum refiner.

While the latest suit by Kansas against Colorado over the Arkansas River, which was filed in 1983, ended with a judgment against Colorado for $34 million in 2005 (Kansas had originally sued for over $300 million), there was still a serious dispute as to how much Colorado owed to Kansas for fees and costs. Kansas claimed $11 million, Colorado offered $1 million. The dispute revolved around a federal statute providing for fees and costs and whether, under Article III, Section 2 of the US Constitution, the statute applied to cases within the original jurisdiction of the Supreme Court (including suits by one state against another). Colorado contended the statute applied; Kansas disagreed. When the US Supreme Court set the case for oral argument, it was the twelfth time in 106 years that disputes between the two states over the Arkansas River had been heard by the Court. I called the Attorney General of Kansas, Steve Six, and suggested that, because the issue was one of statutory and constitutional construction and not a highly complex water law question, he and I should argue the case. He agreed.

Preparing to argue a case before the US Supreme Court is a daunting task. I did three moot court arguments. One was at the National Association of Attorneys General office in Washington, DC before a panel of Supreme Court practitioners. They beat me up pretty good but gave me confidence that I had a good sense of how the court would approach the issue.

On Monday, December 1, 2008, I walked into the Supreme Court for the morning arguments. Dan Domenico, the Colorado solicitor general, and the two water lawyers who had handled the lengthy underlying case, accompanied me. Janet, our daughter Alison (now a lawyer), and my sister-in-law Jane McGrath sat in the front row.

Prior to the argument, counsel are briefed by the clerk of the court in a room close to the courtroom. On the wall are paintings of famous Supreme Court advocates, including Daniel Webster. It's an atmosphere that caused me to think *What the hell am I doing here?*

The Supreme Court Chamber is relatively small. The podium where arguing counsel stand is only about five feet in front of the chief justice, who sits in the middle of the nine-member court, all of whom are peering down during the argument. The podium is raised or lowered by a hand crank. It's said to be the oldest piece of furniture still used by the federal government, well over 200 years old. Tradition also dictates that everyone who argues before the Supreme Court receives a quill pen.

In my half-hour argument I was asked about twenty questions. General Six was asked even more. One of the cardinal rules of a Supreme Court argument is: Don't try to be funny. Without really trying to be funny, I nevertheless generated considerable levity. Justice Stephen Breyer tended to pose fairly long hypotheticals. He did so to me, suggesting it established a proper basis to find for Kansas. He concluded by saying, "What do you think of my hypothetical, General Suthers?" Without hesitation, I responded, "not much." Before I could elaborate, everyone in the chambers, including all the justices (thank goodness!) burst out in laughter. "That's fair," said Breyer, who then allowed me to elaborate.

It was an incredible experience to argue before the US Supreme Court, an experience that very few lawyers are privileged to have. It was certainly one of the highlights of my very eventful legal career. The experience was made all the more memorable in March of 2009 when the court issued its opinion and found for Colorado on a 9-0 vote. Solicitor General Dan Domenico also argued two cases before the US Supreme Court during my tenure as attorney general.

In 2009, I argued a very interesting case in front of the Colorado Supreme Court. Theater companies had brought suit alleging the statewide smoking ban passed by the Colorado legislature, which prevented them from using real cigarettes in theatrical productions, violated their First Amendment rights of free expression. Although I thought the theatrical ban was stupid, I had no problem arguing it was no more a violation of constitutional rights than requiring actors to use fake guns, fake wounds, and fake fire. The court clearly thought the case was factually interesting and chose it to be part of a special session held in front of high school students in Alamosa, Colorado. The state prevailed 6-1.

Colorado law requires the attorney general to review any transfer of the assets of a nonprofit hospital whether the transfer is to a for-profit hospital or another nonprofit. The law was passed in the 1990s when there were a number of sales of nonprofits to for-profit hospitals and much concern about whether fair market value was received, whether proceeds remained available for charitable purposes and whether there was self-dealing by hospital trustees. If the transfer was to a for-profit hospital the proceeds had to go into a charitable trust to be used for health care purposes. In the case of a transfer to another nonprofit, the statute directed the AG to determine if there was "a material change in charitable purpose." If not, the transfer was to be approved. When I became attorney general, I had no idea how much time we would spend reviewing hospital transfers. It became a major part of our oversight of charitable organizations.

In 2008 we were asked to review a hospital transfer that proved very controversial. Three Denver-area hospitals, St. Joseph's, Lutheran, and Good Samaritan, were owned by a partnership between the Sisters of Charity of Leavenworth and the Community First Foundation, which operated the hospitals through an entity called Exempla. The hospitals needed a large infusion of cash for necessary upgrades and improvements. The Sisters of Charity owned several hospitals and were in the best position to finance the improvements but were reluctant to do so without management control of the hospitals. Community First Foundation desired to get out of the hospital business and become a strictly grant making foundation. So, they proposed to transfer their interest in the hospitals to the Sisters of Charity for $310 million.

By agreement of the partners, only one of the hospitals, St. Joseph's, had operated under the Catholic health guidelines, which prevented abortions and tubal ligations that were not necessary for the health of the mother. Upon the transfer of all three hospitals to the Sisters of Charity, they would operate under the guidelines. That fact caused a storm of opposition to the transfer. From what I could tell, the vocal opponents were a combination of pro-choice advocates and people with a strong anti-Catholic bias. My office was flooded with letters, emails, and phone calls urging me to bar the transaction as not in the public interest. But our review centered on the question whether there was a "material change in charitable purpose." We found that the delivery of health care services was the charitable purpose and, because abortions and tubal ligations were only 0.3 percent of all inpatient services and even less of total services, there was no "material change." We also found there were not significant barriers to market entry for entities wanting to provide abortion and family planning services for the areas served by the hospitals. Liberal activist lawyers sued me, the Sisters of Charity, and Community First Foundation. The court upheld the transfer, but I was accused by segments of the legal community and several Democrat legislators of being a pawn of the Catholic Church. Interestingly enough, the usually vocal pro-life forces seemed oblivious to the controversy. It was not until 2012 that the transfer was finally completed.

We also advised the Colorado Springs City Council that if they sold the city-owned Memorial Hospital to a for-profit entity, they were required under Colorado law to put the proceeds of the sale into a trust to be used for health care related purposes and could not use such proceeds for regular city functions. In 2012 the city granted a long-term lease of the hospital to the University of Colorado Health System and my office approved the nonprofit-to-nonprofit transfer. The voters of Colorado Springs chose to put the proceeds of the sale in a newly formed Colorado Springs Health Foundation, which would give grants to advance public health in the Pikes Peak region. In 2011 we also reviewed a very large and very complex transfer of interest in several hospitals. A for-profit hospital system, Health One, wound up paying $1.4 billion to the Colorado Health Foundation for their interest in the hospitals. The foundation immediately became one of the largest in the country. Our oversight of Health One's obligations under the agreement continued for several years.

While I worked hard to perform my duties as attorney general in a bipartisan manner, I did get publicly contrary with Governor Ritter and the Democrat-controlled legislature on a few issues. Upon taking office, Ritter asked my staff for advice as to how he could, by executive order, create "employee partnerships" (i.e., unionize state employees). Pursuant to my obligation to competently represent the governor we presented him with an extensive legal memo telling what he could and could not do by executive order. But, without violating any client confidence, I also exercised my prerogative as an independently elected constitutional officer to publicly criticize the decision as bad public policy. Unionizing Colorado state employees, who were among the highest paid in the country (except for elected officials like me who were among the lowest), was a solution in search of a problem, I said. The governor's decision cost him much of the support of the business community that had been instrumental in his election. It also got him off to a bad start with *The Denver Post* editorial board from which he never completely recovered.

In 1992 the Colorado voters had passed a TABOR that limited the annual growth in government revenues to a percentage equal to inflation plus population growth and requiring any increase in taxes to be approved by voters. In the years following the passage of TABOR the state legislature created a statutory formula in the state's School Finance Act to ensure that school districts did not collect more property taxes than they were allowed under TABOR. As property values went up, mill levies (tax rates) would automatically go down to ensure the increase in revenue didn't exceed TABOR limits. Unfortunately, in my opinion and that of many others, the voters then approved a citizen initiative, Amendment 23, that constitutionally required the budget for kindergarten through twelfth grade education (about 45 percent of the entire state budget) to grow by inflation plus 1 percent each year, regardless of whether state revenues were growing or declining. Because of significant declines in revenue from 2001 to 2003, and other budget demands, Colorado had to use more and more income and sales tax revenue to backfill for shortfalls in local property tax funding of schools. By 2007, the governor and the legislature understandably wanted to increase the local property tax revenue of the school districts and thereby reduce the state tax revenues required to meet the funding requirements of Amendment 23. But under TABOR, a tax increase required a vote of the people. Unwilling to ask the voters, the Democrats chose another route. They passed a statute freezing the property tax rate and suggesting no tax increase was involved. In fact, of course, but for the tax rate freeze, the rate would have declined as property values increased. The effect of the change would be to generate several billion dollars in additional revenue over the next several years.

Because the Colorado Constitution required any change in tax policy that resulted in increased revenue to the taxing entity to be voted on, my office advised the governor and legislature in a written memo that we believed the legislation violated the TABOR. They passed it anyway. When the Mesa County Commissioners and several individual taxpayers sued alleging the legislation violated TABOR, the governor understandably didn't want my office to defend the suit. Pursuant to statute, the governor hired outside counsel. The trial court found the legislation violated TABOR. But the Colorado Supreme Court had a very liberal majority that had long been hostile to the TABOR, and I had no illusion they would follow the clear constitutional directive requiring a vote of the people. But even I was surprised how they got around the plain language of the state constitution. They held that if the resulting revenue from a tax increase or change in tax policy did not cause the state to exceed the total TABOR limit, then the increase did not require a vote of the people. Because the $150 million increase in revenue the first year would still leave the state below its TABOR revenue limit, no vote was required. In other words, they simply read into the constitution a requirement that wasn't there. Not surprisingly, in the 2010 legislative session the Democrats used the Supreme Court decision to repeal various business tax credits, claiming that the resulting increase in tax revenue did not require a vote because the millions in revenue the first year did not cause the state to surpass the TABOR limit.

This was the only case during my tenure as attorney general where I did not defend a law passed by the legislature. I felt very strongly that the attorney general has a duty to defend the state's laws unless the highest court with jurisdiction has issued an unequivocal on-point ruling invalidating it. Even when I vehemently disagreed with laws passed by the Colorado legislature, including several gun control laws, my office defended them. And when several Democrat attorneys general around the nation refused to defend their state's constitutional bans on gay marriage, I wrote an op-ed for *The Washington Post* arguing it was the attorneys general's obligation to defend the bans until the US Supreme Court issued an on-point decision declaring them unconstitutional or declined to take a circuit court case that did so. I said, "Refusing to defend unpopular or politically distasteful laws will ultimately weaken the legal and moral authority attorneys general depend upon. We will be viewed as simply one more player in a political system rather than as legal authorities in a legal system. The courts, the governments we represent and, most importantly, the people we serve will treat our pronouncements and our arguments with skepticism and cynicism."

The op-ed got lots of attention nationally and led to US Attorney General Eric Holder appearing at a national attorneys general meeting in Washington, DC three weeks later and announcing to the AGs and the national media that it was acceptable for an attorney general to refuse to defend a law if he or she *thought* it was unconstitutional. That caused him much criticism and simply heightened the national debate. Eventually, in the fall of 2014, same-sex marriage became the law in Colorado when the US Supreme Court refused to review a 2-1 Tenth Circuit decision finding a ban on gay marriage violates the Fourteenth Amendment's equal protection provisions. In 2015 the US Supreme Court struck down all state bans on same-sex marriage on a 5-4 vote, declaring them in violation of the equal protection clause. Given the great shift in public sentiment, it was clear that same-sex marriage would be embraced legislatively in America. But I viewed dictating it by court decree a dramatic triumph for a "living constitution." I'm quite certain that courageous members of Congress who drafted the equal protection clause to prohibit racial discrimination after the Civil War would be surprised to learn of its modern-day application.

In September of 2017 the University of Notre Dame Law School gave me its St. Thomas More Award as "a public servant with uncompromising integrity and rigid adherence to principle." That largely stemmed from my advocacy for the principle that government lawyers have a duty to defend the law, even when the law is unpopular and it's politically risky to defend it.

In the 2010 legislative session, medical marijuana was at center stage. In 2000 the voters of Colorado approved a constitutional amendment allowing patients with a "debilitating medical condition" to grow small amounts of marijuana or, if they were unable to do so, a "primary caregiver" could grow it for them. By health department guideline, a caregiver could not have more than five patients. By 2007 there were only about 1,700 patients on the health department registry. But then two things happened to energize the pro-marijuana forces. First, the state health board failed on a 4-3 vote to enact a formal rule limiting caregivers to five patients. That caused marijuana advocates to suggest they could be the caregiver for hundreds, if not thousands, of patients. And they could recruit such patients through aggressive advertising. Secondly, upon his election as president in 2008, Barack Obama fulfilled a campaign promise by having the Department of Justice instruct US attorneys not to federally prosecute people acting in compliance with state medical marijuana laws, despite the fact all such activities violated federal law. By the fall of 2009, Colorado was experiencing a "gold rush" of marijuana dealers setting up shop as "caregivers" and the rolls of "patients" swelled to 60,000. Everyone looked to the legislature to deal with the problem.

I led a broad coalition of law enforcement, drug treatment, and medical professionals who wanted the legislature to simply clarify the 2000 constitutional amendment and statutorily limit caregivers to no more than five patients. We argued that publicly visible dispensaries would drastically lower adolescents' perception of the risk of the drug and that youth consumption rates would rise. We also predicted Colorado would become a major supplier of marijuana to other states. We looked to Governor Ritter, generally a law enforcement ally, for leadership. Unfortunately, none was forthcoming. Ritter, who was contemplating seeking reelection at the time, told me he didn't want to get crosswise with liberals in his party who controlled the judiciary committees. The result was a bill that legislatively approved a system of medical marijuana dispensaries and related grow operations that popped up all over the state to supply the "patients" that quickly numbered well over 125,000. It was clear that only a very small fraction actually had a *debilitating* medical condition. Most of the patients were under forty and 70 percent were men. It was the same demographic profile as users of illicit drugs. Throughout the debate and in subsequent years, I was the highest profile critic of Colorado's marijuana industry. As adolescent use of the drug rose and it became clear accessibility to medical marijuana was the cause, and as marijuana from Colorado grow operations was diverted all over the country, I tried to educate the public. I became enemy number one of the industry and they were not a respectful group. I was routinely booed and hissed at public appearances and the subject of death threats. One angry advocate spit on me. After a debate at the University of

Denver Law School, I needed a police escort to safely exit the campus.

In my opinion, the medical marijuana fiasco, particularly the legislature's embrace of dispensaries, helped convince Colorado voters to give up on any prohibition and support an initiative on the ballot in 2012 that legalized recreational possession of small amounts of marijuana as well as large wholesale grow operations and retail distribution stores. The initiative passed 55-45 percent and caused Colorado to spend the next several years developing an industry that operated in violation of federal law. I remain convinced the state will pay a high social cost with higher rates of adolescent marijuana use, particularly of products with very high THC content, leading to greater overall drug abuse related problems in the coming years.

My consolation for the abuse I took from marijuana proponents was the respect of many I admire. The drug investigators in Colorado gave me a special award for my courage. National columnist, George Will, a conservative voice I have long admired, wrote a column about the medical marijuana debate in Colorado and called me "an honest and thoughtful man trying to save his state from the hypocrisy that is medical marijuana." Being called honest and thoughtful by George Will (I had breakfast with him on two occasions) was worth a lot of abuse. Gil Kerlikowske, the nation's drug czar, called me on a couple of occasions to thank me for my opposition to the marijuana industry.

Bill Ritter's vacillation on the medical marijuana issue was, in my opinion, indicative of his challenges as governor. I had worked closely with Bill when he was a Denver district attorney and liked him a lot. I authored a widely read book about the prosecution function that was published in 2008 and he wrote the foreward to the book. I think Bill Ritter is one of the best human beings I've known. He is honest, sincere, and a truly dedicated public servant. He was probably the most genuine and affable of the three governors I worked with as attorney general. But his personal qualities did not translate to political effectiveness. Because I knew him well, and shared a prosecution background with him, I paid close attention to how he governed. Bill had been an effective prosecutor because he was passionate, imminently fair, and largely non-ideological. But his desire to be fair and his lack of a clearly defined political ideology did not work well as governor. He would side with labor on one issue and business on the next. The result was a loss of support from both.

Ritter lost favor with editorial boards across the state, particularly *The Denver Post*, and by January of 2010, three years into his term, he suffered from high unfavorable ratings in the polls. It was not wholly surprising to me that he chose not to seek reelection. He cited family concerns, but I knew from experience that a family's reaction to politics has a lot to do with how popular one is as a politician.

In the course of my first full term as attorney general I assumed several leadership positions among the nation's AGs. I had served as chair of the Criminal Law Committee of the National Association of Attorneys General (NAAG) during my first three years as AG and had done a good job. I also represented the AGs on a committee that, with US attorneys and district attorneys, met quarterly with the US attorney general to discuss law enforcement issues. My contributions led to an appointment to the Executive Committee of NAAG in 2007 and I was reappointed or elected to the committee each year thereafter until 2013. I was part of a controversy in 2007 when I became a critical vote necessary to remove the longtime executive director of NAAG, Lynne Ross. NAAG President Lawrence Wasden of Idaho sought her removal. Several AGs actively opposed the move. Many AGs, including myself, considered Lynne a friend. And many were loyal to her despite multiple performance audits that showed she had serious shortcomings as a manager of the NAAG staff. I was convinced the NAAG staff deserved a better manager and joined in the 7-4 Executive Committee vote to replace her. Fortunately, our choice to replace her, Jim McPherson, a retired Navy Admiral who had headed the JAG corps, did a great job and virtually all the AGs came to recognize the wisdom of the move.

Through NAAG and my committee work I had numerous interesting opportunities to meet with national leaders. In March of 2010 I joined other AGs at a meeting with President Obama and Treasury Secretary Tim Geithner in the Roosevelt Room of the White House to discuss financial regulatory reform. I found the president self-confident to an extreme and dismissive of some very serious issues we raised about the pending Dodd-Frank legislation. When I asked the president why small community banks were ensnared in the new Dodd-Frank regulations when they had nothing to do with the foreclosure crisis and economic recession, he simply responded, "Everyone has to feel the pain." I expected a more thoughtful response. We met with then Vice President Joe Biden on a couple of occasions. His son, Beau, served as the Attorney General of Delaware, before his untimely death from brain cancer. Beau frequently called on me for advice on criminal justice issues. Because of my membership on the law enforcement working group that met quarterly with the US attorney general, I was on a first name basis with all the US attorneys general that served from 2005-2015. My personal observation of Alberto Gonzales is consistent with his public perception. He was an incredibly nice guy but was in way over his head as AG. His mishandling of the firing of US attorneys in 2007 was symptomatic of his impotence as a leader of the department. I was initially impressed with Eric Holder. He was an experienced prosecutor who appeared to bring professionalism to a department much in need of image repair. Unfortunately, he lost credibility with me by shedding responsibility for an ill-conceived firearms investigation along the border with Mexico and by the way he handled the federal response to Colorado's legalization of marijuana in 2012. In the last few years of his tenure, he took a very highly politicized posture on race related issues that I thought was unbecoming of a US attorney general.

Governor Hickenlooper and I called General Holder the same week the voters of Colorado approved the marijuana legalization initiative in November of 2012 and told him the federal government needed to set forth its position promptly before the state expended resources implementing policy in violation of federal law. He promised a prompt response that did not occur. In the last week of February 2013, I publicly confronted him on the issue at a meeting of the NAAG. He said a response was imminent. In fact, it was clear President Obama was making the decision and no federal position was announced until September of 2013. While he had an obligation to be loyal to the president, his lack of candor was disturbing to many of us in law enforcement.

Whether the issue was enforcement of federal marijuana laws, statutory deadlines in the Affordable Health Care Act (Obamacare), or immigration reform, the Obama administration, frustrated that a divided Congress would not act, would simply enact executive orders or publicly decree that it would not enforce the law rather than wait for Congress to change it. Holder was a co-conspirator by directing US attorneys and federal law enforcement not to enforce a wide variety of federal laws. When Holder then sanctioned the refusal of state attorneys general to defend certain laws they didn't like, I came to seriously question his commitment to the rule of law.

I was elected chairman of the Conference of Western Attorneys General (CWAG) for 2009-2010. CWAG consisted of the AGs of fifteen western states and the Pacific territories of Guam and American Samoa. But other AGs were auxiliary members because we had great annual meetings at beautiful locations in the West. The organization addressed some issues of particular interest to the western states. During my presidential tenure, my initiative was on water, and I hosted a conference on that complex issue at the Broadmoor Hotel in my hometown of Colorado Springs. In 2013 I hosted the annual conference of CWAG that drew more than 850 people to the Broadmoor.

CWAG also became a very important player in US-Mexico relations. The organization was the recipient of millions of dollars in US government funding to train hundreds of Mexican prosecutors and investigators who were converting to a public, adversarial court system in order to stem rampant corruption. My office was very involved in such training efforts from 2008 to 2014 and I recognized that the effort could have profound ramifications for the future of Mexico and its relationship to the United States.

In an effort to stem border violence and drug, weapon, and human smuggling between our countries, western attorneys general met with the Mexican federal AG and the attorneys general of the Mexican states on several occasions. I traveled to Mexico for such meetings several times, the most memorable of which was in Mexico City and nearby Cuernavaca. The security was incredibly heavy because of the threat of Mexican cartels. Heavily armed escorts accompanied us when we traveled, and helicopter gunships hovered over our meeting locations. Janet and I took a trip to the pyramids outside of Mexico City and had no fewer than six armed security guards to accompany us. I became acquainted with Mexico Attorney General Eduardo Medina Mora and was sad when President Calderon replaced him in 2010 because of lack of progress in stemming cartel violence. We renewed our acquaintanceship when he became Mexican ambassador to the United States in 2013. He was subsequently appointed to the Supreme Court of Mexico but resigned in 2019 when it was revealed he was under investigation for financial dealings.

Beginning in the fall of 2007, I became an adjunct professor at the University of Denver Law School. Each fall semester for the next eight years I taught a Thursday night seminar entitled The Prosecutor as Protagonist. It was an in-depth look at the role of the prosecutor in the justice system. It was a very popular course. I got high ratings as a teacher and the students got to hear from an incredible group of speakers that included the governor, Supreme Court Justices, trial judges, district attorneys, and the best defense attorneys in Colorado. I was heartened by the fact several of my students subsequently credited my course with inspiring them to begin their legal career as a prosecutor. In the spring of 2010, I began teaching a class as a Scholar in Residence at the University of Colorado at Colorado Springs (UCCS). I taught undergraduate courses in the Criminal Justice Section of the School of Public Affairs. I greatly enjoyed the teaching opportunities. It allowed me to think both theoretically and practically about the work I'd been doing throughout my career. I believe I positively impacted the students I was teaching, and it gave me an opportunity to stay in touch with what students were thinking about. It also allowed me to earn an additional $30,000 per year. My paltry AG salary of $80,000 was significantly less than the average salary of lawyers in my office and $60,000-$70,000 less than my top deputies. It was also the second lowest AG salary in the country. Holding a night job became a practical necessity.

In 2013 the UCCS School of Public Affairs created a John Suthers Endowed Scholarship Fund. I helped raise the initial endowment of $100,000 and helped it grow significantly over subsequent years to assist numerous UCCS students.

In 2008 I also wrote a book entitled *No Higher Calling, No Greater Responsibility: A Prosecutor Makes His Case*. It contained my observations about the justice system based on experiences as a district attorney, US attorney, and attorney general. The book was published by Fulcrum Publishing and would gain national popularity among prosecutors and law students. A Denver-based law firm, Holland and Hart, purchased a copy for each of the approximately 1,500 prosecutors in the state. The modest royalties I received were also helpful.

In 2008, when Barack Obama was elected president of the United States, he shortly thereafter nominated Colorado Senator Ken Salazar to be Secretary of the Interior. That meant Salazar would vacate his US Senate seat with two years left in his term. Governor Ritter shocked virtually everyone, and perhaps

Democrats more than Republicans, by picking Michael Bennet, the Denver Public School Superintendent, to replace him. Bennet had come to Colorado a decade earlier to work for Phil Anschutz and subsequently as Denver Mayor John Hickenlooper's chief of staff, before being appointed school superintendent. In appointing Bennet, Ritter had passed over some seasoned, and frankly more popular, Democrat candidates like Speaker of the House Andrew Romanoff. The general sense was that both Ritter and Bennet would be vulnerable in the 2010 election and a great deal of speculation began as to whether I, the only Republican in statewide office, would run for governor or US Senate in 2010. What ensued was two months of somewhat tortuous introspection that ultimately led me to learn a lot about myself.

The decision about running for governor was easy at first. I feel strongly that an attorney general should not run against an incumbent governor for ethical reasons. The governor is the AG's client. How do you give the best possible legal advice and representation to someone you're running against and avoid any appearance of impropriety? How do you avoid the appearance you're using information gained from the attorney-client relationship in the campaign? The simple answer is you can't. Other AGs may have tried, but not me. The Senate race, on the other hand, I thought long and hard about. I did believe Michael Bennet was vulnerable and that I would have an excellent chance of winning. Polling looked very favorable. It was likely to be a good Republican year. Many people, including Colorado Republican party chair Dick Wadhams, were very encouraging. I had three phone conversations with US Senator John Cornyn from Texas, the chairman of the Republican National Senatorial Committee, who was actively recruiting me to run. I consulted Janelle Domenico, a top-notch fundraiser who had worked in several US Senate campaigns. She laid out for me what a Senate campaign would mean in terms of a time commitment. She suggested I needed to raise an average of $15,000 per day every day for twenty-two months. That meant traveling out of state for fundraisers about 150 nights and spending several hours per day on the phone. Essentially that meant not really functioning as the attorney general for two years. And that's what led me to an epiphany. The notion of walking away from my work as AG was very distressing to me and it caused me to carefully evaluate what I did and did not like about my life in public service over the past twenty years. What I liked first and foremost was the lawyering and management I'd done as DA, US attorney, and attorney general. Enforcing the law affords one the opportunity to be righteous and avoid some of the rawness of politics. What I liked least was the fundraising. Janet made a profound observation that I found accurate and ultimately convincing. "I've watched you closely throughout your career, John," she said. "The reality is that you're a law and order guy. You're Eliot Ness masquerading as a politician." She knew me well. What I really cherished was my role as a lawyer/public servant; much more so than my role as a politician. I loved being attorney general, as I had loved being district attorney and US attorney. I got into politics because I wanted to be district attorney. I didn't run for DA because I wanted to get into politics. The same could be said for my campaigns for attorney general. In February of 2009, I released a public statement as to my intentions for 2010. I thanked people for their support in suggesting I run for governor or US Senate. But I explained that I simply did not want to give up my work as attorney general to run. It was a role that I truly enjoyed, and I had therefore decided to seek reelection as attorney general. Even when Bill Ritter decided in January of 2010 that he wouldn't seek reelection as governor, I didn't seriously reconsider. I wasn't willing to give up even a year of interesting work as AG to run for governor.

In the early stages of the 2010 attorney general campaign, the Democrats once again had trouble finding a viable candidate to challenge me. The vice-chair of the state Democrat Party, Don Slater, announced at one point, but then withdrew when he got little traction. A few others toyed with the idea, but by the end of February 2010, no strong candidate had emerged. That all changed in March of that year.

Congress, largely along party lines, passed comprehensive health care reform and President Obama signed the bill on March 23rd. Within hours after the Patient Protection and Affordable Health Care Act became law, a dozen states, including Colorado, filed a lawsuit alleging that an important part of the bill, called the "individual health insurance mandate" was unconstitutional. Under the mandate, beginning in 2014 Americans would have to prove to the federal government on their annual tax return that they had purchased health insurance which conformed to federal rules and regulations or pay a fine of up to two-and-a-half percent of their adjusted gross income. Health insurance is obviously a good thing and because of the bill's elimination of pre-existing conditions as a basis for denial or higher premiums, a large pool of healthy young people in the insurance pool was absolutely essential. So "what's the problem?" the media, the public, and liberal law professors asked. The problem was the fact that the expansion of federal power evidenced by the mandate threatened an essential principle of the US Constitution—federalism.

Federalism is the concept enshrined in our Constitution that says the federal government can exercise only the enumerated powers granted to it in the Constitution and, by the express terms of the document, all powers not expressly given to the federal government are reserved to the states and the people. Article I, Section 8 of the Constitution sets out the enumerated powers. Needless to say, there is no health care power in the Constitution. The founders never envisioned the federal government would be in the health care business. Congress and President Obama expressly justified the individual mandate on the basis of the commerce power. And therein lay the problem. Over the past 200 years, Congress and the courts had broadly construed the commerce clause and it had been the vehicle for the greatest expansion of federal power. But it had heretofore always been used to regulate economic activity impacting interstate commerce. This was the first time in American history Congress sought to use the commerce power to punish individuals who dared to defy the government by being economically inactive—by *not* buying a product or service the government wanted them to buy. If the government could invoke the commerce power to force people to buy health insurance, it could invoke the power to force them to buy all kinds of things it thought were good for them, like fuel efficient cars, solar panels, and healthy food. Previously the federal government was content to merely encourage such beneficial purchases by offering tax deductions or credits for those who made such purchases. I was convinced that if Congress could use the commerce power to control the economic decision-making of individual Americans, federalism was dead. I gladly joined with other attorneys general and governors who were similarly convinced. Eventually, more than half the states would challenge the constitutionality of the individual mandate.

A second claim in the states' lawsuit challenged a huge expansion of Medicaid contained in the Affordable Health Care Act. Up to twenty million additional Americans would be eligible for Medicaid coverage and, beginning in 2016, states would have to assume a share of the additional cost. Congress said if a state didn't accept the additional enrollees, it would lose all Medicaid funding. The states alleged this all-or-nothing approach was so coercive to the states as to violate federalism.

Critics wasted no time in lambasting me. Governor Ritter and the Democrats in the legislature issued statements criticizing me. They didn't contest my authority to bring the suit, but rather alleged it was a frivolous case and a waste of time. Liberal law professors around the country called the suit laughable. *The Denver Post* and other editorial pages around the country also called the lawsuit *frivolous*. Over the next two weeks I heard from over 10,000 people by letter, phone, email, and petitions that I was thwarting the public will. One such critic was Stan Garnett, the Democrat Boulder district attorney, who had been elected in 2008 after a lengthy career as a trial lawyer with the prestigious Brownstein firm in Denver. Stan had gone out of his way during the previous few years to tell me what a good job I was doing as AG and I suspected he might want to pursue the job when I vacated it. He sent me a few emails saying my joining the health care lawsuit was cynical and partisan and he was withdrawing his support of me and searching for a strong Democrat candidate to run against me. His search was short and within two weeks he announced his candidacy for AG. Frankly, I wasn't naive and fully expected that joining the suit would lead to the Democrats targeting me. And they did.

Garnett hired a well-known retired newspaper and TV reporter as his communications director, and he spent all day every day trying to plant stories with his buddies in the media. Garnett's son, Alec, served as his campaign manager. Garnett was a well-connected lawyer, and he actively pursued fundraising from trial lawyers with considerable success. The political pundits were convinced the AG's race would be close.

But a funny thing happened. Over the next few months my office heard from about 30,000 Coloradans in favor of the lawsuit. And polls showed about 56 percent of the state agreed with me. I found that as I spoke to groups, even hostile ones, their attitude changed when I explained that the case wasn't about health care, it was about the federal government's ability to control their lives. When the trial judge in our case, and in a similar case brought separately by Virginia, denied the federal government's motion to dismiss the cases, it became apparent to the media and the public that the suit wasn't frivolous but rather a serious constitutional issue that was destined for the US Supreme Court.

As Garnett's reason to challenge me became less viable as a campaign issue he took on other causes. I was weak on consumer protection, he claimed. The trouble was I could document we had been more aggressive in that area than any AG before me and he got no traction with the media. Then he attacked me for taking contributions from people in the payday lending industry. That had some legs until I pointed out in a television debate that two-thirds of his money was from trial lawyers and another big chunk was from the medical marijuana industry. I also pointed out that the payday loan industry had just sued me for new regulations my office had imposed, so their political support hadn't helped them much.

About six weeks before the election, a poll showed me up by 16 percent. At that point Garnett's campaign turned extremely negative. They decided to run a TV ad accusing me of having unleashed a serial killer when I was US attorney. A guy named Scott Kimball had been in federal custody for check-related offenses. Apparently, the FBI came to an assistant US attorney in the drug unit and asked if Kimball could be released one month early to act as a confidential informant in a case they were investigating. The head of the drug unit approved the deal, but it was not run by the head of the criminal division, the first assistant US attorney, or me. Given the nature of Kimball's criminal record, and the very limited concession involved, that wasn't unusual or surprising. Unfortunately, over the next several years Kimball had killed three people in drug related dealings in Boulder and was prosecuted by Garnett's predecessor. Garnett had become DA by the time Kimball was eventually sentenced to seventy years in prison as part of a plea bargain. His campaign ad featured the father of one of the female victims blaming me for her death.

I had never heard of Scott Kimball when *The Denver Post* ran a front-page Sunday headline story that was obviously planted by Garnett's campaign. In the article, he essentially called it the worst deal ever struck in the history of criminal justice and said it evidenced my detached management style, apparently inferring that if he was US attorney he would have been personally involved in the case and told the FBI that Kimball couldn't be released a month early. A few days later *The Denver Post* ran a great editorial defending me and criticizing Garnett. But the case became the lynchpin of his TV campaign.

Garnett put $125,000 of his own money in his campaign and spent about $375,000 on television. Luckily, I raised over $700,000 in my campaign and had $380,000 to wage a good counter TV campaign. My ad spent ten seconds citing press criticism of Garnett for his misleading ad and twenty seconds on a positive message. "Public safety will always be my highest priority," I said.

While Garnett always put on a polite and professional front, he became increasingly negative toward me throughout our ten formal debates. It appeared he was prepared to say anything to get elected. That had never been my style.

While some in the media played up the negative campaign against me and maintained it was a close race, our campaign's polling said otherwise. We polled the night before Garnett's ad began to run three weeks before the election. We were up by 15 percent. A week and a half later we were still up by 15 percent. His ad was not moving the numbers. As one of my advisors suggested, "Portraying John Suthers as soft on crime is not a formula for success."

We also ran a good campaign in other respects. The Starboard Group did my fundraising and hired Andrew Cole to manage the campaign. Andrew was a Regis College graduate with a master's from George Washington. He'd worked for a few Congressmen and was politically astute. We did a lot of retail campaigning at parades and on street corners. We also spent $20,000 to send a mailing to every unaffiliated voter in the key counties of Arapahoe, Adams, and Jefferson.

I got all the major newspaper endorsements except for the ultra-liberal *Boulder Daily Camera*. I was particularly heartened to know several newspapers that criticized my participation in the health care lawsuit, including *The Denver Post*, nevertheless endorsed me, saying I had done a good job as AG and my participation in the suit stemmed from sincere beliefs. Several of the newspapers praised me for being a lawyer first, and a politician second.

On November 2, 2010, I won overwhelmingly. I received 961,000 votes, the most ever in Colorado in a non-presidential election year. I carried fifty-four of sixty-four counties, including several traditional Democrat counties like Pueblo and Adams. We won 57 percent to 43 percent. While I tried hard not to personalize the opposition campaign, it made it a particularly satisfying win. Many years later, in May of 2021, Alec Garnett, who had become the Democrat Speaker of the House in Colorado, went out of his way to apologize to me for the campaign he'd run against me in 2010. "I'm embarrassed by it," he said. "I was very immature."

The 2010 election had been very successful for Republicans nationwide, with the GOP gaining control of the US House and gaining several governorships. Republicans had gained six attorney general positions. But while we had gained the Secretary of State and Treasurer offices in Colorado, we had lost both the governor's race and US Senate race. The "establishment" GOP candidate for governor, Scott McInnis, had imploded in a plagiarism scandal and the Republican nomination went to a laughably unqualified candidate. Denver Mayor John Hickenlooper was elected governor. In the Senate race our strongest candidate, former Lieutenant Governor Jane Norton, lost a close primary to Weld County DA Ken Buck, a Tea Party favorite. Buck got only 39 percent of the female vote in the general election and Democrat Michael Bennet won by a very narrow margin. Despite these developments, I had no regrets about my decision to remain as attorney general.

On the morning of January 11, 2010, a frigid day in Colorado, I stood on the west steps of the state capitol and, for the third and final time, took an oath to faithfully serve the citizens of Colorado as their attorney general. That afternoon my campaign paid for a catered lunch for all the employees of the AG's office. I thanked them for all the work they'd done to make me look good and to secure such a high level of public confidence in the office.

All This I Saw, and Part of It I Was

In the fall of 2010 the head of my State Services Section, Monica Marquez, applied for an opening on the Colorado Supreme Court. Monica was brilliant and fair-minded, and I was glad to publicly champion her for the job. Bill Ritter appointed her to the court. Because she was a Democrat and openly gay, my support raised some Republican eyebrows. But they were raised even higher when I selected her replacement to head the State Services Section.

I wasn't entirely happy with the first round of applicants for the job and wound up taking a bold step. Bernie Buescher had been a high-profile Democrat legislator from Grand Junction. When Mike Coffman resigned as secretary of state to assume a seat in Congress, Buescher was appointed to the job by Governor Ritter. As secretary of state, my office found Buescher, a lawyer, to be knowledgeable and easy to work with. When Buescher lost the 2010 secretary of state's race to Scott Gessler, I asked him to apply for the job as Deputy AG for State Services. He was clearly the best applicant. His appointment caused much consternation among Republicans. I thought he did a great job.

Other changes in the office included the appointment of David Blake, a former long-standing US Department of Justice employee, as Deputy AG for Legal Policy and Michael Dougherty, a former top manager in the Manhattan DA's office, as head of the Criminal Justice Section. Blake did a good job both lobbying the legislature and playing a key role in many important projects, including the implementation of Amendment 64, the legalization of marijuana in Colorado. Dougherty was a terrific prosecutor and would eventually leave to become the assistant DA in Jefferson County in January 2013 and subsequently became the district attorney in Boulder.

In many ways, my final term as Colorado's attorney general would be the most interesting and challenging. I had some seniority among the nation's AGs and had earned significant credibility in the National Association of Attorneys General. That led to the assumption of leadership positions in several very high-profile matters and to some fascinating opportunities.

When the states that challenged the constitutionality of certain aspects of President Obama's health care reform prevailed in the trial court, an executive committee of six AGs was formed to manage the case going forward. As one of the six, my office was instrumental in the hiring of Paul Clement to argue the case for the states in the Eleventh Circuit Court of Appeals and in the US Supreme Court. Clement had been the S.G. of the United States in the second George W. Bush administration and was generally regarded as one of the premier Supreme Court advocates. He clearly wanted to argue the case and agreed to do so for $250,000. The going rate was between one and two million dollars. Clement did an outstanding job.

The Eleventh Circuit found the individual mandate was an unconstitutional exercise of the commerce power in a 2-1 decision. The federal government petitioned for certiorari to the US Supreme Court. The states sought certiorari as to the Eleventh Circuit's holding that the Medicaid expansion was constitutional. It really wasn't until the US Supreme Court granted certiorari on both petitions and set the case for an unprecedented six hours of argument in March of 2012 that the legal intelligentsia had to acknowledge this was a historic constitutional confrontation.

On March 26, 27, and 28 of 2012, the court heard arguments on four issues: 1) Was the challenge to the individual mandate premature because the penalty was really a tax and could not be contested under the federal Anti-Injunction Act until it was imposed in 2014? 2) Was the mandate in the Patient Protection and Affordable Health Care Act that all Americans buy health insurance or pay a penalty a constitutional exercise of the commerce power? 3) If the mandate was unconstitutional, was it severable from the rest of the act or did the entire act fail? (The trial court had found the mandate unseverable and the entire act unconstitutional. The Eleventh Circuit found it severable.) 4) Was the way Medicaid was structured and expanded by the act so coercive to the states that it violated federalism?

As a member of the Executive Committee managing the health care lawsuit, I was privileged to be in the Supreme Court for what was now among the most memorable arguments in history. Seating in the court was so limited that the twenty-six plaintiff states were only given six seats. Some AGs managed to secure seats through other channels and there were about ten state AGs present for each of the four arguments.

The atmosphere around the Supreme Court each day was electric. Thousands of people protested in front of the court and on both sides of the issue (and miscellaneous other issues). Thousands of national media people were present, despite the fact only a couple dozen would get inside the courtroom. The court chambers were packed for each of the four sessions with US Senators, cabinet members, and the nation's most renowned lawyers and law professors.

At the hearing on March 26th, it appeared none of the nine justices had any appetite to call the mandate a tax and avoid ruling for another two years. Both the conservative and liberal members of the court commented that Congress had justified the mandate as an exercise of the commerce power and that the president said it wasn't a tax. Justice Ginsburg commented that the purpose of the mandate was not to raise revenue but rather coerce conduct, and that therefore, it was a penalty and not a tax. As we all exited the court that day, I heard one noted constitutional law professor say to another, "at least we know one thing—they won't find the mandate a tax." Little did he know.

The tension in the court was palpable on Tuesday, March 27th when the court heard arguments on the constitutionality of the mandate. The audience hung on every word. The US solicitor general, Donald Verrilli, Jr., had no sooner started his argument than Justice Kennedy, who many perceived to be a swing vote, zeroed in on the essence of the states' argument. "The Constitution gives the federal government the right to *regulate* commerce," he conceded, "but does it give the government the ability to *create* commerce by forcing Americans to buy a product or service? If we rule that it does, aren't we fundamentally changing the nature of the relationship between the federal government and the individual?" he asked. Justice Scalia reiterated the iconic question in the case, "Can the government mandate you to buy broccoli, because it's good for your health, and penalize you if you don't?" There was much discussion about whether there was a limiting principle that assured Americans the government won't try to solve a variety of national problems by mandating them to buy a product or service. As in the lower courts, the federal government had a tough time answering the question.

Paul Clement, arguing for the states, was nothing short of brilliant. Lawyers on both sides conceded that point. The March 28th argument about the constitutionality of the Medicaid expansion was particularly revealing. The states had not prevailed on that issue in the lower courts, but it was clear after Clement's argument that the Supreme Court was not dismissing it.

All the AGs who were plaintiffs in the case were heartened by the arguments. The court was clearly focusing on the issues as we had framed them, and they were giving them serious consideration.

After each session of the court, I walked down the front steps of the Supreme Court into a throng of TV, radio, and newspaper reporters. Each day I did a dozen or more interviews for national and Colorado media outlets. On the afternoon following the individual mandate argument, I had a short and friendly radio debate about the issue with Walter Dellinger, a Duke law professor who was the former US solicitor general under Bill Clinton. Several million people heard it on *National Public Radio*.

Between the March 2012 arguments and the issuance of the opinion on the last Thursday in June, there was much speculation about the result. There were lots of predictions, but none I heard proved accurate. The decision was surprising given the course of the arguments. In an opinion written by Chief Justice Roberts, a majority of five justices sided with the states and found the individual mandate unconstitutional under the commerce clause. The court found that the commerce power did not allow the government to punish economic inactivity and force citizens to buy a product or service. But somewhat shockingly, Roberts joined with the four liberals on the court to uphold the mandate as an exercise of the taxing power. It was a tax, even though Congress said it wasn't, but because Congress did not call it a tax, the Anti-Injunction Act didn't apply, and the decision did not have to be delayed until the tax was imposed in 2014. A *very* curious result.

To the surprise of many, the court also found by a vote of 7-2 that the Medicaid expansion and its all-or-nothing dictate to the states was unconstitutionally coercive. So, the bottom line was the states had prevailed on both the claims in our case but had lost the war in that the mandate had been upheld. Many conservative commentators, including George Will and Charles Krauthammer, called the case a great victory for federalism because of its limitations on the commerce power and the spending power. They speculated that there would not likely be future mandates of this nature, because Americans would be more resistive to exercises of the taxing power than exercises of the commerce power. Given that the case essentially held that Congress could now mandate Americans to buy broccoli and tax them if they didn't, I came slowly to calling it a victory. Only time would reveal the significance of the case. And time has brought me to the conclusion that the court's refusal to expand the commerce clause to include government mandates to purchase a product and for the first time, strike down a coercive federal spending program were, in fact, significant victories for federalism.

Congress subsequently eliminated the mandatory penalty or "tax" for failure to purchase health insurance. That caused Texas and many other states to once again challenge the mandate to purchase insurance, because it could no longer be justified as an exercise of the taxing power. In a 2021 opinion, the Supreme Court, by a 7-2 vote, adroitly sidestepped the issue by holding that without a penalty for non-compliance, the mandate was toothless and could not be enforced by the government. Therefore, the residents of the plaintiff states suffered no injury and had no standing to contest the law. While Democrats hailed it as a victory for Obamacare, the legally sophisticated understood the decision left intact the court's earlier determination that Congress could not use the commerce power to force Americans to buy a particular product or service. I found that consoling.

In late 2010, a new scandal confronted the nation's largest banks. Bank of America, Citibank, J.P. Morgan Chase, Wells Fargo, and Ally handled the servicing of about 62 percent of the nation's mortgages. In the course of court cases in which people were challenging the foreclosure of their mortgages, it became apparent that there was serious misconduct by the banks in the servicing and foreclosure of mortgages. Many foreclosure documents, including affidavits filed with courts, were being "robo-signed." In other words, the representations to the court that files and documents, including assignments of loans, had actually been reviewed and were in good order were false. Further, many loans were being "dual tracked" by the banks. While one part of the bank was negotiating a modification of the loan, another part was going full speed ahead on a foreclosure. My office had over a hundred well-documented complaints about dual tracking. The banks were also miscalculating fees and improperly forcing borrowers to buy mortgage insurance from them. When the state AGs opened a nationwide investigation, I was named to a six-person executive committee to negotiate with the banks. I traveled to Washington a half dozen times, but Andrew McCallin, a first assistant attorney general in the Consumer Protection Section of my office, spent the better part of a year in the very difficult negotiations.

There were memorable moments. At one point at the settlement table, the banks made an offer to settle for $5 billion. I instinctively responded that I found the offer so inadequate as to be insulting. That evening, as I lay in my hotel bed, I thought to myself, *when I was in law school, did I ever envision calling a $5 billion settlement offer insulting?* Obviously not.

The executive committee eventually negotiated a settlement with the five banks worth $25 billion. Twenty billion dollars would be in the form of credits for loan forgiveness, modifications, principal reductions, "cash for keys," etc. Because the credits were not dollar for dollar, the actual credits were approximately $50 billion. Five billion dollars would be cash payments to aggrieved borrowers and to the states. Colorado eventually got over $450 million in credits and $52 million in hard cash. The banks would also have to conform to stringent servicing standards going forward. I thought the settlement was a good deal for the states for several reasons. Federally chartered banks were largely exempt from state regulation at that time and it was unlikely states could fare nearly as well in litigation. Further, we had negotiated a limited release, and the states would still be able to proceed against the banks for various non-servicing misconduct. But it fell to me, as a Republican member of the executive committee, to convince other Republican AGs to join the settlement. That was a tall order given the public criticism of settlement negotiations by some of them. I held group and individual phone conferences with all the Republicans. I worked closely with HUD (Housing and Urban Development) Secretary Shaun Donovan and Associate US Attorney General Tom Perrelli in making the case to my colleagues. Iowa AG Tom Miller, who had spearheaded much of the negotiations, played a similar role with the Democrats. As the deadline to sign on to the settlement came closer, I felt a bit like a college football coach at recruitment time. I had verbal commitments that I was trying to convert to letters of intent. As it turned out I convinced twenty-four of twenty-five Republicans to sign on and a total of forty-nine state AGs approved the deal. Only Scott Pruitt, the Oklahoma attorney general, who would subsequently become EPA director under President Trump and resign after allegations of fiscal impropriety, refused to join the settlement.

On February 9, 2012, I joined US Attorney General Eric Holder, HUD Secretary Donovan, and several of my AG colleagues at the US Department of Justice to announce the settlement. A White House press conference with President Obama followed. In my remarks I commented that it was the most satisfying cooperative effort I'd had with federal law enforcement, largely because of the incredible efforts of Donovan and Perrelli.

I met privately with Colorado Governor John Hickenlooper and the legislative Joint Budget Committee well in advance of the settlement and told them that the $52 million payment to Colorado should go for further relief to homeowners and not to the cash-hungry general fund. They were cooperative and joined in an effort to find the most effective way to utilize the money. Two public hearings were held before I announced how the money would be distributed. Several newspapers, including *The Denver Post*, praised the process and the result.

In the summer of 2012, at the National Association of Attorneys General meeting in Anchorage, Alaska, I was shocked but pleased to be awarded the Kelley-Wyman Award, the highest annual award given by NAAG to the state attorney general who had done the most to further the work of the AGs. It's essentially a most valuable player award selected by peers and I was genuinely touched by it. Only about 1 percent of people who serve as state attorney general are so honored. No doubt my work on the mortgage servicing settlement, in addition to my NAAG Executive Committee work, played a big part in the selection by my peers.

Another major case in Colorado spanned almost my entire tenure as attorney general. In 1876 when Colorado became a state, Congress was requiring all territories who sought to become a state to create a public school system as a condition of statehood. Accordingly, the original Colorado Constitution had a two-sentence paragraph declaring the state would have a "thorough and uniform system of gratuitous public education." No documentation remains to indicate what was meant by thorough and uniform. Only the second sentence in the paragraph gave any clue. It said there should be at least one school in every school district and all students should attend for at least three months a year. The clause certainly didn't refer to state funding, because from the outset public school funding was accomplished through local property taxes. Until 1950, there were no state tax dollars involved in public education. As late as 1993, 65 percent of public school funding was from local taxes and the remainder from state appropriation. But by 2005, the state was funding 65 percent and local property taxes, 35 percent. In fact, 45 percent of the state general fund was going to K-12 schools. Nevertheless, in 2005 rural public school students brought suit against the state alleging that their schools were underfunded and they were being deprived of a thorough and uniform public school system. The case of *Lobato v. Colorado* would prove highly contentious.

In defending the state, my office asserted that what constituted a thorough and uniform public education system was a non-justiciable political question to be determined by the Colorado legislature and voters of the state, not by the courts. We prevailed in the trial court and the Colorado Court of Appeals. But in a 4-3 decision, with a vigorous dissent, the Colorado Supreme Court said the case *was* justiciable and remanded it for trial. A five-week trial was held in August and September of 2011. It was largely a battle of experts. The bias of the trial judge was thinly disguised. She issued an order that was virtually verbatim to one proffered by the plaintiffs. She found the Colorado public education system unconstitutionally underfunded and each and every school district in the state *unconscionably* underfunded. She agreed with the plaintiffs that K-12 spending should be essentially doubled from its current level of $3.2 billion per year. That would be almost 90 percent of the state's general fund. In Colorado, under the state's TABOR, only the voters can raise taxes and in November of 2011, they had once again overwhelmingly refused to increase state taxes for K-12 schools. My office once again appealed the case to the State Supreme Court with the prospect of a constitutional crisis if the court affirmed the trial court. The matter was once again argued before the court on March 7, 2013, and in late May, the Supreme Court finally resolved the matter. The court reversed the trial court and held 4-2 that the evidence in the trial showed the current school financing system was rationally related to the thorough and uniform funding requirement. The state was thereby saved from decades of court interference with the public school system that several other states have endured.

The Criminal Justice Section of the office continued to do great work. In 2011, upon referral from the State Department of Revenue, we secured an indictment against Douglas Bruce, the most high-profile anti-tax proponent in Colorado. Bruce had authored the TABOR that the voters had put into the state constitution in 1992. Bruce was charged with evading income taxes and failing to file tax returns. He spurned numerous chances to resolve the case short of trial and wound up being convicted by a jury of several felonies. He was sentenced to six months in jail and six years of probation. He subsequently violated the probation and was sentenced to prison.

We were appointed by the governor to prosecute Patrick Sullivan, the retired sheriff of Arapahoe County. Sullivan had been one of the state's highest profile and most flamboyant lawmen. After his retirement, he had pursued a clandestine lifestyle that included trading methamphetamine for sex with younger men. He wound up pleading guilty to possession of meth and soliciting prostitution. When he violated his probation, he was sent to prison.

In 2010 my office, in conjunction with the Denver District Attorney's Office, applied for and received a grant from the Department of Justice for a DNA exoneration project in which we reviewed cases where inmates maintained their innocence and DNA testing was not available at the time of their conviction. We were the only prosecution agencies to receive such a grant. In 2012 that process resulted in the exoneration of Robert Dewey. He had been convicted of murder in Grand Junction sixteen years earlier. The DNA testing pointed to another individual that was incarcerated for another murder. Frankly, no law enforcement or prosecutorial misconduct had been involved. Lots of circumstantial evidence pointed to Dewey. This was a sobering but very satisfying experience for a veteran prosecutor like me. Prosecutors should be as zealous to exonerate the innocent as they are to convict the guilty, and DNA is a very valuable tool in that regard. In the 2013 legislative session I worked with the legislature to pass a bill providing for compensation of wrongfully convicted defendants.

In October of 2011, I was asked by the National Association of Attorneys General to travel to St. Petersburg, Russia to speak to Russian prosecutors and judges about how the United States dealt with hate crimes. Hate crimes, particularly by skinhead groups, had become a big problem in Russia. A rule of law organization in the country, Citizen's Watch, was concerned that the hate crime problem be dealt with without violating free speech rights and wanted me to promote the American approach to the problem. It was a fascinating experience, but I came away believing that Russia had largely squandered all the potential it had for democratization after the revolution of the early 1990s. Subsequent events confirmed my impressions. However, I greatly enjoyed taking in the sights and the incredible history of St. Petersburg.

In the spring of 2006, a political supporter of mine in Denver had invited me to a dinner with Mitt Romney, who had recently stepped down as Governor of Massachusetts. Romney told me at the dinner he was considering running for president in 2008 and was meeting with political leaders throughout the country. I was very impressed with Romney as a person and with his record of accomplishments, and when he called me a few months later to ask for my support in a presidential bid, I gladly signed on. I worked hard for Romney in Colorado and spent considerable time with him on campaign visits. He overwhelmingly won the Republican caucuses in the state in March of 2008, but he eventually lost the party's nomination to John McCain. I was the only Republican AG to actively support Romney throughout the primary.

When Romney ran for president in 2012, I was once again a Colorado honorary co-chair for the campaign. This time I helped convince most of the Republican AGs in the country to join the effort early on. I was a Romney delegate to the Republican National Convention in Tampa. After he won the nomination, I introduced Romney at several campaign events in Colorado, including to a crowd of 24,000 three days before the election. I was also a guest of the campaign at the first presidential debate in Denver, which appeared at the time to swing the momentum to Romney. Colorado and some national media speculated I might be a possible candidate for US attorney general in a Romney administration. My conversations with his top advisors led me to believe a top job in the Department of Justice was a possibility. The liberal *Huffington Post* even took the time to do a four-part hatchet job on why I wasn't a good choice for attorney general. It was comical in its lack of sophistication and all the material appeared to come straight out of my 2010 opponent's campaign brochure. I have reason to believe the articles were done at the behest of a company that, because of its economic interests, was angry about my opposition to marijuana legalization in Colorado and my criticism of their commercial website as a vehicle for sex trafficking of minors. But all the speculation went for naught when Romney lost a tight race to Barack Obama. I was particularly disappointed that Colorado went for Obama in 2012. I believe Mitt Romney would have been an excellent president. The fact a man of his caliber did not get elected president and Donald Trump got elected four years later struck me as the ultimate confirmation that in politics the best man does *not* always win.

In my tenure as Colorado attorney general, I had the privilege of representing and working with three Colorado governors. I had a good working relationship with all of them. But unlike Bill Owens and Bill Ritter, who I had worked with extensively before I was their attorney, I had no such prior history with John Hickenlooper. When he was Denver Mayor and I was AG, we had some contact in regard to the development of projects along the South Platte River funded by recoveries in the Rocky Mountain Arsenal litigation and had conversations about the settlement of litigation between the state and Denver regarding the Lowry Landfill. As soon as he took office, I told him the same thing I told Owens and Ritter. Because I was his attorney and needed his trust and confidence, I assured him I would not run against him if he sought reelection. He and his top staff obviously believed me, and we had a very constructive relationship. In many ways he was the best client. He had been a brew pub entrepreneur and not a lawyer and tended to sincerely seek out legal advice and follow it. In the first two years we worked together, I believe my office was of considerable help to him in working through several problems including dealing with the Occupy Denver protestors that had camped on state land in front of the capitol, finding a legal way for the state to get compensation above liability caps to victims of the North Fork Fire that was caused by lack of oversight of a controlled burn by state foresters, and quelling several novel ideas by the legislature that were legally dubious. I also ingratiated myself to Hickenlooper by letting his office be very involved in the process of determining how $52 million of settlement money in the mortgage servicing litigation would be spent in the state. He was able to take considerable credit for the assistance it provided. He was publicly very complimentary of me.

Our strongest differences of opinion tended to center around criminal justice issues. He had no background in the area and had more liberal views than I on issues such as prosecution of violent juveniles as adults, solitary confinement of dangerous inmates, and the death penalty. Hickenlooper was an optimist and "hail fellow, well met" and seemed to be very uncomfortable confronting the existence of evil in society. This discomfort culminated in his granting a reprieve to a death row inmate, Nathan Dunlap, who had executed four fellow employees at a pizza restaurant twenty years earlier. I was very public in my severe criticism of the decision.

Governor Hickenlooper had a self-deprecating sense of humor and, in combination with his very informal dress (he rarely wore a tie) and "aw-shucks" demeanor (he relished the moniker of "Hick" which the press gave him), he had a very sincere and appealing presence. But make no mistake about it. He was a very savvy politician. As the 2014 election approached, he failed to support several measures (including the first pay raise in twenty years for the attorney general) because he was averse to the political risk. Hickenlooper understood business and was very supportive of it. His resulting popularity with the Denver business community was much more politically valuable than whatever lack of support it caused on the far left of his own party. Because I got to personally like Hickenlooper, I was saddened when he and his wife, Helen Thorpe, separated in the summer of 2012. Janet and I had socialized with them on a couple of occasions. The governor remarried a few years later, and Janet and I enjoyed getting to know his new wife, Robin.

The governor and I not only liked each other, we trusted each other. I was touched when he declared October 18, 2014, my sixty-third birthday, John Suthers Day in Colorado. My good working relationship with Governor Hickenlooper would later pay large dividends during his second term and my first as mayor of Colorado Springs and when he was elected to the US Senate in 2020.

In January of 2012, the Colorado Attorney General's Office moved a block to the newly constructed Ralph L. Carr Colorado Judicial Center. Over the course of thirty-eight years the office grew to occupy the entire State Services Building and had run out of room. The State Services Building was also inadequate from a technological standpoint. As providence would have it, the Colorado Supreme Court had similar issues and was looking to build a new courthouse and office complex. They needed an anchor tenant such as the AG's office to make the office building financially viable. The timing was perfect, and we agreed to take over five of the twelve floors in the office building. I commented to AG employees and the public at large that the move marked the start of a new chapter in the 150-year history of the Colorado Attorney General's Office. It was a great morale boost for AG employees. It also meant a beautiful new office for me which included a private bathroom, something I had missed since my days as US attorney.

Office morale was also enhanced in July of 2013 when AG employees got a substantial salary raise, their first in five years, as Colorado's budget benefited from an improving economy. Lawyers in the office got a very large boost, bringing them in line with a salary survey of public law offices in the Denver Metro area. Only the elected AG didn't get a raise.

In early March of 2013, Jack Finlaw, Governor Hickenlooper's Chief Legal Counsel, informed me that Homaidan Al-Turki, the Colorado inmate whose conviction in 2006 had resulted in my going to Saudi Arabia to meet with the King and other officials, was seeking to transfer his sentence to Saudi Arabia under an international treaty. He said lawyers and political consultants hired by the Saudi government had been heavily lobbying the governor's office and he thought the executive director of the Colorado Department of Corrections, Tom Clements, was inclined to grant the transfer. I strongly suggested Clements should speak with me, the DA who tried the case, and the US attorney before making a final decision. Clements did so. The US attorney and the FBI met with Clements to discuss classified information the Bureau possessed. *The Denver Post* ran an editorial objecting to any transfer, apparently at the behest of the DA that tried the case. I met with Clements in my office on March 11th. I gave him the history of the case and told him that on the basis of my observations about the influence of Al-Turki's family in Saudi Arabia, I suspected he would be treated very favorably by the Saudi government. We also discussed at length the fact that Al-Turki had never acknowledged responsibility for his crime and had refused to enter a sex offender treatment program, despite the fact that it could be made culturally sensitive for Muslim inmates.

On Wednesday, March 13, 2013, Clements had a letter delivered to Al-Turki denying his transfer request. The next morning, I got a phone call from the Saudi ambassador to the US, Adel al-Jubeir. He expressed disappointment at the denial of the transfer and asked my thoughts. I told him I thought Al-Turki needed to acknowledge his responsibility and complete a sex offender treatment program. He said he would inform Al-Turki and his family.

At 8:35 p.m. on Tuesday night, March 19, 2013, Tom Clements answered the doorbell at his home north of Colorado Springs and was shot twice, dying almost instantly. Several days later a white supremacist gang member, Evan Ebel, who had recently been released from prison in Colorado, was killed in a shootout with police in Texas. It was quickly determined by ballistics testing that Ebel's gun was used to kill Clements. It was also determined that on the Sunday before Clements's murder, Ebel had murdered a Domino's Pizza delivery man and taken his uniform shirt and hat. The uniform and a pizza box were found in his car and had apparently been used when Ebel went to Clements's door.

Police suspected Ebel had been directed by another person to kill Clements and investigated whether Al-Turki could have been involved. Several circumstances fueled their suspicions, including the fact Al-Turki had been arrested by an FBI agent who used a pizza delivery disguise to lure him to the door and that Ebel had spent time in the same prison cell block as Al-Turki.

I was in Mexico for a meeting with the Mexico attorney general on the night of Clements's murder. I received a call at 8:55 p.m.

(twenty minutes after the murder) from Jim Davis, the head of the Colorado Department of Public Safety and ex-FBI special agent in charge in Denver. He was well aware of my history with the Al-Turki case. Within thirty minutes, Janet was escorted by local police from our home in Colorado Springs and spent the night at a friend's house under police protection. I caught a 6 a.m. flight from Mexico City and was back in Colorado on Wednesday morning.

Prior to Clements's murder, I had a security detail only in response to specific threats or at particularly contentious public appearances. But after his assassination, that changed dramatically. I was under 24/7 protection for about a month and the level of my security concerns was significantly elevated for the remainder of my tenure as attorney general. No one other than Ebel was ever formally implicated in Clements's murder.

The 2013 legislative session was a particularly difficult one for conservatives and for law enforcement. The Democrats had comfortable margins in both the House and Senate and a very liberal agenda was the result. They passed gun control measures and other controversial legislation that I did not agree with but was legally obligated to defend. The gun control measures, a limit of fifteen rounds in a magazine and universal background checks, proved sufficiently controversial that two Democrat state senators were recalled and a third resigned to avoid the possibility. My office defended the gun control laws in a trial before a federal district court judge, and she upheld the laws in a June 2014 decision. The saving grace of the 2013 session for my office was the passage of a bill mandating reporting of physical abuse or financial exploitation of persons over seventy years of age. People in medical and financial positions of trust were required to report the suspected abuse. The bill passed after two previous unsuccessful attempts. Prior to 2013 Colorado was only one of three states that did not have mandatory reporting of elder abuse. My office played an important role in public education efforts about the elder abuse law.

In 2013 my Consumer Protection Section filed a suit against Standard & Poor's (S&P), an investment rating service. S&P's A+ rating of securitized mortgages had played an important part in the financial collapse that had signaled the beginning of a deep recession five years earlier. The A+ rating was important because many institutional investors, including governmental entities and pension funds, could not invest in anything with a lower rating. S&P's represented in its public documents that its rating of investments was wholly objective and uninfluenced by financial considerations. But whistleblowers had alleged otherwise, contending it liberalized its rating criteria in order to retain market share in the rapidly growing area of mortgage securitization. We alleged S&P's public representations of objectivity constituted false advertising under the Colorado Consumer Protection Act. Standard and Poor's eventually settled with several states for a billion dollars, with Colorado receiving a large share.

In the summer of 2013, our antitrust case against Apple and several book publishers went to trial in federal court in Manhattan. The US Department of Justice and several states, including Colorado, alleged that the defendants had engaged in a price fixing conspiracy that caused the price of e-books to rise significantly. Amazon had a monopoly on e-books for several years and had used a pricing model that kept the price of e-books low (usually $9.99) to encourage sale of the e-book reader Kindle. When Apple launched an e-book reader, its chairman, Steve Jobs, didn't like the pricing model Amazon used and was determined to change it. Jobs was dying of cancer and was impatient. He called all the book publishers together and convinced them to use a pricing model that meant more money for all of them. But it could only work if they all forced Amazon to use the same model by otherwise refusing to do business with them. As a result, the price of all e-books rose immediately. Several book publishers settled before trial. At the trial, the Department of Justice and the states presented overwhelming evidence of the conspiracy. Jobs, who had died in the interim, had essentially confessed to the scheme to his biographer. The district court found an antitrust violation occurred. The decision was upheld on appeal. The states sought and secured substantial refunds for e-book users who had been victimized by the price fixing conspiracy.

Advocates of greater government spending in Colorado had long been frustrated with the TABOR, which the voters had put in the state's constitution in 1992. TABOR required a vote of the people before taxes could be raised and public school advocates and others felt state spending on government services was too low. In 2012 a group of current and former legislators, almost all Democrats, brought a very creative lawsuit. They alleged that TABOR violated Article IV, Section 4 of the US Constitution, which provided that "The United States shall guarantee to every state in the union a republican form of government." The plaintiffs alleged in federal court that a republican form of government required that legislative bodies have the power to raise and appropriate revenue as required to meet governmental needs and that Colorado voters had unconstitutionally deprived its legislature of this power.

The AG's office responded that the essential elements of a republican form of government were 1) ultimate power in the people, either directly or indirectly, 2) an accountable executive, and 3) the rule of law. We cited case law indicating challenges to the initiative process were political questions, not appropriate for judicial resolution. The plaintiffs were temporarily gleeful when a federal trial court and panel of the Tenth Circuit Court of Appeals denied our motion to dismiss the case. The case wasn't finally decided until December of 2021. After years of wrangling about jurisdictional issues, the Tenth Circuit Court of Appeals finally ruled on the merits, finding that voters giving themselves the right to vote on tax increases did not violate the constitutional requirement that states have a republican form of government. It was the result I was very confident would occur. It just took much longer than I expected to reach the merits of the case.

In early 2014 my chief deputy, Cynthia Coffman, announced she would run for attorney general to replace me when I was term limited out of office in January 2015. She initially had a Republican opponent, but his support dissipated after the State Republican Assembly in April 2014. In the general election, she faced Don Quick, who had been a former district attorney in Adams and Broomfield Counties and had been chief deputy attorney general in the last few years of Ken Salazar's administration. Quick was well qualified and it was a contentious race. But Cynthia ultimately prevailed by a large margin. While she had run a good campaign, I honestly believe her success also stemmed from the fact that the citizens of Colorado had come to have a very favorable view of the AG's office. Coffman served only one term as AG. Veterans of the office indicated to me that she struggled in the top role. She ran for governor in 2018 and failed to make the Republican primary ballot.

By 2014, my tenth and final year as attorney general, the office had grown to 450 employees, including 275 attorneys. We had a $69 million annual budget, but over the last ten years we'd recovered over $5 billion for the people of Colorado. I had traveled about 250,000 miles around Colorado during the last decade and given about 2,500 speeches. Having practiced law for thirty-seven years and managed three of Colorado's largest public law offices, I'd had the chance to influence a lot of lawyers. Well over 5 percent of Colorado's 22,000 practicing attorneys had worked for me at one time or another and about 100 of them had or would become judges or elected public officials. A half dozen were elected district attorney in various places in Colorado and one was appointed US attorney. Three women who worked for me in the Attorney General's Office, Allison Eid, Monica Marquez, and Maria Berkenkotter were appointed to the state Supreme Court. Eid subsequently was appointed by President Trump to the Tenth Circuit Court of Appeals. My SG, Dan Domenico, was appointed a federal district court judge. He joined four of my former US Attorney's Office employees on the federal bench. My top assistant DA, Jeanne Smith, had succeeded me as district attorney and my chief deputy attorney general, Cynthia Coffman, had succeeded me as attorney general. I was proud of the fact that lawyers who worked for me had made such an impact on the profession.

As my tenure as Colorado attorney general concluded, I was convinced I had accomplished my principal objective. The office was better than when I had taken over its management ten years earlier. Not only was it respected by the citizens of the state, but it was also viewed as an excellent public law office on the national level.

In the course of my decade as attorney general, I had worked with dozens of other state attorneys general. Many of them became governors, US Senators, and federal agency heads. In fact, several spent their entire tenure as AG positioning for higher office. Others, the ones I admired most, realized what an important job they had and their highest allegiance was to the law, even if that adversely affected their chance for reelection or another elected office. I established some enduring friendships with those I admired, including Lawrence Wasden from Idaho and Wayne Stenejhem from North Dakota.

The various personalities I encountered have also left me with some great stories. At meetings of the National Association of Attorneys General the AGs sat around a large rectangular space in alphabetic order according to state. That means I sat next to the attorney general from California. So for four years I sat next to Jerry Brown, who served twice as governor of California and had a well-earned nickname of "Governor Moonbeam." He had what I suggested was adult attention deficit disorder. And for the next four years I sat next to Kamala Harris. We also traveled to Mexico together in an AG delegation. We were on different planets politically, but I found her cordial, charming, and smart. But she had acquired a reputation for being difficult to work with and for.

She was also very ambitious. An AG colleague prophetically suggested she was intent on being the first woman president of the United States. Several AGs had outsized personalities. In many respects it's the people I've met along the way that have made my career so interesting.

As the November 2014 elections approached, there was a lot of speculation about whether I would seek another office. As Governor Hickenlooper's popularity waned after his reprieve of a death row inmate, I received much encouragement to run for governor. Dozens of people contacted me to make the case. I was given two polls showing me statistically tied with the incumbent governor. I was contacted by emissaries of a few wealthy Republicans in Colorado and across the country who were prepared to do what it takes financially to help me succeed in a governor's race. But, as previously indicated, I had long since resolved that an attorney general could not run against his client, an incumbent governor, and avoid an appearance of impropriety. Once again, my lawyerly instincts overcame any political ambition. At this point I also had no interest in pursuing a legislative position, including a Congressional or US Senate seat. My lengthy tenure in the executive branch, making decisions and acting quickly and decisively, had helped to convince me I would not enjoy the legislative process. And the dysfunction of the US Congress made it wholly unappealing to me. So, I began to consider the other options available to me and to assess how each of these options would help or hinder me in reaching my goal of being a good ancestor.

Chapter XIX
The Mayor

During the year leading up to the end of my decade-long tenure as Colorado attorney general in January of 2015, I was contacted by approximately twenty law firms who asked me to consider joining their firm. I narrowed the list and met with four national or regional firms who either had an office in Colorado Springs or were willing to open one if I joined their firm. Janet and I had decided that after fourteen years working in Denver, while still residing in Colorado Springs, it was time to shorten my commute and return my full focus to the hometown I loved. But I wanted to be part of a large national or regional firm so I could take advantage of the many state and national relationships I had developed during my legal career. All the firms made very enticing offers.

But as tempting as a lucrative private practice would be, another intriguing public service opportunity presented itself. In 2010 the voters of Colorado Springs had decided to move from a council/manager form of government to a strong mayor. They had apparently become convinced that the city, which was then the forty-second largest in America, needed greater leadership in establishing and pursing its priorities and economic development ambitions. The first strong mayor elected in 2011, Steve Bach, had been a successful marketing executive and real estate broker, but had no previous political experience. He also had a less than diplomatic personality. Over the next few years his repeated clashes with the city council, which also had some very problematic personalities, led to a widely held perception that city hall was dysfunctional. The city failed to address serious infrastructure problems, particularly deteriorating roads and stormwater systems. It was widely believed that Mayor Bach's opposition to a proposed stormwater fix through a property fee assessment, which the council had supported, led to its narrow defeat by voters. Further, the city's economy continued to lag behind most of Colorado. There had been little or no job or wage growth over the previous decade. As Janet and I watched with dismay as Colorado Springs struggled, we began to pay more attention to suggestions from various community members that I consider running for mayor in April of 2015.

By the summer of 2014, as I was being heavily courted by law firms, and there was increasing public speculation about a possible mayoral run, I resolved to make a decision by Labor Day. I thought long and hard about my options and Janet and I had many discussions about it. She understood that being the mayor's wife would involve a great time commitment on her part. I also took the time to do some research about how mayors were succeeding in making transformational changes to their cities. Much was being written about the way local governments were positively impacting the quality of life of citizens in a way that state and federal governments were incapable of doing. In the final analysis, our love for Colorado Springs and desire to see it succeed triumphed over financial considerations. As it had several times before, public service seemed like the better path to becoming a good ancestor. On September 2, 2014, the day after Labor Day, I indicated to the press that I would run for mayor of Colorado Springs, although I would not formally kick off a campaign until January, after I left the Attorney General's Office.

While my announcement generated considerable press attention, it certainly didn't deter other candidates from getting into the race. I was invited to breakfast on Labor Day morning by Amy Lathen, an engaging and capable county commissioner. She was clearly trying to talk me out of running. She told me running for mayor was her destiny. When I told her I'd probably announce the next day, the breakfast ended abruptly, and she sent out a press release that afternoon announcing her candidacy. A month or so later, a well-respected former mayor, Mary Lou Makepeace, announced her candidacy. She indicated that the stars were aligned for a successful campaign. The most outspoken and controversial city councilman, Joel Miller, announced he was resigning from city council to run for mayor, declaring himself the only true conservative in the race. Two other less-known candidates also announced, rounding out a six-person field.

My entry into the race was probably a significant deterrent to the incumbent mayor, Steve Bach, seeking a second term. Bach knew I would secure a great deal of support from the business community. After I raised a substantial amount of money in October and November, he announced in December he would not run for reelection. The other three viable candidates formally kicked off their campaigns before Christmas of 2014. Our decision to wait until January proved to be a good one. By the time I stood before 300 friends and volunteers on January 17th, we had already raised $150,000 and the community was ready to focus on the mayoral race.

Although the election was a non-partisan one, the first phase of it certainly had the feel of a Republican primary. Mary Lou Makepeace was the only left-of-center candidate and could be confident of securing at least 20-30 percent of the vote. The three right-of-center candidates, including myself, would fight for the rest. What made things very interesting from a strategic point of view is that Colorado Springs had a runoff system for mayoral elections. If no candidate received more than 50 percent of the vote on April 7th, the two top finishers would compete in a runoff on May 19th. With six candidates it seemed unlikely anyone would garner 50 percent of the votes, so everyone geared their campaigns to make the runoff. We set our goal to be the top vote getter in the first round and beat Makepeace in the runoff.

Lathen and Miller attempted to position themselves to the right of me. Miller took on the position of the anti-establishment candidate. He was aided by Douglas Bruce, an anti-tax activist who was hell bent on defeating me because my AG's office had convicted him of tax evasion, and by Dudley Brown, a radical pro-gun activist who was angry that I, as attorney general, had successfully defended gun laws passed by the Colorado legislature. Both spent a significant amount of money on vindictive mailings and robocalls.

Throughout the campaign, I hammered on three priorities I would pursue as mayor: 1) Change the political climate in the city by creating a collaborative relationship between the mayor and city council and between Colorado Springs and other governmental entities in the Pikes Peak region. 2) Invest in the city's critical public infrastructure, particularly roads and stormwater systems. 3) Aggressively promote new job creation. These were issues that had held the city back over the past decade and our campaign polling showed the priorities resonated with city residents.

The enthusiasm of the business community and the public at large for my candidacy was reflected by the fact we raised over $450,000, more than my opponents combined. The Starboard Group, who managed my successful attorney general campaigns, also managed the mayoral campaign. Kitt Smith, a Starboard employee from Colorado Springs, served as campaign manager. A friend, Katie Lally, was deputy campaign manager and a Republican activist, Karla Heard-Price, was the volunteer coordinator. Because everyone's name began with K, I called them my Special K Team. We had over forty neighborhood meet and greets and spent over $250,000 on radio and TV ads. We also sent at least one mailing to all eligible voters.

After a dozen debates, including two on prime-time television, the voters had a month to return their mail-in ballots. A poll my campaign commissioned showed us getting close to 40 percent of the votes with Makepeace a solid second with 30 percent. In fact, we garnered 46 percent of the vote and Makepeace got 23 percent. Joel Miller finished with 16 percent and Amy Lathen finished fourth with 13 percent.

The runoff election also went according to plan. Two more television debates with Mary Lou Makepeace went very well. I knew she was getting desperate when she supported legalizing recreational use of marijuana as a means of paying for road repairs. "Pot for potholes" became her mantra. We continued saturation-level radio and TV ads. Our poll three weeks before the election showed us leading 57-32 percent with 11 percent undecided. So we were delighted to win by an even larger landslide, 68-32 percent.

At an enthusiastic victory party at a downtown hotel, I told the crowd of over 300 that the election had special significance for me. My adoptive parents chose to move from Detroit to Colorado Springs after World War II because they loved the beauty of the place. In the short time I had with them before they died, they instilled in me their love for Colorado Springs. I told the crowd: "If my parents were alive today, I hope they would be proud of what Colorado Springs has become, and I'm very confident they would be pleased that tonight their son was elected mayor of this great city."

Between the election and my swearing in as mayor, I met with outgoing mayor Steve Bach. He showed me a graph that plotted city revenue and expenses over the last ten years and predicted the city would go broke (i.e., exhaust all reserves) by 2019. He told me he had a group of financially sophisticated community members study the city budget and they had concluded the city had a revenue problem, not a spending problem. He lamented that he had been unable to remedy revenue shortfalls that led to the inadequate roads and stormwater infrastructure.

On June 2, 2015, a beautiful sunny day, I put my left hand on our now well-used family Bible and was sworn in as the forty-first mayor of Colorado Springs. I told the crowd on the steps of the old El Paso County Courthouse (now the Pioneers Museum) that we were indebted to our predecessors who had guided the city as it had grown to 460,000 people. "It is our enduring challenge," I said, "to continue to build a city that matches our scenery."

One of my first official acts as mayor was to appoint Jeff Greene as my chief of staff. Jeff had spent the previous nine years as El Paso County Administrator, essentially running the day-to-day operations of the county and was well regarded in the community. He knew the issues and he knew the people and could help me navigate through the challenges that lay ahead. He would prove to be incredibly effective in managing the mayor/city council relationship. He made sure a lot of bad ideas never got to the point that required my veto. Jeff and I interviewed the managers of all the major departments of city government in the two weeks prior to taking office and were generally pleased with the team my predecessor had assembled. I did select a new communications director, Jamie Fabos, as that job was vacant when I took office and within the year, I would replace the fire chief. Everyone else adapted well to the transition. In fact, they became a cohesive team that did great work in the ensuing years.

Within two weeks of taking office, I met in a half-day work session with the nine members of city council, which had three new members. Council member Merv Bennett had been elected President of the Council. I gave the council an extensive list of various objectives and asked for their support and legislative sponsorship of them. They included moving code enforcement from the Police Department to the Planning and Land Use Department, eliminating the business personal property tax which had been a deterrent to attracting new businesses, enacting an ordinance to keep transients from sitting or lying on downtown sidewalks, which also was a deterrent to commerce, regulating marijuana clubs and residential growing of marijuana, and further professionalizing the municipal court. Within a year all of those objectives would be achieved.

But the greatest focus of the work session was how to deal with the city's deteriorating streets and inadequate stormwater infrastructure. Public works indicated we had at least a $1.5 billion infrastructure deficit. The Streets Division demonstrated at the work session that 60 percent of the city's roads were in poor condition. When Colorado Springs had suffered a 16 percent decline in revenue during the recession beginning in 2008, the city manager and council chose not to cut police and fire, which consisted of more than half the budget, and road maintenance and repair took a big hit. Current funding levels were inadequate to change the trajectory. In 2009, the citizens of Colorado Springs had been convinced by anti-tax activists to pass a citizen initiative that eliminated a stormwater fee on residential and commercial properties and as a result of inadequate funding the city now had a large backlog of stormwater projects. Unfortunately, just seven months earlier the voters had rejected an attempt to reinstate a stormwater fee.

The council and I agreed we would do some polling to determine how the public felt about possible approaches to resolving the city's infrastructure problems. That proved to be very informative. Not surprisingly, the citizens cared a lot more about streets than they did stormwater. Eighty percent were very concerned about roads, only 14 percent were very concerned about the city's stormwater program. Most citizens do not understand the necessity of a good stormwater system in terms of flood control and water quality. The poll respondents indicated they would be willing to pay additional taxes for street repairs. They also indicated a strong preference for sales tax over property tax, despite the fact their property taxes were significantly lower than virtually every other large city in America. That stemmed from the fact that nearly one-third of sales tax would be paid by non-residents, including tourists.

With the poll results in hand, I proposed to the council that they refer a ballot measure to voters raising approximately $50 million per year for five years through a 0.62 sales tax increase, to be used exclusively for road repairs, and that we would make significant general fund budget adjustments to greatly increase stormwater spending. My hope was we could build public confidence with city residents and revisit the stormwater issues in subsequent years. The council voted 8-1 to refer the tax increase to the voters in November of 2015.

Colorado Springs is heavily Republican and fiscally conservative. Historically, it's been difficult to pass tax increase measures in the city. Immediately after the ballot measure was referred, anti-tax groups and individuals began attacking it. Americans for Prosperity argued it was unnecessary, relying on an ill-informed report by an out-of-state accountant. Anti-Tax activist Doug Bruce, and his city council ally, Helen Collins, alleged the money would be diverted to other purposes despite the language of the measure to the contrary. Business groups in the city, led by Colorado Springs Forward, put together a campaign in favor of the ballot measure and raised about $380,000 to fund it. I spent my time talking about the necessity of the measure, from both a public safety and economic development perspective, and specifically rebutting the contentions of its opponents. My first State of the City Speech on September 9th centered on the infrastructure challenges.

On November 2, 2015, when the votes were counted, the issue passed by a 65-35 percent margin. Another measure allowing the city to retain $2.1 million dollars and use it for park trails instead of being refunded to taxpayers, also passed with over 70 percent of the vote.

While the result was wholly consistent with the polling we'd done, many pundits were shocked by the margin of victory in tax-resistant Colorado Springs. At a victory party, I assured the citizens of the city that they would continue to enjoy the lowest tax burden of any major city in Colorado and congratulated them for recognizing the importance of critical public infrastructure in creating a great city. "Colorado Springs is moving again," I proclaimed.

But the same week of the victory on roads, the stormwater issue became more challenging. In 2008 the city-owned utility had successfully negotiated with Pueblo County to secure a permit to build the Southern Delivery System (SDS). SDS would be a massive water distribution system pumping millions of gallons per day from Pueblo Reservoir on the Arkansas River to Colorado Springs and providing for fifty years or more of growth for the city. As part of the agreement, Colorado Springs promised to have a viable stormwater program that would help control downstream flooding in Pueblo. But in 2009, Colorado Springs voters had defunded its stormwater program and Pueblo had been threatening to revoke the permit authorizing SDS. In May of 2015 they had directed attorneys to pursue a legal action to stop the $825 million water system from going online in April of 2016, if resolution of the dispute could not be negotiated. In the first week of November 2015, Colorado Springs received a letter from the US Department of Justice indicating it was bringing a claim against the city on behalf of the Environmental Protection Agency alleging that the city's inadequate stormwater spending had caused it to be in violation of an MS-4 permit issued by the EPA. An MS-4 permit requires cities to take measures to mitigate water pollution. In essence, this legal development was a great boost to Pueblo's claims, and the city's ability to turn on the Southern Delivery System in April of 2016 was in considerable jeopardy.

Over the next five months, I joined Colorado Springs Utilities' executives and attorneys in intense negotiations with Pueblo County trying to resolve the impasse. After much back and forth we reached an intergovernmental agreement whereby Colorado Springs and its utility agreed to spend $460 million over the next twenty years on its stormwater program, including approximately seventy infrastructure projects. Essentially, Colorado Springs agreed to spend the amount it would have if the stormwater fee was still in place. That was Pueblo's objective. The Colorado Springs City Council and the Pueblo County Commissioners approved the agreement approximately one week before SDS became operational. It was an emotional moment when, with a click of a computer mouse, the water started flowing. The agreement put a serious strain on the city's general fund budget, but there was little choice in the matter.

Not everything went well during my first year in office. On the Friday after Thanksgiving in 2015 I was home decorating our Christmas tree when I got a call from the police chief, Pete Carey, about an active shooter situation at a local Planned Parenthood clinic. After a few phone conversations with the chief the situation had not been resolved, and I drove to the Emergency Command Center that had been set up near the scene. A dramatic five-and-a-half-hour standoff ensued. A fifty-eight-year-old loner who lived in a small trailer in the mountains sixty-five miles west of Colorado Springs had gone to the clinic to stop it from "killing babies." Using an assault rifle, he killed two patients and a police officer who was among the first to arrive. He also wounded nine others, including five police officers. From the Command Center, I observed the SWAT team commanders (who were monitoring the movements of the perpetrator on a security camera feed from the clinic), advise the SWAT team members who were in the clinic as to his whereabouts. This facilitated the safe evacuations of two dozen people from the clinic and allowed the officers to set up for a final assault to neutralize the shooter. Just before it was executed, we watched as the perpetrator surrendered himself and the highly intense drama finally came to an end.

Colorado Springs became the focus of the national and international media and over the next forty-eight hours, I gave about fifty interviews, many of them broadcasted widely. I talked to the White House and had a joint press conference with Governor Hickenlooper. Janet and I visited injured officers in the hospital and attended funerals of the victims. I spoke at the funeral of Police

Officer Garrett Swasey. My job was to be the consoler in chief and ensure that our city was not defined by this incident of domestic terrorism but rather by our response to it, including the heroism of the police officers involved. It was an exhausting ordeal but an opportunity for strong leadership.

My objective to promote new job creation in Colorado Springs was aided by an improving economy as well as tax incentives and bureaucracy reduction. The result was beyond my most optimistic projections. In 2015 the city added about 8,000 new jobs. We added another 8,000 jobs in 2016, and a total of over 50,000 jobs from 2015 to 2023. The city had only averaged 3,000 new jobs per year for the previous decade. Unemployment fell to 2.3 percent in March of 2017. That was the lowest since records were kept. The job growth was across many business sectors. The State of Colorado decided to locate a National Cybersecurity Center in Colorado Springs to aid our effort to become a cybersecurity hub for the nation. I would serve as Chairman of the Board of the NCC for several years. My close relationship with Governor Hickenlooper was critical in making that happen. Janet and our daughters found it very humorous when their technologically-challenged husband and father was named the Technology Advocate of the Year for his efforts to establish the Cybersecurity Center.

Over a billion dollars in new health care infrastructure was announced during my tenure as mayor. Our two hospital systems were expanding, and a new Children's Hospital was built. We were able to attract several new businesses to the Commercial Aeronautical Zone and Business Park at the City airport, including a four-million-square-foot Amazon Distribution Center with over 2,500 jobs. The increased revenue from airport leases allowed us to lower fees paid by commercial carriers.

Existing airlines increased destinations and frequency of flights. Passenger enplanements began to increase dramatically for the first time in many years. That would set the stage for Southwest Airlines to enter the market in 2021 and become the dominant local carrier. Colorado Springs also became one of the nation's hottest real estate markets. Tourism expanded dramatically beginning in 2016. Hotel/motel vacancies reached record lows. Downtown Colorado Springs became more dynamic with more people living and working there. The city's positive trajectory was evidenced by *US News and World Report* rating it the most desirable city in America, and *Money Magazine* naming it the best big city in the west.

Keeping with my commitment that the city would be more collaborative with other local governments and economic development entities in the Pikes Peak region, my staff and I worked hard to establish close working relationships with El Paso County, surrounding municipalities, Colorado Springs Utilities and the Colorado Springs Chamber and Economic Development Corporation (EDC). The selection of Aram Benyamin as the CEO of Utilities led to much closer cooperation between the city and utilities in economic development matters than had previously existed. Dirk Draper was appointed CEO of the Chamber and EDC shortly before my election as mayor and over the next seven years we worked very closely to foster new economic development opportunities. When Draper retired in 2021, his successor, Johnna Reeder Kleymeyer, brought extensive experience and great enthusiasm to the city's economic development efforts.

In the summer of 2015, I was honored by being elected a member of the board of the Daniels Fund, one of the largest foundations in Colorado with $1.7 billion in assets. Its benefactor, Bill Daniels, made his fortune in Cablevision and left it to the benefit of the citizens of Colorado, New Mexico, Utah, and Wyoming. The board met quarterly and distributed about $70 million annually in grants and college scholarships. Grants went to organizations serving the elderly, disabled, homeless, youth development, including youth sports, and those which were involved in education reform. I was only the second person from Colorado Springs to serve on the board. No doubt my experience overseeing charitable organizations as Colorado attorney general had a lot to do with my selection to the board.

In the spring of 2016, I was awarded the Colorado Citizenship Medal, the highest honor given to a citizen of Colorado for excellence in public service. I was nominated by Governor Hickenlooper "in recognition of outstanding service as attorney general and for putting Colorado Springs on a very positive trajectory."

A municipal election took place the first week in April of 2017. Six of the nine city council seats represent geographic districts within the city and three of the seats are at large. All six of the districts' seats were up for election. Three of the four incumbents that ran were reelected. That wasn't surprising considering that polls showed voters were happy with the direction of the city and the only council member that lost, Helen Collins, had opposed virtually every measure that had passed in the previous two years. Several candidates backed by the business community did not fare well, and because the overall philosophical makeup of the council moved left, media outlets hailed the election as a victory for progressives. I thought a better explanation was that the hardest working candidates won the open seats and the status quo otherwise prevailed. The philosophical shift was evident however when Merv Bennett, who had done a very good job as council president the past two years, was replaced by Richard Skorman. Richard had once again been elected to council after serving a previous stint and unsuccessfully running for mayor in 2011. While I was disappointed that Merv was replaced, I had always found Skorman a very practical liberal and was confident I could work well with him.

The only issue I was personally invested in during the April 2017 city election was Issue 2, which asked the voters to retain up to $12 million of "excess" revenue over the limit allowed by the Colorado TABOR and invest it in stormwater projects. The usual anti-tax forces opposed the measure. Radio ads called me a "tax and spend liberal." The fact we'd made a lot of progress educating the voters about the stormwater issue was reflected in the overwhelming passage of the measure with 66 percent of the vote. But we still needed a long-term solution to the stormwater problem.

At a mayor/city council work session right after the election, the police chief gave a compelling presentation showing our police force significantly understaffed for the size of the city and that this was beginning to be reflected in longer response times to critical incidents. We needed to add as many as 120 officers in the next few years. But that wasn't possible because we had to spend up to about $15 million per year from the general fund to meet our stormwater related legal obligations. I suggested to the council that we do some updated polling to see where we stood on stormwater with the voters. The polling was once again very helpful. It showed that, largely because of the EPA lawsuit and the negotiations with Pueblo, more citizens understood and were concerned about the issue. It also showed that because of all the work being done to fix the roads over the past two years, two-thirds of the voters had a high level of confidence in city government. Fifty-four percent of those polled now said they were willing to reinstate a stormwater fee.

I asked the city council to refer a stormwater fee measure to the ballot in November 2017. While the fee could be reinstated without a vote, given that the previous fee had been abolished by voters, it seemed appropriate to ask them to reinstate it. With the benefit of Council President Skorman's support, the council voted 6-3 to refer the measure and an intense campaign ensued. The opposition, once again funded by Americans for Prosperity, ran radio ads labeling me a taxaholic. I was clearly the face of the pro-campaign. The campaign was run by the Chamber of Commerce and its government affairs manager, Rachel Beck. But I did the fundraising with the help of Kitt Smith. The business community responded, and we raised $475,000 to run a very strategic campaign of targeted mailings and demographically targeted radio ads. On November 7, 2017, our polling proved very accurate, and the stormwater measure passed 54 percent to 46 percent. The initial $15 million that would be raised annually would grow over time. And while that money could only be spent on stormwater infrastructure, maintenance, and operations, the general fund that would now be freed up would allow the city to meet other critical needs, including adequate police and fire staffing. We would add 138 police officers and seventy-six firefighters over the next five years. It was one of the most satisfying election victories of my career, largely because so many political pundits said it couldn't be done.

In many ways my first three years as mayor of Colorado Springs were the most meaningful of my long public service career. It certainly was in terms of political leadership. We had accomplished so many things that were quite difficult. I felt my years of experience in various public and private endeavors had prepared me well for the job and the challenges I faced. Being a lawyer made me better able to understand and work through various significant legal issues. I think the city attorney appreciated that. The opportunity to exercise leadership exceeded my expectations. I was laser focused on my priorities of improving the political climate in the city, investing in critical public infrastructure and new job creation, and we'd made tremendous progress on all three fronts. The city's major newspaper, the *Gazette*, who had endorsed me for mayor, was effusive in its praise for what had been accomplished so quickly. Even my critics during the mayoral campaign conceded the direction of the city had been changed dramatically and positively in a relatively short period of time.

I had worked very hard throughout my career. Long hours were nothing new to me. But the combination of managing a large city and meeting all the ceremonial and promotional responsibilities of a big city mayor resulted in my working longer hours than ever before. Fourteen-hour days were the norm. Weekends were typically booked solid. My executive assistant, Wendilyn Guidotti, did an outstanding job as my scheduler. I often joked that she was the "de facto mayor of Colorado Springs" because she told me where to go and what to say. I was only half joking. The diversity of speaking engagements made me very reliant on the City's Communication Department for research and speech writing. They did an excellent job. While I used a security detail less than my predecessor, they proved very helpful at large, heavily advertised events that attracted folks with an axe to grind. As mayor, I had a much higher public profile than ever before. Even trips to the store meant posing for pictures or listening to constituents' opinions about current city issues.

Fortunately, Janet was able to join me at many social and ceremonial obligations. She also continued to embrace a great deal of volunteer work on various community boards. Together with Doug Price, CEO of Visit COS, she led the effort to brand Colorado Springs as Olympic City USA. Over a forty-year period, the city had become the home of the US Olympic Committee, the largest US Olympic Training Center, twenty-five Olympic sports governing bodies, and the home of the US Olympic and Paralympic Museum and Hall of Fame. Several thousand people now worked for sports related organizations, and sports was now a major part of our local economy, generating approximately $500 million per year. The city had earned the brand of Olympic City, USA and the US Olympic Committee authorized us to pursue it. The mission of the branding effort is to create sustained economic growth and enhance civic pride. A great deal of work went into the effort and the brand was quickly embraced by the citizens. In April of 2016, Janet and I traveled with a group of Colorado Springs residents to Ancient Olympia Greece for the torch lighting ceremony leading up to the Summer Olympics in Rio De Janeiro. Ancient Olympia has become a sister city of Colorado Springs. On opening night of the 2016 games, 30,000 people jammed the streets of downtown Colorado Springs to celebrate the Olympics and Colorado Springs's designation as Olympic City, USA.

In June of 2017 Janet and I again led a delegation of Colorado Springs residents, including eight high school students, to visit

Colorado Springs's longest standing sister city, Fujiyoshida, Japan. In 1962 the two cities, which were similar in size at the time, became sister cities because both were situated at the base of a famous mountain: Mt. Fuji, in the case of Fujiyoshida and Pikes Peak, in the case of Colorado Springs. I planted a tree to mark the fifty-fifth anniversary of the relationship. It was located close to a large birch tree planted by a predecessor as Colorado Springs Mayor, Eugene McCleary, forty-seven years earlier. At a banquet attended by about 200 local officials and businessmen, I was awarded the title of Special Honorary Citizen of Fujiyoshida. We also spent time in Tokyo promoting economic development relationships that subsequently proved beneficial to the city. Panasonic became the city's smart-city consultant and contributed greatly to exhibit design at the Olympic Museum. In the fall of 2022, the mayor of Fujiyoshida came to Colorado Springs to mark the sixtieth anniversary of our sister city relationship.

In February of 2017, I once again agreed to be roasted—this time as a fundraiser for Cheyenne Village, an excellent local nonprofit which provides residential services for adults with development disabilities. Roasting the mayor proved to be a big draw as well over 600 people attended and about $250,000 was raised. My brother-in-law, Ben Gill, was once again a big hit as a roaster. And both our daughters, Alison and Kate, got big laughs describing what it was like growing up as the kids of the district attorney. Kate said to this day when she walks into an empty restaurant she whispers to her husband, "this place has to be a front for drugs," something she heard often from her cynical prosecutor father.

In May of 2017 a strange twist in national politics put me in the media spotlight for a thankfully brief period. It all began when Donald Trump abruptly fired FBI Director James Comey. Trump said he did so because Comey was a showboat, was incompetent, and had lost the confidence of the agency. These assertions didn't hold up well and the public perception was that the president was trying to deter an FBI investigation of his campaign's and administration's ties to Russia. Trump later acknowledged that the "Russian thing" was part of his motivation. Apparently, Trump fired Comey with no thought of who would replace him. During the next week, Colorado's junior US Senator Cory Gardner was having dinner with Vice President Mike Pence. They were former colleagues in the Congress. Pence was lamenting the situation and suggesting the president should appoint an outsider that could attract bipartisan support. Senator Gardner told him, "I know just the guy" and proceeded to tell him about me. Gardner told Pence he would talk to me and determine if I was willing to have my name provided to the White House Counsel, Don McGahn. When Gardner called me, I told him the only three jobs in Washington I had any interest in at this point in my life were attorney general, deputy attorney general, or FBI director. But I also alerted Gardner to my admiration for Jim Comey, stemming from contact I had with him while I was US attorney for Colorado and he was both a US attorney for Manhattan and deputy attorney general, and questioned whether President Trump would be impressed by my by-the-book reputation. But I agreed that Gardner could provide my name to the White House Counsel, and he did the following morning. That afternoon I got a call from an underling in the White House Counsel's office saying only that they would probably do some preliminary vetting. Based on that, I was very surprised the next day when the White House released a short list of eleven people as possible FBI director, and I was one of them. National, state, and local media inquiries exploded. I had to put out a statement saying only that I was honored to be on a list with several outstanding law enforcement professionals, but any further comment would be premature. Over the next several days the media was reporting that several people on the short list were being interviewed by the attorney general or the president and I was not one of them. Then I had another phone conversation with the same underling at the White House Counsel's office. He asked me about my relationship with Jim Comey and Bob Mueller, a former FBI director and deputy attorney general, who had recently been named special counsel to investigate Trump's ties to Russia. I indicated that while I had limited exposure to both during my time as US attorney, I had enough to have respect for them. I suspect that sealed my fate. That and the fact I had not supported Trump in the Republican primary. But I was also shocked to hear the interviewer express frustration that the selection process was a mess, and the president and the White House Counsel's staff were not on the same page. It was consistent with media reports that surfaced over the next few days about dysfunction at the Trump White House. That was the last I heard about the FBI director matter from the White House. A prominent lawyer in Denver had an additional conversation with a lawyer at the White House about my qualifications. Several weeks later, President Trump nominated Chris Wray, a well-qualified individual, as FBI director. He has done an admirable job. It certainly appeared to me that I had never seriously been considered, at least by the president. But it was a hectic couple of weeks.

In August of 2017, I once again heard from the White House. They wanted to talk to me about possible appointment as head of the Consumer Financial Protection Bureau (CFPB). The Bureau had been set up during the Obama administration and was very controversial. It had immense power over businesses that provided financial services to consumers, including credit cards, consumer loans, etc. The controversy stemmed from the fact that the Bureau was not dependent on funding from Congress. It was unclear if the president could fire the director, and the initial director, Richard Cordray, was extremely aggressive. Republicans viewed him as extremely anti-business. Cordray had been the Attorney General of Ohio when I was AG in Colorado and I had worked with him on several cases when he became the director of the CFPB. Cordray was a very smart guy. I agreed with him on several things, including the continuing abhorrent behavior of the big banks towards consumers, and disagreed with him on others, including his opposition to arbitration clauses in consumer contracts.

I interviewed with several people at the White House in September of 2017. I was in Washington, DC on other business at the time. While we had a good discussion, I was pretty firm in letting them know I was not interested in giving up my job as mayor and moving to DC for that particular job. My low regard for President Trump certainly factored in. But that did not stop the White House from re-contacting me in January of 2018, after Cordray had resigned, and asking me to meet with Mick Mulvaney, the acting head of the CFPB, and the president regarding the CFPB job. Again, I indicated that I was not interested in taking on that job at this point in my career. In hindsight, I'm certain I was one of many dedicated public servants who shied away from service in the Trump administration.

Over the next two years I had two brief meetings with President Trump when he came to Colorado Springs for an Air Force Academy graduation and a political rally. I also had a brief conversation with him at the White House. Trump had established a new branch of the military, US Space Force, and Colorado Springs was competing with five other cities to be the permanent home of US Space Command, the combatant command for the Space Force. Colorado Springs was the provisional home of Space Command, and it was clear to us that top brass in the Air Force favored Colorado Springs as the permanent home. While such basing decisions were usually non-political, Trump insisted in our brief meetings that he'd make the decision himself and he would do it after the 2020 election. I knew as soon as he said that it would be a political decision. But I was nevertheless part of an orchestrated lobbying campaign. We were obviously concerned that three of our competitors were in states that, unlike Colorado, had widespread support for Trump, but we felt we did very well in site visits and in a presentation to an Air Force site selection committee. As the president continued to say and do some pretty outrageous things, I worked hard to refrain from public criticism of him, lest it draw his ire and hurt my city's chances to be selected. That proved very difficult when on January 6, 2020, just days before the administration's Space Force decision, the president incited a mob to storm the US Capitol building in an attempt to disrupt Congress in the process of confirming the election of Joe Biden.

But my diplomacy by restraint was to no avail. Trump had lost Colorado by 13 percent. He won Alabama by 28 percent. A week before he left office, the Trump administration named Huntsville, Alabama as the permanent home of Space Force beginning in 2025. It was my biggest disappointment as mayor from an economic development standpoint. And while political appointees in the Air Force insisted it was a merit-based decision, it didn't pass the smell test. Six congressional members from Alabama had just voted not to recognize electoral votes for Joe Biden and Huntsville's Congressman, Mo Brooks, had been Trump's warm-up act at the rally before the Capitol building was stormed, exhorting the crowd to go to the Capitol and "kick ass." Brooks and newly elected Alabama Senator, Tommy Tuberville, a Trump devotee, told their constituents they'd made a deal with Trump to get Space Command. In August of 2021, Trump bragged to an Alabama audience that he single-handedly made the decision to move Space Command to Huntsville. Both the Government Accountability Office (GAO) and the Department of Defense Inspector General conducted investigations of the decision. The reports they issued gave Colorado Springs a lot to argue about. The GAO report called the selection process seriously flawed, saying it lacked transparency and credibility. I joined the Colorado Congressional delegation in an all-out effort to get the decision reversed by the Biden administration. I personally lobbied a number of U.S. Senators. The city hired a top-notch lobbying firm to aid the effort. A final resolution of the issue was pending when this book went to press.

In 1988, Colorado Springs had annexed 24,000 acres, known as Banning Lewis Ranch. It was the largest annexation in the city's history. The developer, Frank Aries, quickly acquiesced in an annexation agreement that was very onerous on developers. As it turned out, Aries and his Arizona lender were engaged in extreme land speculation. Aries eventually absconded to Belize and left his non-recourse lender high and dry. Because the annexation agreement made development of the property economically untenable, the vast area remained virtually undeveloped over the next thirty years. Development leap frogged the Banning Lewis property into the county, causing the city to lose billions of dollars of economic development. By 2016, there were fewer than 5,000 acres of undeveloped land in the city, other than Banning Lewis. We therefore made it a high priority to negotiate an amended annexation agreement that would allow development of the ranch. It was a two-year process, but an updated agreement was finally approved by the city council on a 7-2 vote in March of 2018. I was convinced it was a major step to ensure a prosperous future for the city. It's estimated that more than 150,000 will eventually live in the annexed area.

As Colorado Springs has continued to grow, more residents have become increasingly concerned about the city's water supply. That's understandable given our location in the arid high desert plains. But the city has historically been bold and visionary in ensuring an adequate water supply to meet its growth. During my tenure as mayor, I became convinced the mayor and city council should pass an ordinance demonstrating to residents that we are very cognizant of our available water supply and current water usage and commit to maintaining a comfortable buffer between the two. My concern was heightened by the ongoing drought in the Colorado River basin, and a possible curtailment of the city's water supply from the river. As a result of those developments, the leadership of Colorado Springs Utilities supported such an ordinance. I wanted to get it passed before I left office and was very pleased the council, which also serves as the city's utilities board, did so in February 2023, despite considerable opposition from some developers. It will undoubtedly be tweaked over time but my hope is that it will make city residents more aware of water issues and "no growth" advocates less effective in citing the city's water supply to promote their cause.

Mayors of large cities could spend most of their time attending various national meetings if they were so inclined. I was not. Just as I had been in my previous jobs, I wanted to be a hands-on manager, although not a micromanager. I tried to attend at least one US Conference of Mayors meeting each year and at least one National League of Cities meeting. There were things to be learned from the experience of other cities, but for the most part, I found my issues much different from that of most large city mayors, the vast majority of whom were Democrats. Their constant mantra was that not enough money was flowing from the federal government to the cities and they couldn't build adequate public infrastructure. I actually found my membership in another organization, Community Leaders of America (CLA), which was Republican mayors and city council members, to be much more productive. The emphasis was on finding non-federal solutions to issues facing cities.

One thing was becoming increasingly apparent to all mayors across the country. The focus and nature of political power in America was changing. Extreme partisanship at the national and state levels of government rendered them impotent in resolving the major challenges facing our nation and our states. It was at the local government level, particularly in our cities, where government, often in partnership with the private and nonprofit sectors, was finding a way to solve problems and get things done. The less reliant the city was on federal largesse, the more likely it was to be successful. Some political observers called this emerging reality the "New Localism." Colorado Springs citizens were typical. Polls showed they had much more confidence in their city government than in their national and state government.

In August of 2018, a young Colorado Springs police officer, Cem Duzel, was dispatched to a shots-fired call just east of downtown. When he arrived at the scene and confronted the suspect, Duzel was shot in the head. His traumatic brain injury was so severe he was not expected to survive. I joined the police chief, Pete Carey, in a vigil at the hospital, expecting the worst. But after several brain surgeries, Duzel miraculously did survive and underwent several years of physical rehabilitation and therapy. I will never forget the day Duzel was transported by ambulance from a hospital in Colorado Springs to a rehabilitation center in Denver. Several hundred law enforcement officers lined the hallways of the hospital and saluted him as he passed by on a stretcher. The only gesture Duzel was able to give in return was a thumbs up. It was my most emotional experience as mayor.

After Labor Day in 2018, I announced I would seek a second term as mayor in the April 2019 election. I again hired Kitt Smith to manage the campaign. We began fundraising while waiting to see if any formidable opposition would surface. In January of 2019, when candidate petitions were submitted, three opponents emerged. One, Lawrence Martinez, had run in 2015 for mayor and had finished fifth in the first round. The other two candidates had lived in Colorado Springs for fewer than three years and had little name recognition. While one, John Pitchford, was on the right of me, and the other, Juliette Parker, on the left, they both had the same theme: Suthers was a corrupt mayor in the pockets of the developers and didn't listen to his constituents. Pitchford, a retired dentist, put over $100,000 of his own money in his campaign as the "anti-corruption candidate for mayor." I stayed very positive, touting our many accomplishments, particularly in improving public infrastructure and new job creation, and never mentioning my opponents.

Eleven candidates emerged to run for three at large city council seats. Two were incumbents. Another, Wayne Williams, was very familiar to Colorado Springs voters. Wayne had served as county commissioner, county clerk and recorder, and one term as Colorado secretary of state before losing in the 2018 general election in which a blue wave of anti-Trump voters swept out every Republican statewide office holder in Colorado.

There was also a very contentious issue on the April 2019 municipal election ballot. City firefighters, through their local affiliate of the International Firefighter Association, had petitioned to get a collective bargaining measure on the ballot. The Colorado Springs City Charter prohibits collective bargaining. In Issue 1, they sought to amend the charter to allow uniformed firefighters collective bargaining rights. Their timing was curious to me. They had endorsed me in the 2015 election despite my opposition to collective bargaining. I promised to meet with them regularly, work hard to ensure they were compensated at market with other big city departments and that we would develop a systemic fleet replacement policy to ensure they had state-of-the-art equipment. Over the previous three years line firefighters had gotten raises averaging 16 percent and the city was spending millions annually on fleet replacement. The city council and I met with the leadership of the firefighters several times a year.

But the firefighters had elected more radical leadership and they contended they needed collective bargaining to ensure they had a seat at the table and weren't subject to the whims of capricious politicians. When the firefighters petitioned the issue on the ballot I, along with the local Chamber of Commerce, led the opposition fight. It was an uncomfortable place for me to be because I had always been very supportive of police and fire. But based on my observations of how unionization of city employees had adversely impacted the finances and efficiency of other cities, I was vehemently opposed to Colorado Springs going down that path.

Initial polling showed we had an uphill battle. Citizens favored Issue 1 by large margins. But the polling also showed most citizens didn't understand collective bargaining and could be swayed to oppose it if they understood city firefighters were well compensated, received a lifetime defined benefit pension, and that unionizing the fire department would likely lead to unionization of other city employees, including police and utility workers. The polling also showed I had high trust levels with the voters and should be the face of the opposition campaign. So, I appeared in TV ads talking about how well paid the firefighters were, and how, if they were successful in unionizing, other city employees would follow. Our opposition campaign raised and spent $380,000, but the firefighters, aided by state and national unions, spent more than twice as much. The debates over the issue were well covered by the media.

Election night turned out to be a good one for me. I was reelected with 73 percent of the vote, and Juliette Parker the second highest with 11 percent. And in a result that shocked everyone, including the firefighters, collective bargaining failed by an overwhelming 67-33 percent margin. That result would become more significant a year later when, in the midst of a national debate about police use of force, police unions were identified as a major culprit standing in the way of quick, efficient, and adequate discipline of police misconduct.

On April 16, 2019, with my hand once again on the family Bible, I was sworn in for my second term as mayor. I'd run for public office seven times and been successful six of those times. But at age sixty-seven, I was pretty sure this was my last political campaign. I would be wholly focused on further transforming Colorado Springs and continuing to build a great city that matched its magnificent scenery.

In the fall of 2018, I had been contacted by Bruce Benson, the President of the University of Colorado, and three chancellors of the CU campuses. They asked me to apply for the presidency of CU, which Benson was vacating. The search committee also contacted me to solicit an application. But the problem was simple. I had already announced my candidacy for reelection as mayor. I would not ask the voters for their support while, at the same time, actively pursuing another position.

Colorado Springs continued to prosper in my second term as a result of both public and private investment. In 2012, Colorado passed legislation known as the Regional Tourism Act. That legislation allowed cities to ask the state Economic Development Commission for state sales tax increment financing for projects that were likely to attract large numbers of out-of-state visitors. In 2013, under my predecessor, Mayor Steve Bach, Colorado Springs applied for and received an award of $120.5 million in state sales tax increment financing over thirty years to support four local projects—a US Olympic and Paralympic Museum and Hall of Fame, a sports medicine facility at UCCS, a downtown stadium and indoor arena, and a new Air Force Academy Visitor Center adjacent to I-25. The four projects were collectively named the City for Champions. But the approval of the projects in December of 2013 was just the beginning. While the state sales tax revenue stream would support about $70 million in bonds for the projects, private financing well over $500 million would be required. The burden fell to my administration to help create the public and private partnerships necessary to succeed. While all the projects were daunting, the easiest to get underway was the Olympic Museum. It received the philanthropic support of foundations, companies, and individuals. It's an iconic structure that will be a boon to our tourism economy and cement our city's brand as Olympic City, USA.

The sports medicine facility also proceeded smoothly. The William J. Hybl Sports Medicine and Performance Center is a partnership between UCCS and Centura Health and also benefited from significant private philanthropy. It promises to be a state-of-the-art facility attracting patients, doctors, and researchers to Colorado Springs.

The other two projects proved more difficult. As late as early 2018, I was quite pessimistic that the downtown stadium and arena could be successfully completed. Feasibility studies showed revenue streams could not support the projects without large private investment. Then hard work and good luck changed the landscape. Colorado College came forward to take the lead in building an arena. They would have their Division I hockey program play there and also make it accessible for use by Olympic sport governing bodies, as required by the city's agreement with the state Economic Development Commission. Then Weidner Apartment Homes, a national developer founded by Colorado Springs native Dean Weidner, partnered with the city's professional soccer team, the Colorado Springs Switchbacks, to make the stadium a reality. I flew to Seattle and met with Dean Weidner to help seal the deal. Weidner will build a residential, commercial, and retail complex around the stadium. The stadium accommodates a wide variety of sporting events and outdoor concerts.

A new Air Force Academy Visitor Center, which had to be constructed without direct investment of federal dollars, also proved to be a major challenge. The solution was to create an Urban Renewal Zone and allow the developer to build a hotel, office, and commercial complex that generated sufficient revenue to support construction of the visitor center. After 9/11, because of security issues getting into the Air Force Academy, traffic at the visitor center declined by a quarter million people per year. The new visitor center, which will be accessed without entering the Academy itself, will dramatically increase visitation numbers.

Overcoming considerable obstacles and successfully completing the City for Champion projects was a great accomplishment and I'm very grateful to my Chief of Staff Jeff Greene, Economic Development Director Bob Cope, and many community leaders for the incredible effort that made it happen.

In addition to the City for Champions projects, the city embarked on a long overdue effort to build a new Summit House on the top of Pikes Peak. The existing facility, built sixty years ago, was little more than a windowless bunker where visitors could buy a donut and a T-shirt. Construction materials had changed and there were now large windows that could withstand 140 mph winds and forty degree below zero temperatures. The new Summit House has a large café, gift shop, and exhibits discussing the ecology and history of the mountain as well as the annual events that occur there, including the Pikes Peak Hill Climb Auto Race and Pikes Peak Marathon. The project took three years and cost $63 million. The city enterprise, Pikes Peak—America's Mountain, which operates the Summit House and highway to the top of the 14,115-foot mountain, receives no taxpayer support, but charges toll fees to drive the highway. That revenue stream financed $50 million of the construction costs, and I worked with a small group of citizens and city employees to privately raise the remainder.

Building at 14,115 feet elevation is a real challenge. Altitude sickness, permafrost, snow accumulation, and lightening are just some of the obstacles. G. E. Johnson Construction CO., a locally-based general contractor who also built the Olympic and Paralympic Museum, did a great job on the project. The building opened to the public in June of 2021, at the same time the Broadmoor Hotel, which operates the 125-year-old cog railway that goes from Manitou Springs to the Pikes Peak Summit, completed a $100 million reconstruction of the railroad. On July 30th Governor Polis joined me and over 300 distinguished guests on a ride up the cog railway for a dedication of the new Summit House. These were great developments in tourism for Colorado Springs.

The optimism of the city was evidenced in the fall of each year by the large crowds that attended my annual State of the City Speech. My first such speech in 2015 at the Broadmoor Hotel drew 600 people, but in subsequent years the crowds grew to a capacity of 1,000. It became an event everyone in the business community wanted to attend. And I found the annual speech a great bully pulpit. In the summer of 2017, the state transportation department (CDOT) announced it would likely be ten years before a heavily burdened eighteen-mile stretch of Interstate 25 between Colorado Springs and Denver could be expanded. In my 2017 State of the City Speech, I called that totally unacceptable and noted it only took eight years after President John Kennedy's challenge to land a man on the moon until that feat was accomplished. Two weeks later, I got a visit from the CDOT director. He agreed with my assessment. After a lot of hard work, the I-25 "gap" was completed in five years!

The 2019 November general election saw more success in continuing the city's momentum. By a 67 to 33 percent margin, the voters approved a five-year extension of the road improvement sales tax. We reduced the tax from 0.62 to 0.57 percent and directed that at least half of the anticipated $55 million in annual revenue would go to fix residential streets. In the first five years of the program, over 90 percent of the funds had gone to arterial streets. The voters also allowed the city to retain $7 million of revenue over the amount allowed by the state's TABOR and use it to upgrade city parks. Half that amount went to refurbish historic downtown parks originally given to the city by its founder, General William Palmer. We made the improvements to the city's historic parks part of the 150th anniversary celebration.

As is so often the case in life, one of the greatest challenges I faced as mayor was one I least expected. In my first five years in that role, I had participated in many emergency exercises. We'd prepared for natural disasters, like wildfires and flash floods, which are common in Colorado. We prepared for cyberattacks and ransomware demands. But one calamity we didn't have an emergency exercise for was a worldwide pandemic. And that's precisely what Colorado Springs and the rest of the world confronted in March of 2020. The COVID-19 epidemic began in China in 2019 and received relatively little attention until it spread to Europe and the United States. Colorado Springs's booming economy came to a sudden halt in mid-March. The governor of Colorado, through the state health department, instituted a stay-at-home order for more than a month and a half. Our local unemployment rate went from 3 percent to 12.6 percent in forty-five days. Forty million Americans lost their jobs. Traffic at our city's airport declined 90 percent at one point. City tax revenues plunged 14 percent in March and 23 percent in April. We had all the ingredients of a complete economic collapse. Over the next twenty-four months, one million Americans would die of COVID, including 12,000 in Colorado and 1,600 in El Paso County. Over six million people would die worldwide.

This was the time for a different kind of leadership. Citizens needed consolation, motivation, and inspiration. They needed leaders to be calm and deliberate. I reread two of my favorite Winston Churchill biographies to gear up on crisis leadership. I had numerous press conferences with local health officials throughout the COVID crisis to educate the public about the virus and urge their compliance with various health guidance and directives. Those directives changed as national health leaders learned more about the virus and its mortality. For the first seven months of the COVID pandemic, I felt it had been managed well given the knowledge of the virus. Governor Jared Polis and I had radically different political philosophies, but I thought he did a good job of balancing health concerns with economic realities. After the initial shutdown we were able to gradually reopen Colorado Springs at an appropriate pace, considering the competing interests. Even when COVID cases spiked around the Fourth of July we were able to avoid reverting to greater restrictions. But with fall and colder temperatures causing people to spend more time inside, managing the crisis became a more daunting task. COVID cases skyrocketed beginning in September 2020 and the daily hospital count of COVID patients in El Paso County went from fifteen to 290 in eight weeks. At one point one in every thirty-two Coloradans was contagious. While most deaths were elderly or persons with health complications, there were exceptions. I made a well-publicized visit to a COVID Intensive Care Unit to showcase the outstanding work being done by health care personnel and our hospitals to manage the surge and to emphasize to the public the gravity of the situation. In late November, the state ordered restaurants to close once again and re-imposed greater business restrictions. It embarked on a color coded scheme that I thought was too complicated and resulted in declining public "buy in" to the directives. It really victimized those restaurants that had done a good job with capacity limitations and did not appear to be a major culprit in the rising case numbers. I joined a letter from various community leaders to the governor asking for relief for the restaurants, allowing them to return to 25 percent capacity. In my conversations with Governor Polis, I also spoke candidly about losing credibility with the public. To his credit, the governor rescinded the restaurant closure the week after Christmas.

By the beginning of 2021, as COVID vaccines began to be distributed, it became apparent that the country was in a race between surging cases and the herd immunity that would come from infections and widespread vaccination of the population. Colorado chose to let the race play out and not resort to economy-crippling restrictions. When state capacity restrictions ended in April 2021, the city chose not to impose any local restrictions, even as the Delta variant and subsequently the Omicron variant caused cases, hospitalizations, and deaths to rise significantly—primarily because more than a third of residents refused to be vaccinated. Despite considerable criticism, I think that was an appropriate decision. Managing the COVID crisis was a stressful time for political leaders responsible for the health and economic vitality of their constituents. While most Americans felt they did not get good leadership from President Trump in the COVID crisis, and only somewhat better from President Biden, polls showed that most Coloradans felt that state and local government had managed the crisis well.

Throughout the COVID pandemic and for some time afterward, I talked to Colorado Governor Jared Polis at least once a week and frequently more often. Our conversations not only involved the evolving pandemic and vaccine distribution efforts, but also other political matters. He was very pleased that, unlike most Republican officials in the state, I supported a Democrat-sponsored transportation bill in the 2021 legislative session that put $5.2 billion in additional general fund and user fees into the state's long-neglected transportation infrastructure. I had been frustrated that the state had failed to deal with the issue for over a decade. While the bill was far from perfect, I felt this was as good a proposal as we would see from the Democrat-controlled legislature and that we couldn't kick the can down the road any longer.

But the governor and I had serious disagreements about legislation I considered anti-business and anti-law enforcement. Like Governor Hickenlooper, Polis had little background in criminal justice issues and, in my opinion, the ACLU and State Public Defenders Office had outsized influence over his agenda and that of the Democrat majorities in the State House and Senate. Public safety in Colorado was suffering at the hands of a far-left agenda.

Polis is an interesting guy. He's a Princeton graduate and plenty smart. He is also somewhat quirky. He always wears tennis shoes, even with a coat and tie. He made a fortune starting a couple of online businesses, including ProFlowers.com, and used it to move up the political ranks, beginning with the State Board of Education. Even according to fellow Democrats, he is a bit aloof, and no one seemed particularly close to him. Unlike most Democrats, he exhibits a Libertarian streak on certain issues.

I first met Polis in 2012 when he was a congressman and I was Colorado attorney general. We were debating legalization of marijuana in Vail, Colorado. The audience very much favored his pro-marijuana stance. But I found his personal enthusiasm for the topic a bit strange, at least until May of 2021 when I met with him in his Capitol office and saw a quart baggie of commercially grown marijuana on his desk.

Despite our dramatic differences, political and otherwise, the governor and I had a constructive relationship. I even convinced him to veto or sidetrack a few bad bills over the years, although that did little to slow the state's march to the left during his tenure.

Much to my relief, the Colorado Springs economy proved to be among the most resilient in the country during the COVID crisis. After large revenue shortfalls in the spring of 2020, by summer city revenues were the same or greater than the year before, and by fall they were significantly higher. General fund sales and use tax revenues actually increased by 0.5 percent in 2020 and the city's total tax revenue decline was only about $10 million, due largely to the shortfall in the lodging and rental car tax. While the average US city suffered a 4 percent economic loss, ours was 1/10 of 1 percent. Residential and commercial construction activity continued at record levels. Online purchasing was up 300 percent from the year before. Residents patronized restaurants and retail establishments as faithfully as health directives allowed. Tourism, while down 40 percent in 2020, was still the best in the country, spurred by visitors that drove to the Pikes Peak region. The city's chief financial officer, Charae McDaniel, did a masterful job of helping the city plan for every contingency. We monitored city revenue very closely and made spending adjustments as necessary. When the COVID pandemic first struck, we imposed a hiring freeze, deferred major capital projects, and cut department operational budgets. We also received $37.5 million of Federal Cares Act funding that could be used to defray COVID-related expenses as well as police and fire payroll. In November of 2020, we successfully asked the city's voters to allow us to sidestep a provision of the state's TABOR and use our 2019 revenue base rather than ratchet down to the lower 2020 base for purposes of determining permissible future growth. That let the city recover from the COVID-caused financial downturn more quickly. While most large American cities suffered layoffs, furloughs, reduced service delivery, and significant revenue shortfalls, Colorado Springs did not. By the beginning of 2022 Colorado Springs had recovered 115 percent of the jobs lost during the COVID crisis (the national average was 80 percent) and the city's economy was humming once again. I was very proud of the way Colorado Springs managed the COVID crisis.

In fact, the COVID epidemic significantly benefited the city's economy in the ensuing years. The crisis caused the United States to comprehend the dangers of relying on foreign manufacturing for essential products, including microchips. Congress passed the "Chips Act" with economic incentives to bring chip manufacturing back to the U.S. That caused several companies to bring microchip related businesses to Colorado Springs and create hundreds of high paying jobs. As a lifelong resident of the city, I was excited to see it return to its high tech roots as "Silicon Mountain."

Resiliency was also needed in other respects in 2020. In May, as we were beginning to reopen the economy after the initial COVID shutdown, a case of police brutality in Minneapolis, in which a white police officer killed a Black arrestee, George Floyd, rocked the nation with ramifications for every large city. Many cities, including Denver, experienced extensive rioting and property damage. But in Colorado Springs I worked hard to effectively communicate with police and protest groups to avoid violence. I had many, many late night communications with police chief Vince Niski. I met personally and privately with a dozen protest leaders and had constructive conversations. We were fortunate to have the vast majority of protestors focused on their cause and dedicated to lawfully exercising their First Amendment rights, as well as a police department focused on their right to do so, while also protecting all of our citizens and their property. Damage done by the protestors was minimal in contrast to other large cities.

The Minneapolis incident came less than a year after a police shooting in Colorado Springs had generated controversy. In August of 2019, two white Colorado Springs police officers shot and killed Devon Bailey, a 19-year-old African American. The officers had responded to a report of an armed robbery by two individuals. Detailed descriptions were given, and the police stopped two individuals that met these descriptions. They were told that one of the two, Devon Bailey, had a gun. They advised him to put his hands up while an officer searched him. He was expressly cautioned not to bring his hands down. Despite that, as an officer approached him from behind to search him, Bailey suddenly brought his hands down to his waist. The police officers' body cameras showed one officer simultaneously reaching for his gun and both officers screaming "hands up." Bailey kept his hands around his waist and was shot four times in a matter of seconds. Because three of the shots entered his back, his advocates claimed he was clearly running away and posed no danger to the officers. Bailey indeed had a fully loaded gun in his shorts. Bailey's cousin, the other person with him, said Bailey had been charged with sexually assaulting two stepsisters and was carrying the gun in case other family members sought revenge. In fact, carrying the weapon was a violation of Bailey's bond conditions upon his release from jail pending resolution of the charges.

Having reviewed dozens of police-use-of-force cases as a district attorney, I knew as soon as I watched the body camera footage that the officers had acted in self-defense and would be criminally exonerated. The local district attorney's office presented the case to a grand jury which found unanimously that the officers acted in accordance to Colorado law. The case was also reviewed by the FBI and the Department of Justice. The DOJ lawyer that reviewed it told me he found there was not a hint of racial animus in the encounter.

Bailey's family and a small group of advocates demanded that the officers be fired and criminally charged. Three local Democratic politicians tried to get the governor to intervene. I had some strong words with Governor Polis about the dangers of politicizing such incidents. I told him it was the duty of public officials to hold the police accountable when they violate the law, but to stand behind them when they act lawfully, regardless of how loud the dissenting voices may be.

All This I Saw, and Part of It I Was

As mayor I tried to be empathetic but also calm and decisive in dealing with protests. I was not going to tolerate any unlawful conduct. While a very small group of residents refused to engage in constructive dialogue, they were the exception. The community dialogue that did take place lead to the city council creating a Law Enforcement Transparency and Accountability Commission to make recommendations to the council and the mayor regarding improvement to police policy, resource allocation, data dissemination, and police/community relations. In the final analysis I felt the way the community responded to the social unrest of 2020 was another indication of its resiliency.

In the spring of 2020, Linda Childears, the CEO of the Daniels Fund, resigned. A few of the board members, including the chairman, approached me about taking the $500,000 per year position. I only thought about it for a very short time. Given the challenges of 2020, the COVID crisis, managing the financial impacts, and dealing with social unrest, resigning as mayor in the midst of such challenges would be a failure of leadership and was simply not an option. I did agree to serve as chairman of the fund upon being elected to the position in May of 2021. The board selected another of its members, Hanna Skandera, to be CEO and she's done a terrific job.

In the April 2021 municipal election, the six city council seats that represent geographic districts were contested. The voters again showed their support for the direction of the city by re-electing three of four incumbents and three fairly mainstream newcomers. The incumbent that lost was David Geislinger. He was beaten by a more conservative candidate, Randy Helms, marking a slight shift by the council to the right.

That was significant because Geislinger had been the swing vote to elect Richard Skorman council president four years earlier. As a result, Skorman was replaced by Tom Strand as council president. The council turned even a bit more conservative less than a year later when Skorman resigned to pursue his business interests full time and the council appointed Stephannie Fortune to replace him. I was pleased that, for at least the remaining years of my mayoral tenure, we could continue to fend off some of the liberal politics that have plagued many large cities.

On Mother's Day, May 9, 2021, Colorado Springs was the scene of another heinous crime that generated national attention. Several Hispanic families were celebrating the birthdays of three members at a home in a local trailer park. A twenty-eight-year-old male, who had been dating one of the attendees, was angry that he had not been invited to the gathering. He burst into the mobile home and in rapid succession shot and killed all six adults present at the time, leaving three children alive, before killing himself. Over the next few days, I did several local and national interviews, including an appearance on CNN. I remarked that the crime scene was a stark reminder that domestic violence can be as deadly as domestic terrorism. Janet and I attended a very emotional funeral service in which all six victims lined the front of the church in open caskets. We met with the victims' families before the service, and I gave brief remarks during it, expressing the community's sorrow and its commitment to help the families cope with the tragedy.

Colorado Springs was founded on July 31, 1871, with a stake driven into the ground at what is now the intersection of Pikes Peak Avenue and Cascade Avenue in the city's downtown. That made July 31, 2021, the city's sesquicentennial, or 150th birthday. We began the lead up to the event two years in advance. Matt Mayberry, director of the city's Pioneers Museum, chaired a committee that planned a wide variety of events including museum exhibits, a then-and-now photo exhibit and a Beards, Bonnets, and Brews celebration at the city's historic Rockledge Ranch, which drew 10,000 people. The sesquicentennial observance culminated in a downtown celebration on July 31. The Parade through Time and other events on that day drew 25,000 people to the heart of the city. I wore 1871-style clothing to several events, as did Janet, who sported a bonnet and matching dress. I also challenged all of the men in the community to grow 1871 facial hair to commemorate the event and felt compelled to answer my own challenge, despite the fact I'd never previously grown a beard and Janet was less than enthusiastic about it. Virtually all the male department heads in the city took up the challenge, as did hundreds of city residents.

I told our citizens that I viewed the sesquicentennial celebration as a great opportunity to recognize and celebrate the people and events that led to Colorado Springs's growth and prosperity, but also an opportunity for introspection about the future. What did we want our city to look like decades from now? What do we need to do to be good ancestors for future generations of city residents? How could we preserve the vision of our city's founder, General William Palmer, that Colorado Springs would always be an aesthetically unique place where its citizens strive to build a city that compliments its splendid natural surroundings.

The city had two issues on the November 2021 ballot, and the results were mixed. Colorado Springs has a tremendous parks system, including world renowned parks such as Garden of the Gods and North Cheyenne Canyon. It's part of the legacy of General Palmer, who donated considerable park land to the city during his lifetime. In 1997 the voters established a Trails, Open Space, and Parks program (TOPS) which utilized revenue from a 0.1 percent sales tax to acquire open space. In the ensuing years, the city had acquired 7,500 acres of open space. Through developers' donation of land or fees, it had also acquired a large number of future park sites. Unfortunately, as the city grew and park use expanded exponentially, it has not been able to maintain general fund revenues sufficient to develop new park land or adequately maintain the parks, trails, and open space it already has. The city council and I agreed we needed a larger revenue stream to solve the problem. Issue 2C on the November 2021 ballot would have increased the TOPS sales tax from 0.1 to 0.2 percent. I had argued to the council that we should not seek to raise the tax higher than 0.15 percent because I felt voters would be more likely to support more incremental increases. But a majority of council members argued for a 0.225 or 0.25 percent tax. We eventually compromised on a tax of 0.2 percent and language for the ballot measure that I thought was too wordy. As it turned out, it was school board elections that drove the off-year election turnout and conservatives came out in somewhat disproportionate numbers because of controversy around Critical Race Theory and COVID impacts on education. The voters rejected the parks issue by 53-47 percent. It was the first time since my election in 2015 that an issue I supported had failed. The council and I agreed that we would pursue an extension of TOPS, without an increase in the tax, in the April 2023 municipal election. We were successful, however, in another important ballot measure. One of the greatest threats to the city from a natural disaster perspective is wildland fire. Because of a large wildland-urban interface, fires have been a big part of our city's history and will be a part of our future. While several cities in Colorado were considering creating special taxing districts to fund wildfire mitigation and prevention, I proposed a creative alternative. In Issue 2D we asked the citizens to allow us to retain $20 million in 2021 city revenue above the cap otherwise allowed in order to create a permanent Wildland Fire Mitigation and Prevention Fund. The fund will earn interest, and no more than 5 percent of the surplus can be spent each year under the directive of the Colorado Springs Fire Department and a citizen's advisory committee. The funds will allow us to increase our annual wildfire mitigation efforts by four to five times. Even the disproportionately conservative electorate in the off-year election liked the idea and approved the measure 58-42 percent. We were still able to refund $15 million to city residents from 2021 sales tax revenue.

In November of 2021, I was yet again approached by a group of wealthy Colorado Republicans asking me to run for governor in 2022, this time against Jared Polis. They offered encouraging poll results and financial support to have saturation-level political ads.

Janet and I discussed the offer for twenty minutes before concluding neither of us had the stomach for another statewide political campaign that would take me away from what we foresaw would be a very productive final year and a half as mayor.

Given that I was sixty-three when I ran for mayor, I knew that meant I would probably not run for higher office. But I feel strongly I made the right choice. Both houses of the state legislature had large Democrat majorities during the time I was mayor. Congress was largely dysfunctional. I am certain I would not have had the opportunity for transformational leadership as governor or in Congress that I had as mayor.

One of my highest priorities for my last year in office was to secure the renewal of the Pikes Peak Rural Transportation Authority (PPRTA) in the November 2022 general election. First passed by the voters in 2004, PPRTA is a 0.55 percent sales tax imposed on virtually all El Paso County residents. It funds major road expansion and traffic congestion reduction projects throughout the Pikes Peak region. The renewal was absolutely essential to ensure that transportation infrastructure keeps up with population growth. I helped raise $400,000 for the campaign and appeared in TV ads promoting the measure. I was very grateful to see it passed by an 80-20 percent margin.

I also felt strongly about the other municipal issue on the November 2022 ballot. Issue 300 was a citizen-initiated referendum, funded by the marijuana industry, to allow recreational marijuana sales in Colorado Springs. After Colorado legalized recreational marijuana in 2012, the Colorado Springs City Council had consistently voted not to allow it in the city. The industry ran a campaign to "let the voters decide." The measure would allow 115 medical marijuana facilities to begin selling recreational marijuana. I, along with local District Attorney Michael Allen, became the faces of the opposition campaign. Our TV ads reversed a large polling advantage for the proponents and resulted in the measure being soundly defeated by 57-43 percent. It is my firm belief that the quality of life in Colorado Springs would have suffered if 115 marijuana dispensaries competed to help our residents get high for recreation.

After the Planned Parenthood incident in November 2015 that left three dead, including a police officer, and nine injured, and the domestic violence episode in May 2021 that left seven dead, I hoped I could complete my tenure as mayor without another heinous crime occurring that would attract national attention to Colorado Springs. It was not to be. Just before midnight on November 19, 2022, a heavily armed twenty-two-year-old male entered Club Q, an LGBTQ+ nightclub, and opened fire with a semi-automatic weapon. He killed five people including two employees and three patrons and wounded another seventeen. It's clear many more people in the club would have been killed but for the heroic actions of two patrons that intervened to stop him. Thomas James, a Navy petty officer stationed in Colorado Springs, tackled the perpetrator, and Richard Fierro, an Army veteran, was able to wrestle a handgun away from him, pistol-whip him, and disable him until the police arrived shortly thereafter and took him into custody.

I received a phone call from Colorado Springs Police Chief Adrian Vasquez about two hours later to inform me of the shocking incident. We held our first press conference at 8 a.m. and the national media descended on Colorado Springs. Over the next four days, I did about fifty interviews. Interviews with the print media included *The New York Times, The Washington Post, The Wall Street Journal,* and *USA Today.* Electronic media interviews included ABC, CBS, NBC, Fox News, CNN, and PBS. I took calls from The White House, the Secretary of Homeland Security, and dozens of mayors, governors, and members of Congress. Janet and I attended vigils and funerals for shooting victims.

My principal task was to once again ensure Colorado Springs was not defined by the horrendous crime that had been committed, but rather by the community's response to it. And I'm proud to say that the community's response was overwhelming, both in terms of support services and financial assistance for the victims and the LGBTQ+ community. Several million dollars was raised. The city received largely positive feedback from local residents and from people throughout the country for the manner in which the tragedy was handled.

The perpetrator was charged with 320 felonies, including first-degree murder, attempted first-degree murder, first- and second-degree assault, and numerous bias-related crimes.

When I finished one of my national TV interviews with a high-profile anchor, she commented to me that it appeared that I had considerable experience dealing with high-profile crimes. Sadly, it was true.

In February of 2023, I made my final sister city visit as mayor to Colorado Springs's newest sister city, Kranj, Slovenia. Kranj had sought out the relationship because of our similar topography, climate, and mutual passion for Olympic Sports. The highlight of the trip was attending the World Ski Jumping Championship in Slovenia.

As my eight-year tenure as mayor of Colorado Springs drew to a close, the numbers told much of the story about the transformation the city had experienced. Since my election, the city had added almost 50,000 jobs. Downtown Colorado Springs had been transformed with 600 new hotel rooms, 3,000 new residential units, a downtown stadium, indoor arena, and Olympic Museum. Enplanements at the city's airport had doubled in eight years. The Gross Domestic Product (GDP) for the metropolitan area had grown from $30 billion to $40 billion annually. In other words, it took 144 years to grow the GDP to $30 billion, but it had expanded by a third during my tenure as mayor. By 2022, the city was the thirty-ninth largest in the country and the metropolitan area was the seventy-eighth largest. In eight short years, we had solved the problem of seriously underfunded critical public infrastructure.

Thanks to the support of the voters, for the first time in three decades, roads and stormwater systems had adequate funding. According to the annual Milken Institute, which rates the economics of America's largest 200 cities, Colorado Springs had one of the ten best economies in the country. Yet Colorado Springs residents still enjoyed a very low per capita tax burden. The city's per capita tax burden was just over $800. The average per capita tax burden for the country's 100 largest cities was over $2,400. For five consecutive years, a broad survey of Americans by *US News and World Report* named Colorado Springs the most desirable city in America to live.

I felt the key to my success as mayor was the level of credibility I had gained with the citizens over many years of public service. I was sixteen for seventeen on ballot issues that I took a public position on as mayor. While not everyone was a fan of mine or the transformation Colorado Springs had undergone, I maintained a high level of community support. I was elected mayor in 2015 with 68 percent of the vote, reelected in 2019 with 73 percent of the vote, and in the last poll taken during my tenure as mayor, I had a very high approval rating. Only 25 percent of those polled had an unfavorable view of their mayor. Given all the difficult and contentious issues I had taken on as mayor, I considered that a great compliment.

I've certainly had my share of critics throughout my career. While I've appreciated constructive criticism, I believe one of my strengths as a public official has been my ability to quietly ignore the less-constructive critics. Early on in my career I framed a copy of Teddy Roosevelt's "Man in the Arena" speech and hung it on my office wall. Roosevelt said:

> It is not the critic who counts; not the man who points out how the strong man stumbles, or where the doer of deeds could have done them better. The credit belongs to the man who is actually in the arena, whose face is marred by dust and sweat and

blood; who strives valiantly; who errs, who comes short again and again, because there is no effort without error and shortcoming; but who does actually strive to do the deeds; who knows the great enthusiasms, the great devotions; who spends himself in a worthy cause...

Excerpted from "Citizenship in a Republic" delivered in Paris,

April 23, 1910

I'm frequently asked which of the public service positions I've held is my favorite. It's a really difficult question for me to answer because I can honestly say I've loved every job I've had, including mowing lawns in high school and college. I've learned a great deal in every job I've had and I'm confident each one made me more effective in subsequent endeavors. But if I had to choose the best job, I'd probably say it was my tenure as Colorado attorney general. It's a position where I wielded a great deal of influence, but because only a small segment of the population really understands what the role is, I operated in relative anonymity, in contrast to a governor or big city mayor. The AG generally doesn't need a security detail and can typically go to a restaurant or other public venue without being incessantly approached by constituents. I was in fewer people's selfies in ten years as AG than I was in my first three months as mayor. For a good lawyer interested in law related public service, attorney general was a dream job.

But as to the most difficult job I've had and the one from which I derived the most personal satisfaction, I'd say it was mayor of Colorado Springs. A mayor, unlike the district attorney, US attorney, or attorney general, can't hide behind the law and explain every tough decision based on assessment of the law and facts surrounding the issue. A mayor has to deal with a lot of raw political issues that go to the core of people's quality of life. Virtually every decision, no matter how major or minor it appears, typically has its detractors. But that's why being mayor also presented the greatest opportunity for political leadership, by communicating effectively with constituents about problems needing to be solved and the best means to solve them. It was the opportunity for political leadership and witnessing the impact of that leadership on my hometown that gave me greater personal satisfaction than any other position I've held.

Chapter XX
The Final Chapter

When I walked out of the Mayor's Office for the final time, I was four months short of my seventy-second birthday. I had spent virtually all of the last thirty-five years as an elected or appointed public official. While I felt my analytical skills were still very good, I was self-aware enough to recognize that I had lost some of the acute memory, verbal acumen, and quickness on my feet that characterized much of my career. I also understood that gracefully surrendering the things of youth, as the "Desiderata" urges one to do, is an essential task of a good ancestor. Thomas Jefferson described the realities of growing old as follows:

> In no circumstances has nature been kinder to us, than in the soft gradations by which she prepares us to willingly part with what we are not destined to retain. First one faculty is withdrawn, and then another, sight, hearing, memory, accuracy, affection and friends, filched one by one, until we are left among strangers... Nothing is more incumbent on the old than to know when to get out of the way, and to relinquish to younger successors the honors they can no longer earn and the duties they can no longer perform.

> Excerpted from *Writings of Thomas Jefferson*

> To Horatio Gates Spafford, 11 May 1819

My career in elective politics was over. I've seen way too many aging people, including politicians, hang on too long, to the detriment of those they serve. I do not want to be one of them. On the other hand, as long as my health is good, I have no desire to completely retire. I feel psychologically incapable of it. I still see something meaningful to do and something to look forward to, as essential to my happiness. Stress and adrenaline have been a big part of my life, and I'm not sure I can give them up cold turkey.

That reality is cause for circumspection. I've noted that many successful people have had a hard time managing the last phase of their life. They've worked hard, achieved occupational and financial success and maybe even taken a victory lap of sorts. But then what? I've seen men in such circumstances do some really stupid things: end a long marriage for the allure of trying to restore their youth, or take financial risks that squander their fortune or otherwise destroy a hard-earned reputation. With that in mind, I'm determined to live the last chapter of my life serving others, embracing my family and friends, and being a good example to others who are in earlier stages of life.

I want philanthropy to be a big bigger part of my life. I'm excited to continue serving on the Daniels Fund Board and helping direct charitable grants to worthy recipients and scholarships to deserving students. I'll carefully consider other meaningful opportunities to serve on profit or nonprofit boards when I'm confident I can meaningfully contribute to their work. Because our children and grandchildren are financially secure Janet and I plan on giving much of our estate to favored causes. For Janet, that's an endowed scholarship fund at the UCCS for nontraditional women students returning to school in hopes of acquiring skills that will help them support their family. I have three favorite causes: an endowed scholarship fund in my name at UCCS for students in the School of Public Service, an endowed tuition assistance fund for Catholic school students in the Diocese of Colorado Springs, and an endowed fund at the Colorado Springs Pioneers Museum to support exhibits that chronicle the history of the city. We hope to generously endow all these funds before we die.

I will take on the status of an Executive in Residence at UCCS and do occasional teaching or lecturing at the university. I also want to remain involved in the law, but not as a courtroom litigator again. I see that as a younger person's pursuit. But I believe my knowledge and experience can be of considerable benefit to clients dealing with issues I'm knowledgeable about. That probably means associating with a relatively large firm.

Janet and I have had some incredible travel opportunities in our life, and we hope to continue to travel as long as our health allows it. As of now I've been to all fifty states and forty-five countries on six continents. Travel broadens horizons and understanding of people. It contributes greatly to a life of the mind.

There are two milestones I hope to live long enough to observe and enjoy. In May of 2026 Janet and I will celebrate fifty years of marriage. That's fifty years of love and partnership that has made life so meaningful. In October 2027, I'll mark fifty years as a lawyer. I love the law and love being a lawyer. It's allowed me to have a fascinating career. For forty-five years I've gone to work every day, sometimes feeling stress, sometimes with genuine apprehension, but never disengaged or uninterested. As a lawyer and public office holder I've given over 6,000 speeches and authored a half dozen books. I feel like I have positively impacted a lot of people. I have absolutely no regrets about my choice to become a lawyer. Because of my marriage, my family, and my interesting career, I can honestly say to myself that I've lived the life I intended to live. How many people can say that? I found the meaning and purpose in life that I set out to find as a fifteen-year-old boy reacting to the trauma of the untimely death of his father.

I've certainly had my share of good fortune along the way. While I've worked hard, it was luck that led me to many opportunities, including a full scholarship to Notre Dame and many important relationships, not the least of which was my adoption as an infant into a loving family and a blind date with Janet Gill. And I'm thankful God has given me the strength to cope with life's adversities, including the premature loss of my parents and the tragic death of our son-in-law, Mark Karla.

I don't know how long I have to live, but I want to take my own frequent advice and run through the finish line. I hope my family and friends will conclude I ran a good race. When it's over I'll be buried next to Janet in Colorado Springs historic Evergreen Cemetery, where General Palmer and so many people who helped build Colorado and Colorado Springs are also buried. Our graves will be about fifty feet from my mother and father and Aunt Joe and Uncle Jim. I'll be about 100 feet from Monsignor Harrington. I've asked that my tombstone include the words *Sic Transit Gloria Mundi*.

Acknowledgments

I hope this book has successfully conveyed the love and gratitude I have for my wife, Janet, and our family. Without the unwavering support of my family, both nuclear and extended, I could not have lived the meaningful and purposeful life I have enjoyed.

Although my adoptive parents, Pat and Bill Suthers, were a part of my life for way too short a time, they were very loving people who gave me the foundation for all the success, personal and professional, that I have found in life.

While I have mentioned a few teachers, like Sister Georgetta and Professor Paul Bartholomew, who were pivotal in the direction I chose to go in life, many other teachers helped create the life of the mind that has enriched it so greatly. The many Catholic nuns who taught me were incredibly dedicated to their ministry.

At every step of my life and career I have had benefactors and faithful supporters. I attended college and law school on scholarships funded by philanthropists. You don't win six elections, including two on the statewide level, without supporters who contributed time and money. And you don't succeed at the task of governance over an appreciable period of time without constituents who value your leadership, even when they don't always agree with you. The people of Colorado Springs, El Paso and Teller Counties, and the state of Colorado have given me the honor of leading my hometown and native state and hopefully making a difference in their lives.

I've had outstanding support from those I chose to assist me in managing large governmental entities. Assistant District Attorney Jeanne Smith, Deputy Director of Corrections Brian Burnett, Assistant US Attorney Bill Leone, Chief Deputy Attorney General Cynthia Coffman, S.G. Dan Domenico, and Chief of Staff Jeff Greene were steadfast and loyal and helped me tremendously in improving the organizations I was privileged to lead.

I have worked with literally dozens of department heads at the District Attorney's Office, Department of Corrections, US Attorney's Office, Attorney General's Office, and City of Colorado Springs. Without exception they were dedicated public servants. Many were truly exceptional. And I've managed about 10,000 public employees whose dedication and pride in their work made me look good. While I'm only able to mention a handful of them in this book, they are all deserving of my heartfelt appreciation.

I've had the joy of working with outstanding personal assistants, including Mary Ann Mann, Renee Massey, Judy Evans, Terri Connell, Wendilyn Guidotti, and Julie Lafitte. They helped manage my life and my work, and they had to patiently tolerate my idiosyncrasies.

In compiling and publishing this book I've been helped by my wife Janet, Wendilyn Guidotti, and Laurie Landers. A special thanks to my publisher GracePoint Publishing, in particular editor Laurie Knight and director Tascha Yoder.

In sum, my universe has been filled with wonderful people that have touched my life in so many ways. They comprise the real content of this book.

Index

Abu Hamza Al-Masri, 213, 214
Adams, Gabriel, 158
Adams, John, 170
Adel al-Jubeir, 261, 306
Allard, Wayne, 174, 198, 199, 200, 220
Allen, Michael, 353
Allison, Jim, 205, 224
Al-Turki, Homaidan, 259, 260, 262, 305
Anderson, Jon, 261
Anschutz, Philip, 219, 221
Arcuri, Ed, 126
Aries, Frank, 334
Armstrong, Bill, 132, 138, 173
Ashcroft, John, 200, 201, 202, 203, 214, 215, 216, 217, 221, 224, 233
Aspinwall, Bill, 154, 155, 163, 164
Atkinson, Daryl, 141
Babcock, Lewis, 209
Bach, Steve, 313, 314, 315, 317, 339
Bailey, Devon, 347, 348
Ball, Ken, 130
Ball, Ron, 100, 101
Ballou, Sullivan, 167, 168, 169
Barkley, Alben, 4
Bartholomew, Paul, 72, 363
Barton, Terry, 211, 212
Baylis, Eugene, 151
Beauprez, Bob, 256, 258, 259
Beck, Rachel, 326
Beckwith, Neil, 113
Beckwith, Scott, 113
Behnke, Katie, 254
Benefiel, Cecilia, 147
Bennet, Michael, 283, 290
Bennett, Merv, 318, 325
Bennett, Tony, 2

Bens, Suzanne, 19, 21
Benson, Bruce, 131, 338
Benyamin, Aram, 324
Berkenkotter, Maria, 310
Berry, Chuck, 162
Biden, Beau, 279
Biden, Joe, 176, 279, 333
Bird, Alan Hamilton, 246
Blackburn, Robert, 209, 224
Blake, David, 291
Bogart, Humphrey, 2
Boggs, Julie, 10, 11, 13, 14, 20
Bonds, Barry, 225
Bonham, Jean, 65, 89
Bonicelli, Eloise, 149
Brando, Marlon, 2
Breyer, Stephen, 269
Brooks, David, 169
Brooks, Mo, 333
Brown, Bob, 141
Brown, Dudley, 316
Brown, Hank, 248
Brown, Jerry, 311
Brown, Robert Charles, 146
Bruce, Douglas, 300, 316
Buck, Ken, 290
Buckley, William F., 73
Buescher, Bernie, 291
Bundy, Ted, 84
Burke, Edmund, 74
Burnett, Brian, 181, 363
Burns, Ken, 167
Bush, George H. W., 132, 190
Bush, George W., 170, 190, 197, 200, 202, 214, 215, 216, 217, 224, 228, 233, 258, 292
Buss, Janet, 136
Cameron, James, iii
Campbell, Ben, 174, 198, 199, 229
Cantwell, Bob, 180

Carey, Pete, 322, 336
Carlson, Linda, 33
Carr, Austin, 69
Cash, Norm, 39
Casper, Dave, 71
Catherine, Sister John, 48
Cavanaugh, John, 12
Chadwick, Florence, 3
Chamberlain, Joshua Lawrence, 168
Cheney, Al, 38
Cheney, Helen, 38
Childears, Linda, 349
Christie, Chris, 207
Chung, Connie, 212
Church, Heather Dawn, 145, 146
Churchill, Winston, 4, 343
Cinquanta, Daryl, 141
Clement, Paul, 292, 294
Clements, Tom, 305, 306
Clinton, Bill, 200, 207, 294
Coffman, Cynthia, 310, 311, 363
Cole, Andrew, 289
Collins, Helen, 320, 325
Comey, James, 207, 329
Comey, Jim, 330, 331
Connell, Terri, 364
Conte, Victor, 225
Cook, John, 161
Coolidge, Rich, 254
Coors, Pete, 229
Cope, Bob, 340
Corbett, Michael, 84, 85, 86
Cordray, Richard, 331
Cornyn, John, 283
Corry, Rob, 236
Cummings, Gordon, 77
Curtis, Steve, 175
Daniels, Bill, 324
Daniels, Cady and Jeanette, 77
Dantley, Adrian, 69

Davis, Jim, 307
de Gaulle, Charles, 27
Dean, Howard, 217
Dean, James, 2
DeCorte, Vince, 39
Dellinger, Walter, 294
DeVito, Danny, 156
Dewey, Robert, 301
Dillon, Marshall, 37
DiMaggio, Joe, 1
Dinnebeil, Bill, 172
Dix, Tim, 124
Domenico, Dan, 263, 268, 269, 310, 363
Domenico, Janelle, 283
Donaldson, William, 221
Donovan, Shaun, 297
Dorschner, Jeff, 226
Dougherty, Michael, 291
Drake, Janet, 264
Draper, Dirk, 324
Dunlap, Nathan, 304
Dunn, Jason, 172, 237, 264
Duprey, Melba, 226
Durant, Will and Ariel, vi
Duzel, Cem, 336
Ebel, Even, 306
Eid, Allison, 238, 263, 310
Enoch, Bart, 117
Estep, Park, 150
Evans, Judy, 364
Fabos, Jamie, 318
Fagan, Renny, 235, 238
Fanning, Dick, 65
Faricy, Mike and Betty, 61, 131
Feeney, Amy, 24
Fenn, Dan, 190
Ferrero, Tom, 145
Fierro, Richard, 354
Figa, Phil, 209
Finlaw, Jack, 305
Fischer, Donald C., 13, 17

All This I Saw, and Part of It I Was

Fischer, Jeanne, 12, 13, 14, 17, 18, 19, 21, 41
Fitz-Gerald, Joan, 235
Fitzgerald, Patrick, 217
Floyd, George, 347
Forbes, Steve, 197
Ford, Whitney, 39
Fortune, Stephannie, 350
Freed, Alan, 2
Freyschlag, Barbara, 149
Fritchle, Louise, 99
Gaouette, Dave, 205
Gardner, Ava, 2
Gardner, Cory, 330
Garnett, Alec, 287, 290
Garnett, Stan, 287, 288
Gasko, Jerry, 181
Geislinger, David, 349
Geithner, Tim, 279
Georgetta, Sister, 57, 58, 59, 169, 224, 236, 363
Gerash, Walter, 223
Gessler, Scott, 291
Gill, Ben, 91, 329
Gill, Bud and Anne, 92, 226
Gill, Janet, 90, 362
Glenn, Freddie, 85, 86
Godec, Bev, 50
Gonzales, Alberto, 279
Gore, Al, 197, 198
Gorsuch, Neil, 209
Gossage, Richard "Goose", 66
Grace, J. Peter, 69
Grammer, Karen, 85
Grammer, Kelsey, 85, 87
Granger, Peter, 35
Greene, Jeff, 318, 340, 363
Gregory, Marge and Payson, 36
Groff, Peter, 236
Grossman, Dan, 236, 255
Guidotti, Wendilyn, 327, 364
Halsey, Orville, 145
Hanifan, Richard, 10, 11

Harrington, Michael, 28, 46, 48, 49, 93, 236, 362
Harris, Eric, 210
Harris, Kamala, 311
Harvey, Marty, 112
Harward, Bob, 154, 155
Heard-Price, Karla, 316
Hearst, William Randolph, 4
Hegarty, Michael, 205, 225
Helms, Randy, 349
Henry VIII, 123
Hesburgh, Ted, 75
Hettrick, Peggy, 265
Hickenlooper, John, 258, 280, 283, 290, 298, 303, 304, 305, 312, 322, 325, 345
Hicks, Hilyard, 67
Hillman, Mark, 259
Hilton, Conrad, 2
Hogan, Ben, 3
Holder, Eric, 274, 279, 298
Holland, Mary Blanche, 25
Holloway, Brent, 147
Holmes, Jeff, 50
Holtzman, Mark, 256
Homan, Joseph H., 18
Homan, Joseph L., 18, 20
Homan, Luke, 18
Honssinger, Cynthia, 230, 237
Hood, Brian, 152, 153, 154, 155, 156
Hood, Diane, 152, 153, 154
Hoover, Herbert, 40
Horton, Kay and Horton, 55
Huarte, John, 49
Hubbell, Kristen, 237
Hudson, Ray, 85
Hull, Dottie, 90
Hybl, Bill, 126, 191
Ind, Jacob, 158
Isaac, Bob, 126
Iuppa, Barney, 127, 129, 131, 132, 133, 149, 150

Jackson, Jeff, 72
Jackson, Joe, 4
James, Sister Myra, 143
James, Thomas, 354
Jarret, Kyle, 102
Jefferson, Thomas, 111, 132, 359
Jobs, Steve, 308
Johnson, Bob, 104
Johnson, Gil, 131
Johnson, Kay and Horton, 36
Johnson, Lyndon, 72
Jones, Marion, 225
Kaline, Al, 39
Kane, Tom, 50, 61, 76, 80, 91, 93, 94
Karla, Isabelle Catherine, 114
Karla, Mark, 113, 362
Kazmaier, Richard, 3
Keating, Frank, 120
Kelleher, Daniel, 49
Kenda, Joe, 159
Kenelly, Orville, 102
Kennedy, John F., 47, 190, 342
Kennedy, Ted, 207
Kerlikowske, Gil, 277
Kerouac, Jack, 3
Kerry, John, 229
Kersten, R. Calhoun, 75
Kezele, Floyd, 74
Kierkegaard, 111
Kimball, Scott, 288
King Abdullah, 261
Kintz, Ed, 54, 65
Kirches, Ed, 83
Klebold, Dylan, 210
Klein, Walt, 132
Kleymeyer, Johnna Reeder, 324
Knaizer, Maurie, 240
Knight, Laurie, ii, 364
Krauthammer, Charles, 295
Krieger, Marcia, 209
Kurzava, George, 39

Lacy, Mary, 247
Lafitte, Julie, 364
Lally, Katie, 316
Lamm, Dick, 90
Landers, Laurie, 364
Lane, Frankie, 2
Lanza, Mario, 2
Larry, Frank, 39
Lathen, Amy, 314, 316, 317
Lee, Bob, 230, 231
Leigh, Vivien, 2
Leone, Bill, 205, 221, 222, 363
Limbrick, Charles, 138, 140
Lindsey, Gregory, 140
Lipkins, Cleo, 157
Loo, Dusty, 191
Loo, Gary, 125
Loo, Miriam, 35, 36
Lusk, Steve, 40
MacArthur, Douglas, 4
Madden, Alice, 255
Madden, Terry, 225
Makepeace, Mary Lou, 315, 317
Mann, Mary Ann, 364
Manson, Charles, 159, 183
Mantle, Mickey, 1, 39
Margolis, David, 199
Maris, Roger, 39
Marquez, Monica, 291, 310
Marrow, Chris, 138, 139
Marshall, John, 204
Martin, Hugh, 147
Martinez, Lawrence, 336
Massey, Renee, 364
Masters, Tim, 265
Mateos, Ricky Ricardo, 100
Matsch, Richard, 209, 212
Mauch, Jim, 10
Mayberry, Matt, 350
Mays, Willie, 1
McCain, John, 302
McCallin, Andrew, 296
McCann, Beth, 238

McCeney, Tom, 64
McCleary, Eugene, 329
McCullough, David, 207
McDaniel, Charae, 346
McFarlane, J. D., 104
McGahn, Don, 330
McGrath, Jane, 268
McInnis, Scott, 290
McMahon, Linda, 133
McPherson, Jim, 279
McVeigh, Timothy, 165
Mead, Matt, 207
Medved, Jon, 191
Megel, Gary, 33
Meyer, Natalie, 125, 173
Miles, Mike, 230
Miller, Bob, 206
Miller, Joel, 315, 317
Miller, Tom, 297
Montana, Monty, 33
Mora, Eduardo Medina, 281
More, Thomas, 124
Morgan, Alison, 185
Mueller, Bob, 207, 331
Mullarkey, Mary, 237
Mulvaney, Mick, 332
Mutzebaugh, Dick, 171, 172
Nacchio, Joe, 221, 222
Nagel, Bob, 81
Ness, Eliot, 284
Nichols, Terry, 165
Niemeyer, Gerhart, 73
Niski, Vince, 347
Nittman, Mary, 89, 90
Norton, Gale, 170
Nottingham, Edward, 209
O'Brien, Fern, 255, 256, 258
O'Rourke, Tom, 205
Obama, Barack, 176, 275, 279,
    280, 282, 285, 292, 298, 302
Oberwetter, James, 259
Ochs, Larry, 142
Olson, Ted, 207

Orrell, Ann, 23
Orren, Gary, 190
Ortega, Delphino, 149
Osama bin Laden, 213, 218
Owens, Bill, 174, 176, 177, 178,
    181, 183, 187, 188, 189, 197,
    198, 199, 206, 217, 229, 231,
    232, 236, 238, 239, 247, 254,
    256, 257, 259, 260, 303
Page, Alan, 49
Page, Patti, 2
Palmer, William, iii, 124, 342,
    351
Parish, Liz, 37
Parker, Juliette, 336, 338
Parseghian, Ara, 49, 69
Patton, George s., 27
Pauline, Sister Anne, 45
Pence, Mike, 330
Pendergast, Thomas, 78
Penrose, Julie, 45, 77
Penrose, Spencer, 28, 45, 124,
    143
Peres, Shimon, 253
Perrelli, Tom, 297
Phillips, Acen, 264
Phillips, Anne, 149
Pitchford, John, 336
Pizzi, Bill, 81
Polis, Jared, 341, 343, 344, 352
Powell, Colin, 189
President Ma, 254
Presley, Elvis, 2
Price, Doug, 328
Pruitt, Scott, 298
Quick, Don, 310
Railey, Matt, 99
Rayburn, Sam, 4
Raynes, Tom, 264
Reali, Ben, 153
Reali, Jennifer, 152, 153, 154,
    155, 156
Redford, Robert, 63

Rehnquist, William, 73
Riorden, Linus, 11
Ritter, Bill, 257, 258, 259, 264, 266, 272, 276, 277, 282, 284, 286, 291, 303
Rivera, Ed, 61, 93
Roberts, Julia, 156
Robinson, Ebony, 148
Robinson, Jackie, 3
Robinson, Jackie and Todd, 148
Rockne, Knute, 69
Rodriguez, Gina, 205, 225
Roever, Theresa, 157, 158
Romanoff, Andrew, 283
Romer, Roy, 132, 160, 171, 188
Romney, Mitt, 301, 302
Roosevelt, Teddy, 356
Rosenberg, Julius and Ethel, 3
Ross, Lynne, 278
Rulo, Mike, 184
Rundle, Cassandra, 149
Russel, Bob, 101, 103, 117, 118, 126, 133, 162
Ruth, Babe, 39
Ryan, Cornelius John, 25, 29
Ryan, Jim, 37, 55, 64, 81
Ryan, Jo, 89, 92
Ryan, Marguerite Ann, 23
Ryan, Pat and Terri, 92
Saccone, Mike, 264
Salazar, Ken, 171, 174, 176, 229, 231, 232, 235, 238, 243, 247, 257, 282, 310
Salinger, J. D., 2
Salk, Jonas, 166
Sayers, Rosie, 54
Scalia, Antonin, 207, 294
Schaffer, Bob, 229
Schmidtke, Layne, 135
Schneebeck, Bob, 61, 72, 74, 93
Schwarzenegger, Arnold, 156
Seibel, Tom, 251
Seikich, Robert, 147

Serra, Myrl, 265
Sharansky, Natan, 253
Shearer, LuzMaria, 265
Shipley, Sharon, 156, 157
Shupp, Gary, 104, 105
Shupp, Liane, 159
Simpson, O. J., 98
Sinatra, Frank, 2
Singular, Stephen, 156
Six, Steve, 268
Skandera, Hanna, 349
Skorman, Richard, 325, 349
Slater, Don, 284
Smit, Lou, 142, 145, 146, 150
Smith, Jeanne, 133, 149, 163, 212, 213, 238, 248, 264, 311, 363
Smith, Joe, 171, 172
Smith, Kitt, 316, 326, 336
Sorin, Edward, 76
Spafford, Horatio Gates, 359
Sparks, Ken, 117, 118, 120, 124, 125, 132, 165
Spitzer, Eliot, 244
Spriggs, Dick, 200, 201
Spurgeon, Alan, 104
Stallone, Sylvester, 94
Stelzner, Tim, 82
Stenejhem, Wayne, 311
Stocker, Rebecca, 136
Strait, Marvin, 191
Strand, Tom, 349
Strasberg, Lee, 2
Stratton, Winfield Scott, 31
Strickland, Tom, 200, 220, 226
Sullivan, Patrick, 300
Suthers, Alison, 100, 107, 108, 109, 110, 111, 113, 114, 134, 135, 174, 197, 198, 205, 258, 263, 268, 329
Suthers, Jeremiah, 23, 24

Suthers, Kate, 49, 76, 108, 109, 110, 112, 113, 134, 135, 172, 174, 187, 198, 263, 329
Suthers, Sharon, 7, 27, 28, 42, 55, 58, 82, 89, 94
Suthers, William Dupont, 23
Suthers, William Terrance, 24, 29
Swasey, Garrett, 323
Taylor, Elizabeth, 2
Theismann, Joe, 69
Thomas, Clarence, 238
Thompson, Bobby, 1
Thompson, Larry, 200, 219, 221
Timkovich, Tim, 113
Toole, Otis, 150
Trujillo, Larry, 178, 180
Truman, Harry, 4
Trump, Donald, 207, 264, 298, 302, 310, 329, 330, 331, 332, 344
Tuberville, Tommy, 333
Udall, Mark, 229
Udis, Laura, 241
Ujaama, James, 213, 214
Ulrich, George, 45
Van Hollen, J. B., 207
Vanderhoof, Richard, 125

Vasquez, Adrian, 354
Vehr, Urban J., 29
Verrilli, Donald, Jr, 293
Wadhams, Dick, 283
Wakin, Mal, 123
Waple, Mary Ellen, 24
Wasden, Lawrence, 278, 311
Washington, George, 204, 289
Webster, Daniel, 268
Webster, Dick, 97
Weidner, Dean, 340
Wells, Jeff, 171, 172, 173
West, Mary, 181
White, Byron, 207
Wiepking, Jack, 61
Wiggins, Robert, 186
Will, George, 189, 277, 295
William, Sister John, 45
Williams, Wayne, 336
Witty, Mike, 156
Woodbridge, Monsignor, 10, 11
Wray, Chris, 331
Yoder, Tascha, 364
Young, Rich, 225
Zavaras, Ari, 178, 180
Zavislan, Jan, 238, 245, 249
Zennon, Carl, 180
Zimmerman, George, 67

John Suthers

John Suthers' memoir combines a compelling personal story with an insightful account of an extraordinary public service career that balances what is right and what is necessary.

Born out of wedlock and adopted as an infant, he lost his adoptive parents at a young age. The trauma of his father's untimely death caused him, as a teenager, to resolve to live a life of purpose and consequence—to become a good ancestor. After attending Notre Dame and the University of Colorado Law School on scholarships, Suthers embarked on a legal career that took him from the local courthouse to the U.S. Supreme Court. He completed the "legal trifecta", serving as district attorney, U.S. attorney, and state attorney general. He was involved in captivating criminal cases, historic civil cases, and in waging the war on terrorism after 9/11.

Starting in May 2015, Suthers served as the mayor of his hometown of Colorado Springs, leading it through a period of unprecedented prosperity, while overcoming challenges ranging from domestic terrorism to a global pandemic. He's encountered many interesting people along the way. John hopes his life story will help inspire others to make it their goal to become a good ancestor.

PEAK PRESS

If you enjoyed reading *All This I Saw, and Part of It I Was,* and purchased it through an online retailer, please return to the site and write a review to help others find the book.

Printed in the USA
CPSIA information can be obtained
at www.ICGtesting.com
LVHW040501260923
759271LV00002B/111